SOCIAL JUSTICE, EQUALITY AND EMPOWERMENT

NATIVE AMERICAN GRAVES AND REPATRIATION

SOCIAL JUSTICE, EQUALITY AND EMPOWERMENT

Additional books in this series can be found on Nova's website under the Series tab.

Additional E-books in this series can be found on Nova's website under the E-books tab.

ETHICAL ISSUES IN THE 21ST CENTURY

Additional books in this series can be found on Nova's website under the Series tab.

Additional E-books in this series can be found on Nova's website under the E-books tab.

SOCIAL JUSTICE, EQUALITY AND EMPOWERMENT

NATIVE AMERICAN GRAVES AND REPATRIATION

KATHY J. BERGMANN
EDITOR

Nova Science Publishers, Inc.
New York

For permission to use material from this book please contact us:
Telephone 631-231-7269; Fax 631-231-8175
Web Site: http://www.novapublishers.com

Additional color graphics may be available in the e-book version of this book.

LIBRARY OF CONGRESS CATALOGING-IN-PUBLICATION DATA

Native American graves and repatriation / editors, Kathy J. Bergmann.
p. cm.
Includes index.
ISBN 978-1-61122-410-8 (hardcover)
1. United States. Native American Graves Protection and Repatriation Act.
2. Indians of North America--Antiquities--Law and legislation. 3. Human remains (Archaeology)--Law and legislation--United States. 4. Human remains (Archaeology)--Repatriation--United States. I. Bergmann, Kathy J.
KF8210.A57N38 2010
344.73'094--dc22
2010038647

Published by Nova Science Publishers, Inc. † New York

CONTENTS

PREFACE

In November 1990, the Native American Graves Protection and Repatriation Act (NAGPRA) was passed heralding a balance to the relationship between the Federal government, museums and the Native American community. No longer would Indian tribes and Native Hawaiian organizations be unable to resolve control of Native American human remains and cultural items located in Federal agency repositories and museum collections around the country. Instead, NAGPRA gave Indian tribes and Native Hawaiian organizations a process for seeking their return. This book is an examination of the healing, revival and trust-building as tribes and Native Hawaiian organizations work with museums and Federal agencies on mutual understanding and respect for Native communities, values traditions and ancestors.

Chapter 1- The Native American Graves Protection and Repatriation Act (NAGPRA) required federal agencies and museums to (1) identify their Native American human remains and other objects, (2) try to culturally affiliate them with a present day Indian tribe or Native Hawaiian organization, and (3) repatriate them under the terms in the act. The National NAGPRA office, within the Department of the Interior's National Park Service (NPS), facilitates the government-wide implementation of NAGPRA. GAO was asked to determine, among other things, the (1) extent to which agencies have complied with their NAGPRA requirements, (2) actions taken by National NAGPRA, and (3) extent of repatriations reported by agencies. GAO reviewed records for eight key agencies with significant historical collections, surveyed agencies to obtain repatriation data, and interviewed agency, museum, and tribal officials

Chapter 2- Passage of the Native American Graves Protection and Repatriation Act of 1990 (NAGPRA) marked a watershed in the long and often troubled relationship between Native Americans and many of this country's educational institutions, museums, and public agencies. NAGPRA provides for the disposition of Native American cultural items human remains, funerary objects, sacred objects, and objects of cultural patrimony removed from Federal or tribal lands to lineal descendants or Indian tribes or Native Hawaiian organizations based on geographic or cultural affiliation. NAGPRA also prohibits trafficking of Native American cultural items. Lastly, NAGPRA provides for the repatriation of Native American cultural items in museum and Federal agency collections to lineal descendants or culturally affiliated Indian tribes or Native Hawaiian organizations.

Chapter 3- The native american graves protection and repatriation act (NAGPRA), 25 U.S.C. 3001, acknowledges tribal sovereignty and the right of Native Americans to human remains and important cultural objects affiliated with their tribe or community. Hailed as a significant landmark in human rights and Indian law, NAGPRA provides museums[1] and Federal agencies with a mechanism for resolution of claims and repatriation. Museums and Federal agencies are required to conduct a thorough assessment of their Native American collections. Cultural objects that may be sacred, objects of cultural patrimony, or unassociated funerary objects are listed in summaries and sent to potentially interested Indian tribes[2] and Native Hawaiian organizations (NHOs) to begin consultation. Interested Indian tribes or NHOs can then consult with the museum on objects of interest and make a claim for repatriation. Human remains and associated funerary objects are subject to an inventory process. Museums are required to contact Indian tribes or NHOs that may be affiliated with their collection and consult together to determine cultural affiliation. Culturally affiliated human remains and agreements to repatriate cultural items are published in the *Federal Register* and are then available to be repatriated to the appropriate Indian tribe or NHO.

Chapter 4- The National NAGPRA Program serves constituents of the law which are all Federal agencies with land or collections responsibilities, museums that receive Federal funds, Native Americans, Indian tribes and NHOs, and the public.

This chapter follows the organization of the National NAGPRA Program and its responsibilities pertaining to collections, excavations/discoveries, regulations, and technical assistance given to Indian tribes and NHOs and the museums and Federal agencies that have obligations for NAGPRA compliance. Throughout the report, the term "tribe" is used, as it is in the law, to refer to federally recognized Indian tribes, Alaska Village corporations and Native Hawaiian organizations.

Chapter 5- Pursuant to 25 U.S.C. 3003(a) each Federal agency and museum which has possession of or control over human remains is required to compile an inventory which identifies the geographical and cultural affiliation of items in its possession based on documentary evidence. The inventories provided by the Federal agencies and museums in compliance with 25 U.S.C. 3003(a) resulted in the classification of over 118,000 individuals as culturally unidentifiable. According to 25 U.S.C. 3001, cultural affiliation is defined as, "a relationship of shared group identity which can be reasonably traced historically or prehistorically…" between a current day federally recognized Indian Tribe or Native Hawaiian group. According to the reporting institutions and agencies 118, 833 Native American human remains cannot be found to have a group identity with any existing federally recognized Indian Tribe or Native Hawaiian Group.

Chapter 6- The official designation of the Committee is the Native American Graves Protection and Repatriation Review Committee

In: Native American Graves and Repatriation
Editor: Kathy J. Bergmann
ISBN: 978-1-61122-410-8

Chapter 1

NATIVE AMERICAN GRAVES PROTECTION AND REPATRIATION ACT: AFTER ALMOST 20 YEARS, KEY FEDERAL AGENCIES STILL HAVE NOT FULLY COMPLIED WITH THE ACT

United States Government Accountability Office

WHY GAO DID THIS STUDY

The Native American Graves Protection and Repatriation Act (NAGPRA) required federal agencies and museums to (1) identify their Native American human remains and other objects, (2) try to culturally affiliate them with a present day Indian tribe or Native Hawaiian organization, and (3) repatriate them under the terms in the act. The National NAGPRA office, within the Department of the Interior's National Park Service (NPS), facilitates the government-wide implementation of NAGPRA. GAO was asked to determine, among other things, the (1) extent to which agencies have complied with their NAGPRA requirements, (2) actions taken by National NAGPRA, and (3) extent of repatriations reported by agencies. GAO reviewed records for eight key agencies with significant historical collections, surveyed agencies to obtain repatriation data, and interviewed agency, museum, and tribal officials.

WHAT GAO RECOMMENDS

GAO recommends, among other things, that the Departments of Agriculture, Defense, and the Interior as well as TVA report to Congress the actions that they need to take to fully comply with the act and that they report the status of their repatriations to National NAGPRA. GAO is also recommending that National NAGPRA make improvements in its facilitation of the act. Agriculture, Interior, and TVA agreed with GAO's recommendations. The Department of Defense did not provide comments on the report.

WHAT GAO FOUND

Almost 20 years after NAGPRA, key federal agencies still have not fully complied with the act for their historical collections acquired on or before NAGPRA's enactment. GAO examined NAGPRA implementation in detail for eight key federal agencies with significant historical collections: Interior's Bureau of Indian Affairs (BIA), Bureau of Land Management (BLM), Bureau of Reclamation (BOR), U.S. Fish and Wildlife Service (FWS) and NPS; Agriculture's U.S. Forest Service; the U.S. Army Corps of Engineers (Corps); and the Tennessee Valley Authority (TVA). First, all of the agencies acknowledge that they still have additional work to do to fully comply with the act's requirements to identify all of their NAGPRA items, establish cultural affiliations when possible, and create summaries and inventories of the items. Overall, the Corps, the Forest Service, and NPS did the most work to identify their NAGPRA items. BLM, BOR, and FWS did some work, and BIA and TVA have done the least amount of work. Second, some of the eight agencies, along with some other federal agencies, have not fully complied with NAGPRA's requirement to publish notices of inventory completion for all of their culturally affiliated human remains and associated funerary objects in the *Federal Register*. Until agencies (1) identify all of the possible NAGPRA items in their historical collections, (2) establish cultural affiliations to the extent possible, and (3) publish the required notices, they cannot repatriate their Native American human remains and objects.

To fulfill the Secretary of the Interior's responsibilities under NAGPRA, National NAGPRA has taken some actions consistent with the act, such as publishing notices in the *Federal Register* and administering a grants program. However, GAO identified some actions of concern. National NAGPRA developed a list of Indian tribes eligible under NAGPRA that was inconsistent with BIA's official list of federally recognized tribes and departmental policy. Furthermore, National NAGPRA did not always screen nominations for Review Committee positions properly and, in a few cases, inappropriately recruited nominees for Review Committee positions.

Through fiscal year 2009, 55 percent of the human remains and 68 percent of the associated funerary objects that have been published in notices of inventory completion had been repatriated, according to agency data and GAO's survey results. Agencies are required to permanently document their repatriations, but they are not required to compile and report that information to anyone. Only three agencies—the Corps, the Forest Service, and NPS—centrally track their repatriations. These three agencies, however, along with the other federal agencies that have published notices, generally do not report any of their data on repatriations to National NAGPRA or to Congress. As a result, policymakers, Indian tribes, and Native Hawaiians organizations do not have access to readily available information about culturally affiliated NAGPRA items that have not been repatriated. According to officials, the remaining items have not been repatriated for a variety of reasons, such as a lack of repatriation requests and financial constraints.

ABBREVIATIONS

ANCSA	Alaska Native Claims Settlement Act

BIA	Bureau of Indian Affairs
BLM	Bureau of Land Management
BOR	Bureau of Reclamation
FWS	U.S. Fish and Wildlife Service
NAGPRA	Native American Graves Protection and Repatriation Act
NPS	National Park Service
TVA	Tennessee Valley Authority

July 28, 2010

The Honorable Byron Dorgan
Chairman
Committee on Indian Affairs
United States Senate

The Honorable Nick J. Rahall, II
Chairman
Committee on Natural Resources
House of Representatives

Many federal agencies and museums have acquired Native American human remains, funerary objects, sacred objects, and objects of cultural patrimony over hundreds of years. When the Native American Graves Protection and Repatriation Act (NAGPRA) was enacted, on November 16, 1990,[1] it was estimated that federal agencies and museums had tens of thousands of such items in their historical collections.[2] NAGPRA required federal agencies and museums to (1) identify their Native American human remains, funerary objects, sacred objects, and objects of cultural patrimony,[3] (2) try and determine if a cultural affiliation exists with a present day Indian tribe or Native Hawaiian organization,[4] and (3) generally repatriate the culturally affiliated items to the applicable Indian tribe(s) or Native Hawaiian organization(s) under the terms and conditions prescribed in the act.[5] However, a June 2008 report by the Makah Indian Tribe and the National Association of Tribal Historic Preservation Officers reported a number of concerns about federal agencies' compliance with the act.[6]

Of the variety of NAGPRA requirements for federal agencies, museums, and the Secretary of the Interior, those most relevant to their historical collections, and which are the focus of this chapter, include the following:

- Having each federal agency and museum, with NAGPRA items in their collections, (1) compile an inventory of Native American human remains and associated funerary objects; (2) compile a summary of Native American unassociated funerary objects, sacred objects, and objects of cultural patrimony; and (3) repatriate culturally affiliated human remains and objects identified through the inventory or summary processes if the terms and conditions prescribed in the act are met.
- Having the Secretary of the Interior establish a Review Committee to monitor and review the implementation of these requirements.
- Having certain duties assigned to the Secretary of the Interior, which are carried out by the National NAGPRA Program Office (National NAGPRA) within the

Department of the Interior's National Park Service's (NPS) Cultural Resources program.

To address the status of NAGPRA implementation, you asked us to determine the (1) extent to which federal agencies have complied with NAGPRA's requirements for their historical collections; (2) activities taken by the Review Committee to fulfill its role under NAGPRA and what challenges, if any, it faces; (3) actions taken by National NAGPRA to fulfill its responsibilities under NAGPRA; and (4) extent to which federal agencies reported repatriating Native American human remains and objects.

To determine the extent to which federal agencies have complied with their NAGPRA requirements for their historical collections, we obtained and verified data from National NAGPRA on all federal agencies' notices of NAGPRA items published in *Federal Register* notices through the end of fiscal year 2009. We examined NAGPRA implementation in detail for eight key federal agencies with significant historical collections: Interior's Bureau of Indian Affairs (BIA), Bureau of Land Management (BLM), Bureau of Reclamation (BOR), U.S. Fish and Wildlife Service (FWS), and NPS; the U.S. Army Corps of Engineers (Corps); the Department of Agriculture's U.S. Forest Service; and the Tennessee Valley Authority (TVA). For each of these agencies we reviewed records on NAGPRA compliance, such as inventories, summaries, *Federal Register* notices, and correspondence. We interviewed both headquarters and field staff for each agency, except TVA, to discuss their NAGPRA implementation. For TVA we interviewed its entire staff responsible for NAGPRA implementation. TVA's NAGPRA staff are located at its headquarters in Knoxville, Tennessee. We also reviewed information for other federal agencies that had published NAGPRA notices and included basic data on their submissions in our analysis. To determine how the Review Committee has carried out its role of monitoring and reviewing NAGPRA implementation and what challenges it faces, we attended two Review Committee meetings and interviewed 10 out of 23 current and former Review Committee members who represented a variety of experiences.[7] We interviewed some federal, tribal, museum, and scientific organization officials on the role of the Review Committee. We also analyzed the Review Committee's recommendations to the Secretary of the Interior on disposition requests for culturally unidentifiable human remains and its recommended resolutions of disputes. To examine how National NAGPRA has carried out its role of facilitating NAGPRA implementation, we reviewed National NAGPRA's list of eligible Indian tribes, Review Committee nomination files, National NAGPRA annual reports, and we interviewed the National NAGPRA program staff. To measure the extent to which federal agencies have repatriated items published in notices of inventory completion, we obtained data from the three agencies that track their repatriations—the Corps, the Forest Service, and NPS. For other agencies that had published notices of inventory completion—four other key federal agencies as well as eight additional federal agencies—we deployed a survey. A more detailed description of our scope and methodology is presented in appendix I.

We conducted this performance audit from July 2009 to July 2010 in accordance with generally accepted government auditing standards. Those standards require that we plan and perform the audit to obtain sufficient, appropriate evidence to provide a reasonable basis for our findings and conclusions based on our audit objectives. We believe that the evidence obtained provides a reasonable basis for our findings and conclusions based on our audit objectives.

Table 1. Five Types of Native American Cultural Items Covered by NAGPRA

NAGPRA item	Definition
Human remains	Physical remains of the body of a person of Native American ancestry. 43 C.F.R. § 10.2(d)(1).
Associated funerary objects	Objects that, as part of the death rite or ceremony of a culture, are reasonably believed to have been placed with individual human remains either at the time of death or later, and both the human remains and associated funerary objects are presently in the possession or control of a federal agency or museum, except that other items exclusively made for burial purposes or to contain human remains shall be considered as associated funerary objects. 25 U.S.C. § 3001(3)(A).
Unassociated funerary objects	Objects that, as part of the death rite or ceremony of a culture, are reasonably believed to have been placed with individual human remains either at the time of death or later, where the remains are not in the possession or control of the federal agency or museum and the objects can be identified by a preponderance of the evidence as related to specific individuals or families or to known human remains or, by a preponderance of the evidence, as having been removed from a specific burial site of an individual culturally affiliated with a particular Indian tribe. 25 U.S.C. § 3001(3)(B).
Sacred objects	Specific ceremonial objects which are needed by traditional Native American religious leaders for the practice of traditional Native American religions by their present day adherents. 25 U.S.C. § 3001(3)(C).
Objects of cultural patrimony	Objects having ongoing historical, traditional, or cultural importance central to the Native American group or culture itself, rather than property owned by an individual Native American, and which, therefore, cannot be alienated, appropriated, or conveyed by any individual regardless of whether or not the individual is a member of the Indian tribe or Native Hawaiian organization and such object shall have been considered inalienable by such Native American group at the time the object was separated from such group. 25 U.S.C. § 3001(3)(D).

Source: NAGPRA and its implementing regulations.

Background

NAGPRA covers five types of Native American cultural items, which we refer to collectively, in this chapter, as NAGPRA items (see table 1).

Since the early 1800s, federal agencies have amassed archeological collections with items numbering in the millions. Some, such as NPS, acquired their collections through archeological excavations intended to advance scientific knowledge and preserve cultural resources. Others, such as the Corps and TVA, have made discoveries during the massive construction projects that are part of their missions.[8] Forest Service officials estimated that an overwhelming majority of the agency's collections resulted from non-Forest Service initiated activities, such as research by museums and universities or as a result of the construction of highways, reservoirs, and pipelines; or mining claims. Interior—with its land-management agencies—has the largest collection outside of the Smithsonian Institution, with an estimated 146 million objects and documents that cover archeology as well as disciplines such as art and zoology. Federal agency archeological collections are currently stored at a variety of repositories,[9] both federal and nonfederal, located throughout the country. For example, BLM's collections are stored at three BLM facilities and 121 other repositories. According to TVA officials, TVA's collections are stored at universities in Alabama, Kentucky, Michigan, Mississippi, North Carolina, and Tennessee.[10] These federal collections include tens of thousands of Native American human remains and hundreds of thousands of funerary objects, sacred objects, and objects of cultural patrimony subject to NAGPRA.

Table 2. Background Information on Eight Federal Agencies with Significant Historical Collections

Federal agency	Date established	Organization structure	Acres managed (in millions)	Estimated number of objects inmuseum collection (in millions)	Fiscal year 2010 total enacted agency budget (in billions)
Department of the Interior[a]					
BIA	1824	12 regions and 83 agency offices	55	5.7	$4.8
BOR	1902	5 regions	6.5	8.3	1.2
BLM	1946[b]	12 state offices and 144 field offices	253	13.2	1.3
NPS	1916	7 regions and 392 park units	84	122.5	3.2
FWS	1940[c]	8 regions, 551 national wildlife refuges, and over 700 field offices	150	6.2	2.8
Corps of Engineers[d]	1802[e]	8 regional divisions and 38 districts	11	[f]	4.6
Forest Service	1905	9 regions, 155 national forests, 20 grasslands, and over 600 ranger districts	193	[g]	6.2
TVA	1933	Independent federal corporation[h]	0.3[i]	[j]	[k]

Source: Data from the eight federal agencies.

[a] The Department of the Interior was established in 1849 and was originally comprised of the General Land Office, the Patent Office, the Indian Affairs Office, and the military pension offices.

[b] BLM was established in 1946 through the consolidation of the General Land Office, created in 1812, and the U.S. Grazing Service, formed in 1934.

[c] FWS was established through the merger of the U.S. Fish Commission, established in 1871, and the Office of Economic Ornithology and Mammalogy, established in 1885.

[d] According to Corps officials, the number of Corps organizational units listed in the table are the units that administer fee title lands and are subject to NAGPRA.

[e] When the Continental Congress organized the Continental Army in 1775, it provided for a Chief Engineer to design and construct military batteries and fortifications. In 1802, Congress permanently established the Corps.

[f] The Corps estimates that the size of its collection is 47,500 cubic feet of objects.

[g] The Forest Service estimates that it manages 589,796 cubic feet of objects in museum collections. Forest Service archeological collections include 377,953 cubic feet of material at the Grey Towers National Historic Site, which is a historic mansion in Milford, Pennsylvania, converted into a conservation education and leadership center.

[h] TVA has four main offices (Knoxville, Chattanooga, and Nashville, Tennessee; and Muscle Shoals, Alabama), regional customer service centers, and offices in seven economic development regions. It manages 11 coal-fired plants, 9 combustion turbine plants, 3 nuclear plants, 29 hydroelectric dams, and a pumped-storage plant, among other things.

[i] According to TVA, it manages one of the nation's largest river systems covering a 41,000 square mile watershed and 11,000 miles of shoreline.

[j] TVA estimates that the size of its collection is 20,954 cubic feet of objects.

[k] TVA is an independent, wholly owned federal corporation and receives no federal funding for its operations. It is funded through power sales and the sales of bonds on the financial markets. It has annual revenues of over $9 billion.

NAGPRA defines a federal agency as any department, agency, or instrumentality of the United States, except the Smithsonian Institution,[11] and defines a museum as any institution or state or local government agency, including any institution of higher learning, that receives federal funds and has possession of, or control over,[12] Native American cultural items, except the Smithsonian Institution.[13] The eight federal agencies with significant historical collections that we reviewed—BIA, BLM, BOR, FWS, NPS, the Corps, the Forest Service, and TVA—manage various amounts of federal land in conjunction with their missions and differ in organizational structure (see table 2). They also have long histories over which they came into possession or control of NAGPRA items.

In addition, the missions of the agencies vary widely. For example, NPS's mission is to preserve unimpaired the natural and cultural resources and values of the national park system for the enjoyment, education, and inspiration of this and future generations. In contrast, the mission of TVA is to serve the Tennessee Valley through energy, environment, and economic development. Because of their varying missions, the scope and treatment of their archeological programs have also differed.

Since 1906, federal agencies have been issuing permits to individuals, universities, and corporations to perform archeological excavation and research on the federal land they manage.[14] Although the permitting system has changed over time, these permits generally allowed the entities conducting the excavation and research to preserve the excavated materials in public museums.[15] Thus, in theory, archeological materials legally excavated from federal lands since 1906 are recorded in agency reports and records, or in permitting records located in agency files, the Smithsonian Institution's National Anthropological Archives, or the National Archives. However, due to the age of some of the permits, the large number of permits, and administrative processes that have changed over time, it can be difficult for some agencies to know where all of their collections are currently located. For example, a recent Interior Inspector General report stated that Interior agencies' collections are held in 625 Interior facilities and at least 1,020 non-Interior facilities, but that four of its agencies were not aware of the location of their collections held in the non-Interior facilities.[16]

NAGPRA Requirements for Historical Collections

NAGPRA's requirements for federal agencies, museums, and the Secretary of the Interior, particularly the ones most relevant to their historical collections, which are the focus of this chapter, include the following:

- *Compile an inventory and establish cultural affiliation.* Section 5 of NAGPRA required that each federal agency and museum compile an inventory of any holdings or collections of Native American human remains and associated funerary objects that are in its possession or control. The act required that the inventories be completed no later than 5 years after its enactment—by November 16, 1995—and in consultation with tribal government officials, Native Hawaiian organization officials, and traditional religious leaders. In the inventory, agencies and museums are required to establish geographic and cultural affiliation to the extent possible based on information in their possession. Cultural affiliation denotes a relationship of shared group identity which can be reasonably traced historically or prehistorically between a present day Indian tribe or Native Hawaiian organization and an identifiable earlier group.[17] Affiliating NAGPRA items with a present day Indian tribe or Native Hawaiian organization is the key to deciding to whom the human remains and objects should be repatriated. If a cultural affiliation can be made, the act required that the agency or museum notify the affected Indian tribes or Native Hawaiian organizations no later than 6 months after the completion of the inventory. The agency or museum was also required to provide a copy of each notice—known as a notice of inventory completion—to the Secretary of the Interior for publication in the *Federal Register*. The items for which no cultural affiliation can be made are referred to as culturally unidentifiable.[18]
- *Compile a summary of other NAGPRA items.* Section 6 of NAGPRA required that each federal agency and museum prepare a written summary of any holdings or collections of Native American unassociated funerary objects, sacred objects, or objects of cultural patrimony in its possession or control, based on the available information in their possession. The act required that the summaries be completed no later than 3 years after its enactment—by November 16, 1993. Preparation of the summary was to be followed by federal agency consultation with tribal government officials, Native Hawaiian organization officials, and traditional religious leaders. The summary was to describe the scope of the collection, kinds of objects included, reference to geographical location, means and period of acquisition and cultural affiliation, where readily ascertainable. After a valid claim is received by an agency or museum, and if the other terms and conditions in the act are met, a notice of intent to repatriate must be published in the *Federal Register* before any item identified in a summary can be repatriated.[19] In contrast to a notice of inventory completion for NAGPRA items listed in inventories, notices of intent to repatriate for NAGPRA items listed in summaries are not published until after an Indian tribe or Native Hawaiian organization has submitted a claim for an item.
- *Repatriate culturally affiliated human remains and objects.* Section 7 of NAGPRA and its implementing regulations generally require that, upon the request of an Indian

tribe or Native Hawaiian organization, all culturally affiliated NAGPRA items be returned to the applicable Indian tribe or Native Hawaiian organization expeditiously—but no sooner than 30 days after the applicable notice is published in the *Federal Register*—if the terms and conditions prescribed in the act are met. Furthermore, the regulations require federal agencies and museums to adopt internal procedures adequate to permanently document the content and recipients of all repatriations.[20]

Review Committee Established by NAGPRA

Section 8 of NAGPRA required the Secretary of the Interior to establish a Review Committee to monitor and review the implementation of the inventory and identification process and repatriation activities under the act.[21] The Review Committee is composed of seven members appointed by the Secretary. Three members are to be appointed from nominations submitted by Indian tribes, Native Hawaiian organizations, and traditional Native American religious leaders. At least two of these members must be traditional Indian religious leaders. Three members are to be appointed from nominations submitted by national museum organizations and scientific organizations. The seventh member is to be appointed from a list of persons developed and consented to by all of the other members. Among other functions, the Review Committee is responsible for (1) upon request, reviewing and making findings related to the identity or cultural affiliation of cultural items or the return of such items;[22] (2) facilitating the resolution of any disputes among Indian tribes, Native Hawaiian organizations, and federal agencies or museums relating to the return of such items;[23] and (3) compiling an inventory of culturally unidentifiable human remains and recommending specific actions for developing a process for disposition of such remains.

The Review Committee is a federal advisory committee subject to the requirements of the Federal Advisory Committee Act and its implementing regulations.[24] The Federal Advisory Committee Act establishes requirements for advisory committees subject to the act, including broad requirements for balance, independence, and transparency. Specifically, the Federal Advisory Committee Act requires that the membership of committees be "fairly balanced in terms of points of view represented and the functions to be performed by the advisory committee." Members of advisory committees subject to the Federal Advisory Committee Act are generally appointed as special government employees or representatives. Special government employees are appointed to provide advice on behalf of the government on the basis of their best judgment and must meet certain federal requirements pertaining to freedom from conflicts of interest.[25] Representatives, in contrast, provide stakeholder advice—that is, advice reflecting the views of the entity or interest group they are representing, such as industry, labor, or consumers—and are not subject to the same conflict of interest requirements. NAGPRA Review Committee members are appointed as special government employees. The Federal Advisory Committee Act also requires the Secretary of the Interior to appoint a Designated Federal Officer for the NAGPRA Review Committee. Among other things, the officer must approve or call the meetings of the committee, approve the agendas, and attend the meetings.

The NAGPRA Review Committee differs from most advisory bodies subject to the Federal Advisory Committee Act in two important ways. First, while most agencies have broad discretion in balancing their committees, NAGPRA limits this discretion because of its requirements both for the types of members that can serve (i.e., the requirement that at least two members be traditional Indian religious leaders) and the entities that can nominate them. Second, according to Interior officials, most federal advisory committees are not tasked with the dispute resolution function performed by the Review Committee.

NPS's National NAGPRA Program Office

NAGPRA also assigned duties to the Secretary of the Interior that are carried out by the National NAGPRA Program Office (National NAGPRA) within Interior's NPS Cultural Resources program. National NAGPRA has a staff of 5.75 full-time equivalent employees and one contractor. Its annual operating budget, which includes the operating expenses for the Review Committee, is about $1 million. One of the duties assigned to National NAGPRA is to help fill vacancies on the Review Committee. National NAGPRA is also responsible for developing NAGPRA's implementing regulations and it provides administrative support to the Review Committee. The main body of the regulations was proposed in 1993 and became effective in 1996.[26]

The Evolution of National NAGPRA

NAGPRA required the Secretary of the Interior to perform a number of functions, which the Secretary initially delegated to the Departmental Consulting Archeologist, a position within NPS that provides coordination, leadership, technical assistance, and guidance to all federal agencies with responsibility for archeological resources. According to agency officials, this position was housed within the Archeological Assistance Division under the Associate Director for Cultural Resources. Officials further stated that, from 1990 to the mid-1990s, the Departmental Consulting Archeologist and other support staff within the Archeological Assistance Division were responsible for facilitating NAGPRA compliance governmentwide (such as reviewing inventories and summaries and publishing notices) and the Anthropology Division, also within the Cultural Resources Program, was responsible for conducting NPS's compliance activities to meet NAGPRA requirements (such as completing inventories and summaries and drafting notices). Both offices reported to the Associate Director of Cultural Resources. Officials said that in the mid-1990s, the Archeological Assistance Division and Anthropology Division were merged into a new unit—the Archeology and Ethnography Program—under the Departmental Consulting Archeologist, who then conducted both activities until 2000.

In 2000, due to concerns voiced by NAGPRA practitioners over a conflict of interest between NPS's facilitation of governmentwide NAGPRA implementation and its own NAGPRA compliance, the Director of NPS split these functions by creating a National NAGPRA office to handle the facilitation of NAGPRA governmentwide and a Park NAGPRA office to handle NPS compliance with the act. However, the two offices still reported to the Associate Director for Cultural Resources. New staff were brought in for National NAGPRA; the Departmental Consulting Archeologist continued to lead Park

NAGPRA efforts and both NAGPRA programs reported to the manager of the Center for Cultural Resources, under the Associate Director for Cultural Resources.

Additional changes were made in 2004 due to continued concerns about the two offices reporting to the same manager under the Associate Director for Cultural Resources. The Secretary removed Park NAGPRA from the Cultural Resources Program and placed it within the Office of Indian Affairs and American Culture in NPS's Intermountain Region; this office then reported to the Regional Director. In addition to being organizationally moved, Park NAGPRA was physically moved from Washington, D.C., to the Intermountain Region located in Denver, Colorado. National NAGPRA was removed from the Center for Cultural Resources and placed directly under the Associate Director for Cultural Resources, but it remained in Washington, D.C.[27] As a result of these changes, the Departmental Consulting Archeologist and the Archeology Program, as it is currently known, no longer has any NAGPRA responsibilities.

National NAGPRA's Grant Program

National NAGPRA operates a grants program established by section 10 of NAGPRA that amounts to about $2 million per year. The grants are for two purposes—consultation and repatriation.[28] Consultation grants are competitively awarded to Indian tribes, Native Hawaiian organizations, and museums to consult and document human remains and objects. They are not awarded for activities related to excavations or inadvertent discoveries under section 3 of NAGPRA, cultural items in the control of a foreign institution, or activities associated with the Smithsonian Institution, among other things. For fiscal year 2010, consultation grant awards can range from $5,000 to $90,000. National NAGPRA issues an annual call for consultation grants that provides a deadline for applications. In contrast, repatriation grants are non-competitive and are awarded to defray the expenses associated with repatriating human remains and objects, such as the packaging, transportation, and documenting the condition and treatment history of cultural items to mitigate potential health risks. Applications for repatriation grants are accepted on a rolling basis year round.

Once received, National NAGPRA staff review the applications for consultation and repatriation grants to ensure they meet the eligibility requirements. For consultation grants, a panel, selected by National NAGPRA and consisting of federal government employees familiar with repatriation issues, reviews and scores grant applications and provides recommendations on which grants to award. The Assistant Secretary of Fish, Wildlife, and Parks ultimately makes the award decisions. According to the National NAGPRA Program Manager, consultation and repatriation grants are neither available to federal agencies nor to Indian tribes or Native Hawaiian organizations seeking to consult with and repatriate items from federal agencies.

Federally Recognized Tribes and Alaska Native Villages

In accordance with NAGPRA's implementing regulations, National NAGPRA has developed a list of Indian tribes and Native Hawaiian organizations for the purposes of carrying out the act. The list is comprised of federally recognized tribes, Native Hawaiian organizations, and, at various points in the last 20 years, corporations established pursuant to the Alaska Native Claims Settlement Act (ANCSA).[29] The term "recognize" means the federal government acknowledges that a particular Native American group is a tribe by conferring specific legal status on that group, establishing a government-to-government relationship between the United States and the tribe, imposing on the government a fiduciary trust relationship to the tribe and its members and imposing specific obligations on the federal government to provide benefits and services to the tribe and its members.[30] National NAGPRA's list has evolved over time as additional tribes have either been granted federal recognition or had their federal recognition restored.[31] Since NAGPRA was enacted, 28 Indian tribes have been newly recognized or restored (see app. II). In addition, hundreds of Indian groups that are currently not federally recognized have expressed an interest to BIA in seeking federal recognition.

Since the enactment of two recognition laws in 1994,[32] BIA has regularly published a comprehensive list of recognized tribes—commonly referred to as the list of federally recognized tribes—that federal agencies are supposed to use to identify federally recognized tribes. As of August 11, 2009, there were 564 federally recognized tribal entities—339 in the continental United States and 225 in Alaska—recognized and eligible for funding and services from BIA by virtue of their status as Indian tribes.[33] Indian groups not included in the list are commonly referred to as "non-federally recognized tribes."

The recognition of Alaska Native entities eligible for the special programs and services provided by the United States to Indians because of their status as Indians has been controversial. Since a 1993 legal opinion by the Solicitor of the Department of the Interior,[34] BIA's list of federally recognized tribes has not included any ANCSA group, regional, urban, and village corporations. These corporations, chartered under state law, were the vehicle for distributing land and monetary benefits to Alaska Natives to provide a fair and just settlement of aboriginal land claims in Alaska.

ANCSA defined Alaska Native villages by referring to the lists of villages contained in sections 11 and 16 of ANCSA. ANCSA required the Secretary of the Interior to review the section 11 list and add or delete villages that did not meet specified requirements. The Secretary's review produced a so-called modified list, which included Alaska Native villages defined in or established under section 11 of ANCSA and the villages listed in section 16. Interior's Solicitor has noted that a number of post-ANCSA statutes have included Alaska Native villages within their definition of Indian tribe by reference to the ANCSA definition of Native village and that these references are to this modified ANCSA list.

Key Federal Agencies Have Not Fully Complied with NAGPRA for Their Historical Collections

While the eight key federal agencies we reviewed generally prepared their summaries and inventories by the statutory deadlines, the amount of work put into identifying their NAGPRA items and the quality of the documents prepared varied widely. For some of the human remains and associated funerary objects that these eight key federal agencies, along with other federal agencies, have culturally affiliated, they have published notices of inventory completion, although some notices have encountered delays. In addition, not all of the culturally affiliated human remains and associated funerary objects have been published in a *Federal Register* notice as required. Officials for the eight agencies also identified challenges that they faced complying with NAGPRA, which included lack of funding and staff only working on NAGPRA compliance for historical collections as a collateral duty.

Key Federal Agency Summaries and Inventories were Generally Prepared on Time, but the Amount of Work Conducted and the Quality Varied Widely

While federal agencies compiled hundreds of summaries and inventories, generally by the statutory deadlines, the amount of work conducted and the quality of the documents prepared varied widely and in some cases did not provide reasonable assurance of compliance with the act. When NAGPRA was enacted, the task facing each federal agency varied depending on several factors, including the size of their historical collections, the extent of centralized records in existence for their collections and institutional knowledge of repositories in possession of their collections, how dispersed their collections were both geographically and among different repositories, and each agency's structure, staffing, and resources available for cultural resources management.

For most agencies, the task of identifying their NAGPRA items within the larger universe of their historical collections was complicated by longstanding challenges with the curation and management of their archeological collections.[35] For example, in 1981, we reported that Interior's efforts to guide and coordinate many federal archeological activities were characterized by "disorder, confusion, and controversy."[36] More recently, a December 2009 report by Interior's Office of Inspector General described similar deficiencies with the management of Interior's museum collections (including NAGPRA items) and stated that Interior is failing to fulfill its stewardship responsibilities over museum collections, which are second in size only to the Smithsonian Institution.[37] The Inspector General report noted that for fiscal year 2007, 53 percent of Interior's museum collections, or 78 million objects, were not catalogued, and that Interior "had little idea" what collections non-Interior repositories held.

Officials at several of the eight agencies that we focused on during our review said NAGPRA compliance involved a large amount of work and because they had different levels of resources to expend, they took varied approaches to meet the act's requirements for their historical collections. Of these eight agencies, the Corps, the Forest Service, and NPS did the most extensive work to identify their NAGPRA items, and therefore they have the highest confidence level that they have identified all of them and included them in summaries and inventories (see table 3). In contrast, relative to the top three agencies, BLM, BOR, and FWS were moderately successful in identifying their items and including them in summaries and inventories, and BIA and TVA have done the least amount of work. As a result, these five agencies have less confidence that they have identified all of their NAGPRA items and included them in summaries and inventories.

Table 3. Examples of Eight Federal Agencies' Activities to Identify NAGPRA Items and Prepare Summaries and Inventories

Agency	Agency activities to identify their NAGPRA items and prepare summaries and inventories
Agencies that have done the most work and have the highest confidence that all their NAGPRA items have been identified	
Corps of Engineers	**Requested funding.** According to Corps staff, before NAGPRA's enactment, the agency proactively requested additional funding to identify archeological collections. As of the end of fiscal year 2008, the Corps' Mandatory Center of Expertise for the Curation and Management of Archeological Collections (Center) for NAGPRA estimated that it had attained about 80 percent compliance (complete summaries and inventories and publication of relevant notices). **Examined records and performed physical inspections**. The Corps' Center staff examined historical records and archeological permits at the Smithsonian Institution, the National Archives, and State Historic Preservation Offices, and performed physical inspections of non-federal repositories. They determined that the Corps has confirmed collections in 166 repositories around the country. **Centralized reporting.** All Corps components must consult with the Center in compiling NAGPRA summaries and inventories, and the Center has prepared full collection audits on non-federal repositories' curation of the Corps units' NAGPRA items. **Maintains compliance data.** The Corps Center maintains agencywide data for the Corps on NAGPRA compliance status and activities, including repatriations. **Funding levels.** For fiscal year 2009, the Corps' Center expended over $1.55 million for NAGPRA compliance activities.
Forest Service	**Region 3 controls most NAGPRA collections.** According to Forest Service staff, 90 percent of the Forest Service's NAGPRA items are under the control of Region 3, which covers portions of the Southwestern United States. Staff also stated that in 1991, the Forest Service hired a NAGPRA coordinator for Region 3, who later became the Forest Service's agencywide NAGPRA coordinator, and expanded the search for archeological permits and collections to all the other Forest Service regions. **Examined records and contacted repositories.** In the early 1990s, the NAGPRA Coordinator retrieved all the archeological records for Region 3 from the Smithsonian Institution and the National Archives that could have involved NAGPRA items. According to the NAGPRA Coordinator, copies of the records were then sent to all the relevant non-federal repositories for verification, and he followed up on discrepancies that emerged from their responses. **Maintains compliance data.** The Forest Service's NAGPRA Coordinator collects and maintains agencywide data for the Forest Service on NAGPRA compliance, status, activities, and completed repatriations. **Funding levels.** For fiscal year 2009 the Forest Service expended $210,000 for NAGPRA compliance work and repatriations.
NPS	**Maintained collections before NAGPRA.** According to NPS officials, NPS units curate a major portion of their archeological collections in their own facilities before and since NAGPRA. This factor gave NPS an initial advantage in achieving NAGPRA compliance, and enabled NPS to compile more complete summaries and inventories.

Table 3. (Continued)

Agency	Agency activities to identify their NAGPRA items and prepare summaries and inventories
	Maintains compliance data. Park NAGPRA maintains agencywide data for NPS on NAGPRA compliance status and activities, including repatriations. **Funding and staffing levels.** Park NAGPRA manages a $850,000 agencywide budget for NAGPRA activities, approximately $500,000 of which it awards to NPS regions through a competitive, needs-based process, according to NPS staff. The office has a Program Manager with collateral duties and one additional full-time employee.
BLM	**Relied on BLM State Offices and the Corps to identify collections.** According to BLM staff, BLM relied on its state offices to contact the repositories in the western states directly and for the eastern half of the country BLM contracted with the Corps' Center to compile a list of non-federal repositories in possession of BLM's archeological collections. Some of these efforts led to successful NAGPRA compliance, but in some cases the agency encountered significant challenges in determining its NAGPRA collections—for example in the states of Utah, California, and Alaska. **Building centralized compliance data.** The first centralized reporting and data collection for BLM NAGPRA compliance was started in 2006. The BLM NAGPRA Coordinator has since been able to create a baseline of data and also stated that the agency has accelerated its efforts to comply with NAGPRA. **Funding levels.** For fiscal year 2009, BLM had a budget over $15.7 million for its cultural resources budget, of which $69,286 was expended for NAGPRA compliance.
BOR	**Identified repositories, but additional work to identify NAGPRA** item remains. According to BOR's Federal Preservation Officer and NAGPRA Coordinator, BOR has been able to identify the non-federal and BOR repositories that maintain archeological collections, but has not verified if the repositories contain NAGPRA items. **Faced challenges in compiling inventories.** Some BOR regions were able to compile complete summaries and inventories. However, the Great Plains and Mid-Pacific Regions have faced considerable challenges in NAGPRA compliance because complicated land ownership issues and discrepancies in land ownership records must first be addressed to determine whether BOR controls the item. **Building compliance data.** There is no centralized BOR tracking of NAGPRA compliance, although BOR's NAGPRA Coordinator said a database is in the process of being developed.
FWS	**Identified repositories, but additional work to identify NAGPRA items remains.** According to agency officials, FWS contracted with the Corps' Center to identify all non-federal repositories in possession of FWS archeological material. The FWS Service Archaeologist (the national NAGPRA coordinator for FWS) stated that 80 percent of FWS's collections have not been comprehensively reviewed (i.e., compared against records, examined, catalogued) to identify NAGPRA items. **Lacks compliance data.** Although FWS did submit summaries and inventories, the FWS NAGPRA coordinator said it is unlikely that the documents are complete because the agency is not fully aware of the contents of its collections.

Table 3. (Continued)

Agency	Agency activities to identify their NAGPRA items and prepare summaries and inventories
	Funding levels. FWS provides approximately $385,000 annually for all museum property management functions, which includes NAGPRA compliance.
Agencies that have done the least work and have low confidence that all their NAGPRA items have been identified	
BIA	**Scope of BIA's compliance responsibility was ambiguous and remains unsettled.** In 1998 BIA headquarters officials requested a legal opinion from Interior's Office of the Solicitor regarding whether BIA owned NAGPRA items removed from Indian lands under the Antiquities Act of 1906 and therefore would have to comply with NAGPRA for those items. The Solicitor has not issued a legal opinion but has discussed the matter with BIA. As a result of these discussions, BIA has, in some cases, issued joint notices with the non-federal repositories in possession of NAGPRA items. BIA reports that in the past it has contracted with the Corps Center to produce reports assessing its nationwide curation needs. **Lacks compliance data.** BIA's Chief of Environmental and Cultural Resources Management (the national NAGPRA coordinator for BIA) stated that BIA Regional Offices act independently to implement NAGPRA and that centralized tracking of NAGPRA compliance data for the agency was started in 1997, but has not yet been completed due to staff turnover and lack of resources. **Funding levels.** For fiscal year 2009, BIA had a budget of $300,000 for its museum program, $150,236 of which funded contracts with museums for NAGPRA compliance.
TVA	**Relied on repositories to compile and submit inventory and summary documents.** TVA relied on its own records and those of its repositories to identify the locations of its archeological collections. TVA generally relied on repositories in possession of its collections to compile the agency's summaries and inventories. The repositories prepared these documents more than 10 years ago. For TVA's collections at the University of Alabama, TVA has not conducted specific consultations on cultural affiliations. As a result, TVA considers its inventories to be preliminary since the required consultations have not yet occurred. **Lacks compliance data and faces other challenges.** According to TVA's NAGPRA coordinator, a database of TVA's NAGPRA collections is being developed. TVA cultural resources management staff stated that due to gaps in communications, a lack of consultations, and other challenges, TVA has not been able to establish final cultural affiliations for any of the NAGPRA items in its historical collections. In addition, for NAGPRA items that were excavated during the course of TVA projects several decades ago, some ambiguity may exist as to which entity—TVA or the museum that curates the items—has legal control over the items, according to TVA. **Funding levels.** As of fiscal year 2009, TVA did not specifically track costs associated with NAGPRA.

Source: GAO analysis of NAGPRA activities for the eight federal agencies.

While some agencies have done more than others to comply with the requirements of the act, it does not appear that any of the eight agencies we reviewed are in full compliance. The act and its implementing regulations did not provide a specific list of activities or actions that federal agencies and museums had to take in order to identify their NAGPRA items. However, the act clearly stated that the summaries and inventories had to contain the NAGPRA items each agency or museum was in possession or control of. We believe that without conducting a level of activities that would provide a federal agency with a reasonable assurance that the summaries and inventories were complete, federal agencies cannot be confident that they have complied with NAGPRA's inventory and summary requirements. Even those agencies that have done the most work acknowledge that they still have some individual units that have more work to do. For example, the Corps reports that as of the end of fiscal year 2009 the Louisville, Nashville, Mobile, and Tulsa Districts have not yet produced their inventories. Additionally, some agencies said they do not know exactly how much work is left in order to be confident that they have identified all of their NAGPRA items.

In addition to the completeness of agency summaries and inventories, we found that two other important requirements affecting the quality of these documents—consultations with Indian tribes and Native Hawaiian organizations and the establishment of cultural affiliations—were also lacking in some instances. We found that the confusion over when consultations should occur and when cultural affiliations should be established appeared to be rooted in the confusion among some NAGPRA practitioners about the differences between summaries and inventories. Specifically, summaries described collections, and consultation was to occur after the summary document was prepared; and cultural affiliations were to be included in summaries where readily ascertainable.[38] In contrast, inventories were item-by-item descriptions, consultation was to occur before the inventory document was completed, and cultural affiliations were to be made to the extent possible. However, we found examples where agency officials treated inventories like summaries in that the consultation occurred and cultural affiliation determinations were made after the preparation of the inventory. Also, several tribal officials stated that the frequency and thoroughness of consultations throughout the NAGPRA process for historical collections varied widely depending on the agency and agency personnel involved. However, agency officials also reported challenges in consulting with tribes, such as certain tribes not wanting to attach any cultural affiliations to NAGPRA items because of deeply-held spiritual beliefs. If agencies did not perform these initial critical steps to fully identify and disclose the NAGPRA items that they have in their historical collections, the repatriation process cannot move forward.

Publication of Some Notices of Inventory Completion Has Been Delayed, and Some Agencies Have not Published All Required Notices

According to information from National NAGPRA's database, as of September 30, 2009, 16,302 Native American human remains, or 55 percent of all the Native American human remains inventoried by agencies, had been published in notices of inventory completion and 13,519 had been listed in inventories for federal collections as culturally unidentifiable (see table 4). Of the associated funerary objects inventoried by federal agencies, 193,324 objects, or 74 percent, had been published in a notice of inventory completion and 66,918 had been listed as culturally unidentifiable.

Table 4. Native American Human Remains and Associated Funerary Objects Published in Notices of Inventory Completion and Those Listed in Federal Agency Inventories as Culturally Unidentifiable, as of September 30, 2009

	Published in notices of inventory completion				Culturally unidentifiable[a]	
Agency	Number of original notices	Number of corrections	Human remains[b]	Associated funerary objects	Human remains[b]	Associated funerary objects
Department of the Interior						
NPS	86	10	4,053	77,927	1,304	14,656
BLM	55	1	1,565	16,615	399	249
BOR	7	2	550	3,330	122	38
BIA	32	1	464	9,621	56	18
FWS	14	0	127	626	765	5,123
Indian Arts and Crafts Board	2	0	2	0	0	0
Subtotal	**196**	**14**	**6,761**	**108,119**	**2,646**	**20,084**
Department of Defense						
Department of the Navy	8	1	3,397	7,734	214	0
Corps of Engineers	27	1	722	40,869	1,508[a]	9,955[a]
U.S. Army	8	2	105	1,557	172	753
U.S. Air Force	4	1	38	85	3	0
National Museum of Health and Medicine	8	0	16	0	158	0
Subtotal	**55**	**5**	**4,278**	**50,245**	**2,055**	**10,708**
Forest Service	47	9	5,246	33,618	757	15,157
Department of Justice	5	0	9	2	2	1
Department of Energy	4	0	6	1,340	20	97
Department of Homeland Security	2	0	2	0	0	0
TVA	[c]	[c]	[c]	[c]	8,030[a]	20,870[a]
Environmental Protection Agency	[c]	[c]	[c]	[c]	9	1
Total	**309**	**28**	**16,302**	**193,324**	**13,519**	**66,918**

Source: National NAGPRA.

Note: In a few cases, notices of inventory completion were published listing culturally unidentifiable human remains after the Secretary made a recommendation in response to a disposition request submitted to the Review Committee.

[a] Numbers in the culturally unidentifiable columns are from National NAGPRA's database, which, as noted in appendix I, may be unreliable. Several agencies that maintain their own data have asserted that the numbers reported for them in this table do not match their own data. For example, the Corps reports 87 human remains and 422 associated funerary objects, and TVA reports that while

they do not have exact numbers, their estimates are not close to what National NAGPRA's reports. Officials from both agencies indicated that they will continue to work with National NAGPRA to reconcile these numbers.

[b] Human remains are counted using the "minimum number of individuals" approach. The minimum number of individuals refers to the fewest possible number of people in a skeletal assemblage. This is often used in forensic anthropology and osteology to determine an estimate of how many individuals are represented in a cluster of bones. While there are formulae that can be applied to determining the minimum number of individuals, making this determination is essentially based on logic. Counts of the minimum number of individuals are based on age, sex, and repeat skeletal elements. For example, if there are three right humerus bones, that implies there were at least three individuals. If those all three happen to be male, and there is a clearly female skull, then that adds one more individual to the count. A count of one could be for a complete skeleton of over 200 bones or one fragment of a bone from one individual.

[c] As of September 30, 2009, TVA and the Environmental Protection Agency had not published any notices of inventory completion. The inventory for the Environmental Protection Agency did not include any culturally affiliated NAGPRA items and therefore no notice was required.

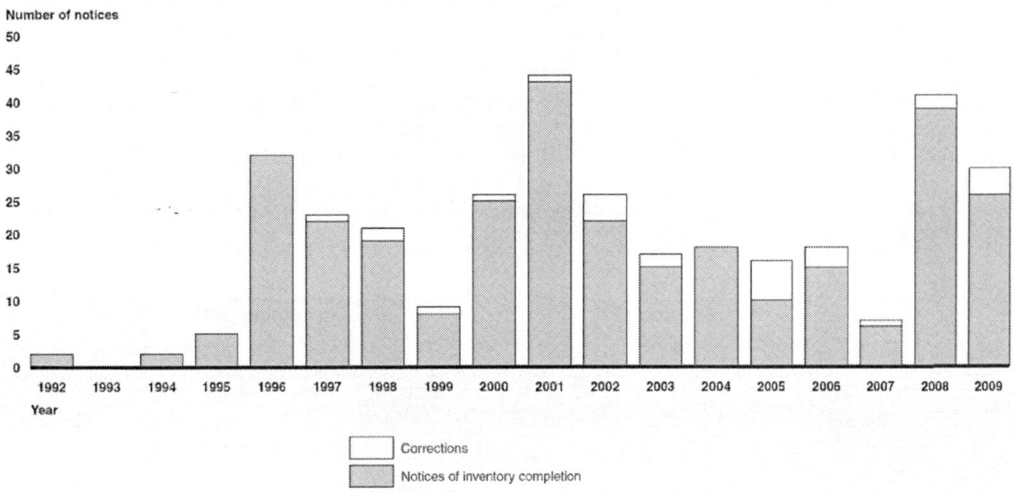

Source: GAO analysis of National NAGPRA data.

Figure 1. Number of Notices of Inventory Completion and Corrections Published by Federal Agencies, by Fiscal Year

However, we found that in some cases the publication of these notices encountered significant delays. When agencies made cultural affiliation determinations for Native American human remains and associated funerary objects listed in their inventories, they were required to notify the affiliated Indian tribe(s) or Native Hawaiian organization(s) within 6 months and at the same time submit a copy of the notice to National NAGPRA for publication in the *Federal Register*.[39] NAGPRA and its implementing regulations do not contain a deadline for when the notice actually had to be published. If a notice of inventory completion is published and later is found to be inaccurate or new information emerges, agencies are to work with National NAGPRA to publish a correction notice. Through fiscal year 2009, federal agencies had published 309 notices of inventory completion and 28 corrections (see figure 1).

According to agency officials and National NAGPRA, several reasons contributed to the delays in publishing notices of inventory completion. First, during its review process National NAGPRA determined that some inventories had not been properly prepared and, as a result, agencies had prepared improper draft notices. For example, one improperly prepared draft notice included unassociated funerary objects, which are to be included in summaries and notices of intent to repatriate. This may have been partly because the regulation for the inventory process was not finalized until December 4, 1995, after the deadline for preparing inventories had passed.[40] National NAGPRA officials said they returned improperly prepared draft notices to the agencies. A second reason for delays in publishing notices, according to some agency officials, was the highly complex nature of their consultations with the tribes, which resulted in the agencies needing additional time to finalize their cultural affiliations before publishing their notices. Third, some agencies treated inventories like summaries and waited for a culturally affiliated entity to request repatriation before submitting a notice for publication. Fourth, some agencies relied on non-federal repositories (such as universities and museums) that held their historical collections to compile the summary and inventory documents and submit them directly to National NAGPRA. According to one former National NAGPRA official, in one case the P.A. Hearst Museum at the University of California, Berkeley was granted an extension to the 5-year deadline for compiling inventories for their own collections, and some agencies believed that this extension also applied to their federal collections held by the museum.[41]

Table 5. Examples of Federal Agencies' Units That Still Need to Publish Notices of Inventory Completion for Culturally Affiliated Human Remains

Agency component	Culturally affiliated human remains that have not been published in a notice of inventory completion[a]
BOR, Great Plains Region, Nebraska-Kansas Area Office	61
BOR, Pacific Northwest Region	15
NPS, Glen Canyon National Recreation Area	13
FWS, Buenos Aires National Wildlife Refuge	4
FWS, Upper Mississippi National Wildlife and Fish Refuge	4
Forest Service, Gifford Pinchot National Forest[b]	3
Department of Defense, Naval Air Station Fallon	2
FWS, Sevilleta National Wildlife Refuge	2
Indian Arts and Crafts Board	1
FWS, Eufaula National Wildlife Refuge	unknown

Source: GAO analysis of National NAGPRA data and agency documents.

Note: TVA officials stated that they consider the cultural affiliations for the 320 human remains in the 1999 inventory for their NAGPRA items at the Alabama Museum of National History to be "preliminary" because the required consultations with the relevant Indian tribes has not been performed. The officials stated that TVA can not move forward with the publication of a notice of inventory completion in the *Federal Register* for these human remains until consultations have occurred and the inventory and the cultural affiliations have been finalized. According to TVA officials, TVA had preliminary discussions with federally recognized tribes regarding TVA's NAGPRA compliance in 2002 and 2007, but there has been no specific consultation with tribes regarding the preliminary cultural affiliations for these items.

[a] Human remains were counted using the "minimum number of individuals" method.

[b] The Gifford Pinchot National Forest has submitted a draft notice of inventory completion to National NAGPRA and it is working with the office on publication of the notice.

Additionally, we found that a number of federal agencies have not fully complied with NAGPRA's requirement to publish notices of inventory completion for all of their culturally affiliated human remains and associated funerary objects in the *Federal Register*, thereby complicating efforts of Indian tribes or Native Hawaiian organizations to make repatriation requests for those items (see table 5). Agency officials provided several reasons for their lack of compliance with this requirement. For example, TVA staff stated that, because of personnel turnover and poor communication—with a repository and with National NAGPRA in the 1990s—320 human remains preliminarily culturally affiliated to the Creek and Cherokee tribes have not yet been published in notices. In addition, an official at BOR's Great Plains Regional Office stated that, even though the office had listed culturally affiliated human remains in its inventory, National NAGPRA rejected the inventory in the 1990s because it was not properly formatted. The BOR official stated that resources have not been available to revise the inventory and publish the required notices.

National NAGPRA and the Makah Indian tribe, with the National Association of Tribal Historic Preservation Officers, have conducted studies to identify culturally affiliated human remains and associated funerary objects listed in agency NAGPRA inventories but for which no notices of inventory completion have been published. However, our analysis has shown that none of these studies has been comprehensive and complete. National NAGPRA is currently in the process of reconciling all the inventories submitted with its electronic database in order to determine which culturally affiliated human remains and associated funerary objects have not been included in a notice of inventory completion. Program officials expect this effort to be completed by October 2010. Until federal agencies have published notices of inventory completion in the *Federal Register* for culturally affiliated human remains and associated funerary objects that they have listed in inventories, items cannot be repatriated according to the provisions of NAGPRA. Although National NAGPRA will have more information on the level of compliance by federal agencies from the reconciliation of data, this may not lead to improved compliance because NAGPRA and its implementing regulations do not provide National NAGPRA or any other federal office with authority to ensure federal agency compliance with the act. See appendix III for a discussion of NAGPRA enforcement.

Federal Agencies Identified a Number of Challenges That Inhibit Their Efforts to Comply with NAGPRA

Officials with the eight agencies that we reviewed identified a number of challenges that their agencies have faced in complying with NAGPRA. First and foremost, officials at all of the eight key federal agencies that we spoke with and a December 2009 Interior Inspector General report all noted that the lack of funding is one of the most significant challenges to complying with NAGPRA. Officials noted that without funding, their cultural resources management programs have not been adequately staffed to comply with NAGPRA. For example, BIA has one curator for the estimated 5.7 million items in its collections across the entire agency, and FWS's Service Archaeologist estimated that it would cost $35 million and take 28 years to properly review all of FWS's historical collections for NAGPRA items. Second, NAGPRA compliance for historical collections is generally a collateral duty among all the other tasks that agency cultural resource staff must perform, including section 3 NAGPRA responsibilities for new intentional excavations and inadvertent discoveries.[42] Officials at almost all of the eight agencies we reviewed confirmed that compliance with sections 5 and 6 of NAGPRA for historical collections is a collateral duty for most federal agency staff that work in this area. For example, BLM staff stated that their state archaeologists prioritize compliance with section 3 of NAGPRA, section 106 of the National Historic Preservation Act,[43] and the National Environmental Policy Act.[44] Even the national-level NAGPRA coordination staff at many agencies, such as BLM, BOR, FWS, and BIA, told us that they do not spend the majority of their time on NAGPRA compliance. Third, as discussed earlier, poor curation practices by agencies and repositories, in general, along with poor historical records and documentation, have also made NAGPRA compliance a challenge.

THE REVIEW COMMITTEE HAS MONITORED COMPLIANCE WITH NAGPRA IMPLEMENTATION, MADE RECOMMENDATIONS WITH MIXED SUCCESS, AND CONTINUES TO FACE CHALLENGES

To fulfill its responsibilities under NAGPRA, the Review Committee has monitored federal agency and museum compliance, made recommendations to improve implementation, and assisted the Secretary in the development of regulations. While the Review Committee's recommendations to facilitate the resolution of disposition requests involving culturally unidentifiable human remains have generally been implemented, recommendations to facilitate the resolution of disputes over the disposition of NAGPRA items have generally not been fully implemented. Moreover, some actions recommended by the Committee have exceeded NAGPRA's scope and, until recently, letters from the Designated Federal Officer informing parties of the Committee's recommendations did not clearly indicate whether the Secretary of the Interior had concurred with the Committee's recommendations after an independent assessment of the disposition request. In addition, the Review Committee has faced a number of challenges, in trying to effectively fulfill its role under the act.

The Review Committee Has Monitored Compliance with NAGPRA Implementation and Made Recommendations with Mixed Success

As part of its role in implementing NAGPRA, the Review Committee has (1) undertaken various activities, such as monitoring compliance with the act; (2) made recommendations on the disposition of culturally unidentifiable human remains; and (3) made recommendations on disputes.

The Review Committee Has Undertaken Various Activities in Its Role under NAGPRA

The Review Committee has undertaken various activities and provided information and advice to the Secretary and Congress on a wide range of NAGPRA issues:

- *Monitoring compliance*. Since its first meeting in 1992, the Review Committee has monitored agency and museum efforts to comply with NAGPRA using data provided by National NAGPRA and from status reports presented by agency, museum, and tribal representatives at Review Committee meetings. National NAGPRA has provided periodic information to the Review Committee on the quantity of agency and museum submissions of summaries, inventories, and publications in the *Federal Register*. Also in two meetings in the late 1990s, the Review Committee heard reports from representatives of more than 13 federal departments and agencies about their efforts to comply with NAGPRA's requirements, consult with Indian tribes, and determine the cultural affiliation of human remains and objects. Officials from some agencies and museums, including NPS and the Forest Service have also regularly attended Review Committee meetings and provided updates on their efforts. The Review Committee has used this information in its annual reports to Congress and has noted that federal agency efforts to comply with NAGPRA have been uneven, complex to measure, and lacking in transparency.
- *Making recommendations to Congress.* In its annual reports to Congress, the Review Committee has recommended several amendments to NAGPRA but none have been enacted to date. For example, first, in its annual reports covering 2002 through 2008, the Review Committee recommended that Congress amend the definition of the term "Native American" to add the words "or was" so that the definition would read: "Native American means of, or relating to, a tribe, people or culture that is, *or was*, indigenous to the United States." [Emphasis added] The members wanted this change made in response to a court case.[45] While legislation has been introduced that would make this change, it has not yet been enacted. Similarly, in its annual reports to Congress covering 1995 through 2001, the Review Committee recommended that Congress amend NAGPRA to include language that would protect Native graves on state or private lands from grave robbing and destructive activities. An amendment adding this language to NAGPRA has not yet been enacted. Finally, to help eliminate some of the barriers to NAGPRA implementation, the Review Committee has made recommendations to Congress about appropriating funding for federal agencies, Indian tribes, Native Hawaiian organizations, and museums to implement the act's requirements.
- *Assisting in the development of regulations.* The Review Committee has assisted in developing regulations to implement NAGPRA. In its early years, the Review Committee, in conjunction with Interior's Office of the Solicitor spent substantial amounts of time developing the main rule. After assisting with the main rule, in 1997, the Review Committee turned its attention to providing input into the rule addressing the disposition of culturally unidentifiable human remains (see app. IV for a discussion of this rule), and in 2002 to the rules addressing civil penalties for noncompliant museums, and the future applicability rule for newly recognized tribes and other situations.

Most Review Committee Recommendations on the Disposition of Culturally Unidentifiable Human Remains Were Implemented, but Some Actions Recommended Exceeded NAGPRA's Scope

Through fiscal year 2009, the Review Committee has made recommendations to the Secretary on 61 disposition requests for culturally unidentifiable human remains. We found that 52, or about 85 percent, of the Committee's disposition recommendations had been fully implemented by the parties after the Secretary concurred with the Committee's recommendation.[46] Of the remaining 9 disposition recommendations, 3 have been partially implemented, 3 have been not implemented, and the status of 3 is unknown (see table 6). Twenty-two of the 61 requests involved federal agencies, and 19 of the 22, were fully implemented. Parties generally agreed in advance to their preferred manner of disposition and, in accordance with the regulations, came to the Review Committee to complete the process and obtain a final recommendation from the Secretary. The two most common recommendations made by the Review Committee were (1) disposition to a federally recognized tribe or group of tribes and (2) the need for additional consultation or documentation.

Table 6. Unresolved Cases of Culturally Unidentifiable Human Remains Brought before the Review Committee as of September 30, 2009

Year	Federal agency or museum	Review Committee recommendation[a]	Status of Review Committee recommendation
Partially implemented			
1997	Baylor University, Strecker Museum	Conduct additional consultation.	Museum attempted to consult with Indian tribe, but received no response.
1997	Henry County Historical Society, Indiana	Conduct additional consultation.	Museum attempted to consult with Indian tribes, but they indicated they were not interested in receiving the human remains.
1998	California Department of Parks and Recreation	Conduct additional consultation.	Museum attempted to consult with non- federally recognized Indian group, but received no response.
Not implemented			
1997	Oakland Museum, California[b]	Conduct additional consultation.	Museum did not attempt to conduct additional consultation with Indian tribes or non- federally recognized Indian groups.
1997	De Anza College, California[b]	Conduct additional consultation.	Museum did not attempt to conduct additional consultation with Indian tribes or non- federally recognized Indian groups.
1997	City of Santa Clara, California	Conduct additional consultation.	Museum determined that human remains were culturally affiliated to a non-federally recognized Indian group, but the human remains are still in the museum.

Table 6. (Continued)

Year	Federal agency or museum	Review Committee recommendation[a]	Status of Review Committee recommendation
Status unknown			
1995	Department of Defense, U.S. Army, Fort Hunter-Leggett	Disposition to non-federally recognized Indian group.	Current staff at agency not aware of status.
1997	Department of Energy, Fernald Site	Agency should retain human remains until identification of mechanism for disposition.	Site closed down and agency office reorganized.
1998	NPS, Fort Clatsop National Memorial	Solicitation of letters of support from federally recognized Indian tribe.	Agency staff stated that non-federally recognized Indian group affiliated with the NAGPRA items declined to work with federally recognized Indian tribes

Source: GAO analysis and museum and federal officials.

[a] Recommendations in this column relate directly to the recommended disposition of the NAGPRA items, and are not inclusive of all of the Committee's recommendations for these requests.

[b] Two requests where museums did not implement the Review Committee's recommendations—Oakland Museum, California, and De Anza College, California—involved the same collection of human remains.

Table 7. Review Committee Recommended Actions for Disposition of NAGPRA Items That Fell Outside the Scope of NAGPRA, 1994 through 2008

Date ranges for when the recommendations were made	Recommendation outside the scope of NAGPRA	Number NAGPRA items
Between 1994 and 2001	Repatriate culturally unidentifiable human remains to non- federally recognized Indian groups.[a]	387 human remains[b]
Between 1998 and 2008	Repatriate culturally unidentifiable human remains to non- federally recognized tribal entities, such as coalitions of tribes.[c]	156 human remains[b]
Between 1994 and 2006	Repatriate funerary objects associated with culturally unidentifiable human remains.[d]	29 associated funerary objects

Source: GAO analysis of Review Committee recommendations.

[a] In *Bonnichsen v. United States*, the district court noted that "a non-federally recognized band is not a proper NAGPRA claimant" and that the Secretary of the Interior had acknowledged that. 217 F. Supp. 2d 1116, 1141 (D. Or. 2002). *Accord* Castro Romero v. Becken, 256 F.3d 349 (5th Cir. 2001). *Cf.* Abenaki Nation of Mississquoi v. Hughes, 805 F. Supp. 234, 251 (D. Vt. 1992) (holding that Abenaki Nation, which is not a federally recognized tribe, meets the definition of "Indian tribe" under NAGPRA, but failing to address the statutory phrase *"which is recognized as eligible for special programs and services provided by the United States to Indians because of their status as Indians"* appearing in NAGPRA's definition of "Indian tribe").

[b] Human remains were counted using the "minimum number of individuals" method.

[c] In *Bonnichsen v. United States*, the district court noted that the Secretary of the Interior's conclusion that a coalition of tribes is a proper claimant contradicts the plain language of the statute, which identifies the appropriate recipient in the singular as the Indian tribe. 217 F. Supp. 2d 1116, 1141-2 (D. Or. 2002). The court noted that, although there may be instances in which two tribes both have valid claims, because, for example, they descended from the same

identifiable earlier group and have a shared group identity, under any circumstance, the claims of coalition members must be independently meritorious. *Id.*

[d] Interior has noted the statute's silence regarding culturally unidentifiable associated funerary objects.

In reviewing the recommendations made by the Review Committee, we noted that some of the actions recommended by the Review Committee were outside the scope of NAGPRA (see table 7). These recommendations were made prior to the new regulation on the disposition of culturally unidentifiable human remains.[47]

We found that the Review Committee recommended actions that fell outside the scope of NAGPRA for four primary reasons:

- Committee members were acting in accordance with the Review Committee's principles of agreement, which outline the criteria that members are to use when considering requests for disposition of culturally unidentifiable human remains.[48] According to former Review Committee members we spoke with, the principles of agreement stated that appropriate repatriation solutions included the return of human remains that were culturally unidentifiable for which there was a shared group identity with a non-federally recognized Indian group. The Review Committee had concluded that NAGPRA intended and did not prohibit funerary objects associated with culturally unidentifiable human remains from being repatriated.
- In instances where human remains were deemed culturally unidentifiable because they were culturally affiliated to non-federally recognized Indian groups, Review Committee members believed that it would be scientifically dishonest to recommend disposition to Native Americans not culturally affiliated with the human remains, thus they recommended dispositions to non-recognized Indian groups.
- Review Committee members recommended disposition of objects accompanying culturally unidentifiable human remains because they had heard from tribal representatives that it was culturally unacceptable to separate human remains from the objects buried with them.
- Some members lacked strong knowledge of the complexities of the law.

Although attorneys with Interior's Office of the Solicitor attend Review Committee meetings and provide legal advice, one attorney stated that the Solicitor's Office allowed Review Committee members wide leeway with regard to their recommendations because the Committee's recommendations are not binding.

Nevertheless, we found that the Review Committee has not recommended dispositions to a non-federally recognized Indian group since 2001, and the Review Committee, National NAGPRA, and Interior officials have generally addressed the issue of the Review Committee recommending actions that are outside the scope of NAGPRA. First, for the culturally unidentifiable associated funerary objects, since 2008, letters from the Designated Federal Officer to the affected parties informing them of the Review Committee's recommendations have included the stipulation that NAGPRA does not authorize disposition of these objects. The letters state that a federal agency or museum may choose to repatriate such objects under other authorities they may have. Under the recently issued rule on the disposition of culturally unidentifiable human remains, agencies may repatriate these objects if state or federal law does not preclude it. Further, an attorney with Interior's Office of the Solicitor reported advising the Review Committee of this in the late 1990s. Second, according to National NAGPRA officials, since the fall of 2008, the Designated Federal Officer has requested that all parties seeking Review Committee consideration describe the issue that they wish to present. The officer reports using this information to help determine what type of issue is being presented and whether the issue is outside the scope of NAGPRA and therefore ineligible for consideration. In addition, with regard to tribal coalitions, attorneys with Interior's Office of the Solicitor told us that they believe NAGPRA authorizes repatriations to coalitions of tribes as long as agency or museum records indicate that actual repatriation was made to a federally recognized tribe.

We also found that, through January 2007, letters from the Review Committee's Designated Federal Officer to the parties receiving a recommendation did not clearly indicate whether the Secretary of the Interior's recommendation was the result of an independent assessment of the facts, NAGPRA, and the Review Committee's recommendations. The importance of whether the Secretary's recommendation is the result of Interior's independent assessment of the request is two-fold. First, the Review Committee is advisory and its recommendations cannot bind the Department or the parties. Second, NAGPRA regulations require that agencies and museums retain possession of culturally unidentifiable human remains pending promulgation of an applicable regulation, unless legally required to do otherwise, or recommended to do otherwise by the Secretary.[49] An attorney with Interior's Office of the Solicitor confirmed to us that the Secretary's recommendation reflects Interior's independent assessment of the disposition requests for culturally unidentifiable human remains, and the Review Committee's recommendations. However, we found that letters sent between 1994 and January 2007 did not clearly state that the Secretary had considered the facts or whether the Secretary had independently assessed the requests in concurring with the Review Committee recommendation. Letters sent since January 2007 have clarified the Secretary's independent assessment of and concurrence with the Review Committee's recommendations and in two cases stated that Interior disagreed in part with the Review Committee's recommendation and did not recommend disposition.[50]

Few Review Committee Recommendations on Disputes Were Fully Implemented

In contrast to the amicable nature of disposition requests, disputes are generally contentious and the Review Committee's recommendations have had a low implementation rate. Through the end of fiscal year 2009, the Review Committee had considered 12 disputes brought by Indian tribes and Native Hawaiian organizations—three against federal agencies and nine against museums. We found agencies and museums usually did not implement some elements of the recommendations in disputes. In particular, the Review Committee recommended four times that agencies and museums revise the cultural affiliation of human remains or the classification of objects, but these recommendations were never implemented. Of the 12 disputes that we reviewed, the Review Committee's recommendations were fully implemented for 1 dispute, partially implemented in 3 others, not implemented for 5, and the status of 3 cases is unknown. Furthermore, three of these cases have resulted in lawsuits, which further illustrates the Review Committee's difficulties in fulfilling its statutory responsibility to facilitate the resolution of disputes. See appendix V for more information on the status of the Review Committee's recommendations on the 12 disputes.

The Review Committee Faces a Number of Challenges in Fulfilling Its Responsibilities under NAGPRA

According to officials of museums and scientific organizations, the Review Committee and its annual reports, the Committee has faced a number of challenges in fulfilling its NAGPRA responsibilities. These challenges fall into the following four categories:

- *Perception that the Review Committee favors tribal interests.* Officials from museums and scientific organizations and some Committee members themselves that we spoke with said that the Review Committee favors tribal interests over the interests of the museum and scientific community. This has led some to question the Committee's objectivity. One official representing a museum that had previously been a party to a dispute considered by the Review Committee stated that she considered engaging with the Committee as one of the least preferred methods to achieve resolution on NAGPRA issues because of the perceived lack of balance. At the same time, some Committee members told us that the Review Committee acknowledges there may be some bias and regarded it as understandable because they believe the intent of NAGPRA was to serve Native American interests and overcome years of bias against tribal interests by museums and scientific organizations. Regardless, the issue of the Review Committee's actual and perceived objectivity is a concern because it could impact the Review Committee's ability to carry out its responsibilities. We have previously reported that to be effective, federal advisory committees must be—and, just as importantly, be perceived as—independent and balanced as a whole.[51] If federal agencies and museums perceive the Review Committee as lacking objectivity and heavily favoring tribal interests, they may disengage from the process.
- *Lack of data on federal agency compliance.* In its annual reports to Congress from 2006 through 2009, the Review Committee has cited the lack of data on federal agency compliance as a significant challenge. From 2006 through 2009, the Review Committee regularly reported that the lack of data prevented it from assessing whether required consultations between Indian tribes and federal agencies were taking place. Further, in its annual report covering 2008, the Review Committee requested that Congress hold open hearings for agencies, as well as museums and tribes to provide the Review Committee and other stakeholders with more information on the challenges that NAGPRA practitioners have encountered. National NAGPRA officials noted that in addition to the biennial reports provided to the Review Committee on the status of NAGPRA compliance, National NAGPRA also produced a 2006 report on the status of Native American human remains in the control of federal agencies.[52]
- *Limited resources.* According to annual reports prepared by the Review Committee and Committee members that we spoke with, the Committee lacks the resources it

needs to effectively fulfill its responsibilities under NAGPRA. According to these sources, the Committee's travel budget only allows it to hold two face-to-face meetings per year; therefore, it is unable to devote the attention needed to adequately cover all the agenda items. Two Review Committee members also told us that given their busy schedules, they have limited time to review particularly voluminous documents for disposition requests and disputes.

- *Lack of administrative support provided by National NAGPRA.* Several current and former Review Committee members expressed dissatisfaction with the level of administrative support provided by National NAGPRA to the Committee. For example, some stated that National NAGPRA did not provide Review Committee members briefing packets in a timely manner. These materials are essential for the proper preparation of meeting activities, particularly for complex disputes and disposition requests.

National NAGPRA officials stated that they make efforts to provide the materials at least 15 days prior to the meeting. To accomplish this, they request that parties provide documents to National NAGPRA 30 days in advance, but, in some cases, presenters have come to the meetings with additional information that must then be provided to Committee members. In addition, two Committee members stated that in the past, National NAGPRA has been slow to reimburse the cost of travel to meetings, which has placed a financial burden on members.

NATIONAL NAGPRA HAS, IN SOME CASES, NOT EFFECTIVELY CARRIED OUT ITS RESPONSIBILITIES

National NAGPRA has taken several actions to help the Secretary carry out responsibilities under NAGPRA. Overall, while most of the actions performed by National NAGPRA were consistent with the act, we did identify concerns with a few actions. Specifically, National NAGPRA has promulgated a number of regulations to implement NAGPRA, but failed to meet the statutory deadline for promulgation. In addition, National NAGPRA has developed a list of Indian tribes for the purposes of carrying out NAGPRA, but at various point in the last 20 years the list has not been consistent with BIA's policy or a Solicitor legal opinion analyzing the status of Alaska Native villages as Indian tribes. Also, National NAGPRA has not always properly screened nominations for the Review Committee and, in 2004, 2005, and 2006, inappropriately recruited nominees for the Review Committee and, in one case, recommended the nominee to the Secretary for appointment.

National NAGPRA Has Taken Actions Consistent with the Act, such as Publishing Notices, Administering a Grants Program, and Supporting the Review Committee

National NAGPRA has taken a number of actions that are consistent with the act. For example, National NAGPRA has published federal agency and museum notices in the *Federal Register*; increasing this number in recent years while reducing a backlog of notices awaiting publication. Furthermore, it has administered a NAGPRA grants program that from fiscal years 1994 through 2009 has resulted in 628 grants awarded to Indian tribes, Native Hawaiian organizations, and museums totaling $33 million. Other actions include the development of publicly available databases and providing training and educations materials to NAGPRA practitioners. See appendix VI for more details on these activities.

Table 8. NAGPRA Regulations and Related Information Published in the *Federal Register*, as of April 2010

Action	Date of publication in the *Federal Register*	*Federal Register* citation
Main rule		
Notice of proposed rulemaking	May 28, 1993	58 Fed. Reg. 31122
Final rule	Dec. 4, 1995	60 Fed. Reg. 62134
Correcting amendments to final regulations	Aug. 1, 1997	62 Fed. Reg. 41292
Final rule; technical amendment	Sept. 30, 2005	70 Fed. Reg. 57177
Correcting amendment	Apr. 3, 2006	71 Fed. Reg. 16500
Civil penalties for noncompliant museums		
Interim rule	Jan. 13, 1997	62 Fed. Reg. 1820
Final rule	Apr. 3, 2003	68 Fed. Reg. 16354
Rule regarding future applicability following statutory deadlines for summary and inventory completion		
Proposed rule	Oct. 20, 2004	69 Fed. Reg. 61613
Final rule	Mar. 21, 2007	72 Fed. Reg. 13184
Disposition of culturally unidentifiable human remains[a]		
Draft Review Committee recommendations	June 20, 1995	60 Fed. Reg. 32163
Draft Review Committee recommendations	Aug. 20, 1996	61 Fed. Reg. 43071
Draft principles of agreement	June 23, 1999	64 Fed. Reg. 33502
Draft principles of agreement	July 29, 1999	64 Fed. Reg. 41135
Review Committee recommendations	June 8, 2000	65 Fed. Reg. 36462
Proposed rule	Oct. 16, 2007	72 Fed. Reg. 58582
Final rule with request for comments[b]	Mar. 15, 2010	75 Fed. Reg. 12378

Source: Federal Register.

[a] In addition to these actions published in the Federal Register, according to the preamble for the final regulation on the disposition of culturally unidentifiable human remains, the Review Committee also (1) sent comments to the Secretary of the Interior on the issue in 2000, 2003, and 2008; (2) considered drafts of the proposed rule at its May 31-June 2, 2002, and November 8-9, 2002, meetings; and (3) reviewed the actual proposed rule at its January 8, 2008, teleconference. 75 Fed. Reg. 12378 (Mar. 15, 2010).

[b] The rule became effective on May 14, 2010.

National NAGPRA, primarily through the Review Committee's Designated Federal Officer, has also assisted the Review Committee in several areas such as developing meeting agendas in concert with the Review Committee Chair and maintaining a list of culturally unidentifiable human remains.[53] To assist parties that wish to bring issues before the Review Committee, National NAGPRA staff have produced templates for needed documents that, according to agency officials, help the parties organize materials for the review, focus presentations before the Review Committee, and simplify committee actions. Other activities have included publishing *Federal Register* notices of upcoming Review Committee meetings, issuing letters conveying Review Committee recommendations to affected parties, and providing logistical support to Review Committee members, such as reimbursing their travel expenses to attend Review Committee meetings. National NAGPRA has also administered the nomination process for Review Committee members.[54]

Some Actions Taken by National NAGPRA Raise Concerns

We have concerns with (1) the time frames in which the regulations have been promulgated and the inclusion of ANCSA corporations as Indian tribes in National NAGPRA's list of Indian tribes for the purposes of carrying out NAGPRA at various points in the last 20 years, and (2) the screening of Review Committee nominations and questionable recruiting practices.

National NAGPRA Was Late in Promulgating NAGPRA Regulations and Treats ANCSA Corporations as "Indian Tribes" Contrary to BIA Policy and a Solicitor Legal Opinion

As shown in table 8, National NAGPRA has promulgated regulations to implement NAGPRA in four main sections. While section 13 of NAGPRA required the Secretary to promulgate regulations within 12 months of the law's enactment, the main body of the regulations was not published in final form until December 4, 1995; several years after the statutory deadline. Also, the regulations were not effective until January 3, 1996, which was after the 1993 and 1995 deadlines for the completion of summaries and inventories, respectively.

In addition, National NAGPRA must still promulgate regulations for two remaining sections—disposition of unclaimed human remains, funerary objects, sacred objects, or objects of cultural patrimony (section 10.7) and failure to claim where no repatriation or disposition has occurred (section 10.15(b)). Furthermore, according to agency officials, National NAGPRA plans to revisit the NAGPRA regulations in their entirety, opening them up for public comment. However, the officials could not provide us with specific dates for when these additional rulemaking activities would occur.

In accordance with the regulations, National NAGPRA developed a list of Indian tribes for the purposes of carrying out NAGPRA that includes federally recognized tribes and, at various point in the last 20 years, ANCSA corporations. National NAGPRA's inclusion of ANCSA corporations in its list of Indian tribes does not appear to be consistent with Interior's legal and policy positions regarding the status of Alaska Native villages and ANCSA corporations. Specifically, the inconsistency stems from the inclusion of village, regional, group, and urban corporations established pursuant to ANCSA that are not on BIA's list of federally recognized Indian tribes or the modified ANCSA list of Alaska Native villages.

NAGPRA's enactment and National NAGPRA's original development of the list of Indian tribes for the purpose of carrying out NAGPRA coincided with an ongoing debate within Interior about the status of ANCSA corporations. Although BIA currently does not recognize any of the ANCSA corporations as eligible for the special programs and services provided by the United States to Indians because of their status as Indians, at various times they have been included in BIA's list of federally recognized tribes. For example, in 1982—the first time Alaska Native entities were included in the BIA list—the ANCSA corporations were excluded because they are not governments. However, the 1988 BIA list included ANCSA corporations, raising a number of questions with respect to the effects of the list, as BIA later recognized. After a 1993 legal opinion by the Solicitor that concluded that ANCSA corporations do not qualify as Indian tribes for the purposes of federal law,[55] BIA published a revised list in 1993 that did not include any ANCSA corporations. Subsequent lists also have not included ANCSA corporations. Accordingly, BIA has not recognized and does not treat ANCSA corporations as federally recognized tribes.[56]

Moreover, none of the ANCSA corporations are included in the modified ANCSA list of Alaska Native villages. The Solicitor has noted that a number of post-ANCSA statutes, such as NAGPRA, have included Alaska Native villages within their definition of Indian tribe by reference to the ANCSA definition of Native village and that these references are to this modified ANCSA list. Therefore, the inclusion of ANCSA corporations in National NAGPRA's list is at odds with the Solicitor's legal position that the Alaska Native villages on the modified ANCSA list are Indian tribes for purposes of federal law. Under this interpretation, the inclusion of Alaska Native villages in NAGPRA's definition of Indian tribe refers to the villages on the modified ANCSA list that were subsequently included in BIA's list of federally recognized tribes and not the ANCSA corporations.

However, because National NAGPRA's list of Indian tribes for purposes of carrying out NAGPRA has included ANCSA corporations, at various times over the past 20 years, the office as well as other federal agencies and museums, have considered them eligible to make nominations for Review Committee positions, receive NAGPRA grants, and request repatriation of NAGPRA items.

National NAGPRA Has Not Always Properly Screened Review Committee Nominations and Has Engaged in Questionable Recruiting Practices

We found that in its administration of the Review Committee nomination process, National NAGPRA has not always properly screened nominees to ensure that they were nominated by one of the required entities specified in NAGPRA. During the first several rounds of nominations, we found numerous instances of this. For example, in 1991, National NAGPRA forwarded to the Secretary the names of a number of nominees that were submitted by ineligible entities, such as individual university staff members, tribal consortia, a non-profit organization, and a federal agency official. We identified similar, albeit fewer, problems in the 1996 and 2000 nominating rounds. As a result of this improper screening, the Secretary has appointed members who were nominated by ineligible entities several times since 1991.

National NAGPRA has taken steps to improve the screening process. For example, in its April 2002 *Federal Register* notice soliciting nominations, National NAGPRA included the requirements for both nominators and nominees and required submission of additional information with nominations.[57] Specifically, the notice required (1) nominations submitted by Indian tribes or Native Hawaiian organizations to be signed by the leader of the tribe or organization and (2) that traditional religious leaders making nominations identify themselves as such. It also clearly stated that nominations from other individual tribal members could not be considered. Also, beginning in 2002, National NAGPRA began to confirm the status of

Native American traditional religious leaders, both as nominators and nominees, by contacting both sources to verify this information. The June 2003 nomination notice further required that nominations from Indian tribes or museum and scientific organizations include a statement indicating that the official is authorized to make the nomination.[58] Moreover, it required that nominations from traditional Native American religious leaders include a statement by the nominator that the nominee is a traditional Native American religious leader. The August 2006 nomination notice further required that the nominator explain how he or she meets the definition of traditional religious leader.[59]

Despite National NAGPRA's efforts to improve the screening process, some issues still remain. For example, two nominees forwarded to the Secretary recently were nominated by ineligible individuals or entities. In the first case, an individual was nominated by a tribe's director of cultural resources and the nomination letter did not include a statement that the director was authorized by the tribe to make the nomination. This individual was appointed by the Secretary and currently serves on the Review Committee. After we brought this issue to their attention, National NAGPRA officials contacted the tribe and obtained an official letter from the chairman of the tribe supporting the individual's nomination. In the other case, a nomination was made by a non-federally recognized tribe. Interior officials confirmed that nominations must be submitted by a federally recognized tribe. Again, we alerted National NAGPRA to this issue, and officials responded that although the individual's name was on the list sent to the Secretary, he was not actually considered because he was not eligible.

In addition to its lack of adequate screening of nominating entities, National NAGPRA has also bypassed the nomination process by essentially making its own nominations. In one case in 2004, National NAGPRA actively recruited a nominee and the nominee accepted the offer 6 months after the deadline for submitting nominations had passed. National NAGPRA then sought and received permission from a nominating entity to use a 7-year-old nomination for the current nominating round even though the entity had already nominated a different individual in response to the solicitation. The Secretary appointed the individual recruited and recommended by National NAGPRA. According to an Interior official involved in this recruitment effort, National NAGPRA became involved in recruiting efforts because the *Federal Register* solicitations had garnered an inadequate pool of nominees,[60] and some National NAGPRA officials believed that the Review Committee had become too weighted toward the interests of the museum and scientific communities and was seeking an individual more favorable to tribal interests. In addition to this case, we identified two other instances in 2005 and 2006 where National NAGPRA recruited nominees. Both were appointed to the Review Committee. The National NAGPRA Program Manager pointed out that in these latter two instances, the nominees initiated the contact and pursued the position.

The lack of adequate screening and recruitment issues surrounding the nomination process has damaged the credibility of both National NAGPRA and the Review Committee and has contributed to the perception of a lack of objectivity cited by some museum officials and Review Committee members that we interviewed. For example, several Review Committee members said that the appointment process is not transparent and fair and some, referred to it as a "black box" because they are not aware of what happens to nominations once they are submitted to National NAGPRA. The National NAGPRA Program Manager clarified that current policy is to collect and forward all of the nomination submissions, to the NPS Policy Office and subsequently to the Secretary of the Interior for further review.

Table 9. Human Remains and Associated Funerary Objects Repatriated for Notices of Inventory Completion Published as of September 30, 2009

Agency	Human remains published in notices[a]	Human remains repatriated[a]	Percentage	Associated funerary objects published in notices	Associated funerary objects repatriated	Percentage
Agency reported data[b]						
Forest Service	5,246	796	15.17	33,618	16,464	48.97
NPS	4,053	3,416	84.28	77,927	37,823	48.54
Corps of Engineers	722	623	86.29	40,869	40,340	98.71
GAO survey data[c]						
Department of the Navy	3,397	1,802	53.05	7,734	7,127	92.15
BLM[d]	1,565	1,056	67.48	16,615	14,237	85.69
BOR	550	550	100.00	3,330	3,327	99.91
BIA	464	443	95.47	9,621	9,609	99.88
FWS	127	63	49.61	626	246	39.30
U.S. Army[e]	105	103	98.10	1,557	1,551	99.61
U.S. Air Force	38	29	76.32	85	61	71.76
National Museum of Health and Medicine	16	10	62.50	0	0	0
Department of Justice[f]	9	2	22.22	2	1	50.00
Department of Energy	6	6	100.00	1,340	1,340	100.00
Department of Homeland Security	2	2	100.00	0	0	0
Indian Arts and Crafts Board	2	0	0	0	0	0
Total	**16,302**	**8,901**	**54.60**	**193,324**	**132,126**	**68.34**

Source: Corps, Forest Service, and NPS databases and agency responses to GAO survey.

Note: The TVA and the Environment Protection Agency have not published any notices of inventory completion so they are not included in this table. The table also does not include any repatriations that federal agencies may have performed prior to the enactment of NAGPRA or for new or inadvertent discoveries and intentional excavations under section 3 of NAGPRA. For example, TVA reported that it repatriated 137 sets of human remains from the Tellico project prior to NAGPRA's enactment.

[a] Human remains are counted using the "minimum number of individuals" approach. The minimum number of individuals refers to the fewest possible number of people in a skeletal assemblage. This is often used in forensic anthropology and osteology to determine an estimate of how many individuals are represented in a cluster of bones. While there are formulae that can be applied to determining the minimum number of individuals, making this determination is essentially based on logic. Counts of the minimum number of individuals are based on age, sex, and repeat skeletal elements. For example, if there are three right humerus bones, that implies there were at least three individuals. If those all three happen to be male, and there is a clearly female skull, then that adds one more individual to the count. A count of one could be for a complete skeleton of over 200 bones or one fragment of a bone from one individual.

[b] These three agencies provided consolidated agencywide data on repatriations.

[c] We surveyed four of the eight key agencies that did not have consolidated repatriation data, as well as eight other federal agencies that had published notices of inventory completion. We did not survey TVA as it had not published any notices of inventory completion through fiscal year 2009.

[d] BLM's California State Office survey response reported repatriating 18 unassociated funerary objects listed in a notice of inventory completion. These were not counted in our analysis because this type of object did not belong in an inventory.

[e] The U.S. Army survey response for Fort Kamehameha, Hawaii, reported 83 more human remains repatriated than the 9 that were published in the notice of inventory completion. An Army official explained that 82 human remains were actually excavated or discovered since November 16, 1990, NAGPRA's date of enactment. We deducted 82 from the total repatriated because they were returned under section 3 of NAGPRA and 1 other because it was not in a corrected notice.

[f] The Department of Justice's Federal Bureau of Investigation office in Louisville, Kentucky, did not respond to our survey with regard to two published notices that included five human remains and one associated funerary object.

Many NAGPRA Items Have Been Repatriated, but Repatriations Are Not Tracked or Reported Governmentwide

According to agency data and our survey results, a total of 55 percent of human remains and 68 percent of associated funerary objects have been repatriated as of September 30, 2009. While agencies are required to permanently document their repatriations, they are not required to compile and report that information to anyone. Of the federal agencies that have published notices of inventory completion, only three have tracked and compiled agencywide data on their repatriations. These three agencies, however, along with other federal agencies that have published notices of inventory completion, do not regularly report comprehensive data on their repatriations to National NAGPRA, the Review Committee, or Congress. Agency officials identified several reasons why some human remains and associated funerary objects have not been repatriated, including a lack of a repatriation request from a culturally affiliated entity, repatriation requests from disputing parties, a lack of reburial sites, and a lack of financial resources to complete the repatriation. Federal agencies have also published 78 notices of intent to repatriate covering 34,234 unassociated funerary objects, sacred objects, or objects of cultural patrimony.

Agencies Have Repatriated 67 Percent of Culturally Affiliated NAGPRA Items, but Repatriations Are Not Tracked or Reported on a Governmentwide Basis

Federal agencies reported repatriating 141,027 of the 209,626 NAGPRA items published in their notices of inventory completion, or 67 percent, as of the end of fiscal year 2009. The repatriation rates by agency ranged from 0 percent to 100 percent and they represent 55 percent of the human remains and 68 percent of the associated funerary objects in federal agencies' notices of inventory completion, according to agency reported data and our survey results (see table 9).[61]

Of the eight key agencies we reviewed, the Forest Service and FWS had the lowest repatriation rates for human remains among the key agencies with published notices of inventory completion. In addition, through fiscal year 2009, TVA has not published any notices of inventory completion and as a result, it has not repatriated any Native American human remains or associated funerary objects.

One of NAGPRA's purposes was to set up a process by which federal agencies and museums receiving federal funds would inventory their holdings and work with culturally affiliated Indian tribes and Native Hawaiian organizations to repatriate certain Native American human remains and objects in their historical collections. However, as noted in the data above only three of the eight key agencies with significant historical collections presently consolidate agencywide data on the extent of their repatriations. In addition, as they are not required to do so, these agencies and others generally do not regularly report comprehensive repatriation data by notice to National NAGPRA, the Review Committee, or Congress.[62] Therefore, policymakers do not have an overall sense of how federal agency repatriation of NAGPRA items is progressing. Similarly, Indian tribes and Native Hawaiian organizations do not have readily available information on which human remains and objects have been culturally affiliated with them but have not been repatriated. Regulations implementing NAGPRA require that federal agencies and museums must permanently document the content and recipients of all repatriations, but do not require museums and agencies to compile these data and make them available to the public or to National NAGPRA.

Because neither National NAGPRA nor the Review Committee receive this information, they cannot include it in their annual reports. Without repatriation data, we believe that National NAGPRA, the Review Committee, and Congress are lacking valuable information on the progress of NAGPRA implementation toward the overall goal of returning control of human remains and objects to affiliated groups.

The 2008 report on NAGPRA implementation by the Makah Indian tribe and the National Association of Tribal Historic Preservation Officers found that Congress has no means of periodically assessing the effectiveness of NAGPRA implementation. The report recommended that federal agencies and National NAGPRA compile information on all completed repatriations reported by agencies and that National NAGPRA develop a database to hold this information.

National NAGPRA has started a "Culturally Affiliated Native American Inventories Database," which is to provide a snapshot on the current status of human remains and associated funerary objects that have been culturally affiliated as a result of consultation with Indian tribes and Native Hawaiian organizations. National NAGPRA reports that all the human remains and objects that are eventually listed in this database should be represented in a notice of inventory completion. National NAGPRA reported that the database was 75 percent complete as of April 1, 2010, and expected it to be fully populated by summer 2010. Completion of the database would provide reports on the minimum number of individuals culturally affiliated but not yet in notices. Because data on completed repatriations of culturally affiliated remains and objects are already being documented by federal agencies, and National NAGPRA already tracks the number of human remains and objects listed in each notice, National NAGPRA staff told us that they could include the repatriation status of the items appearing in each inventory and notice in their database. National NAGPRA staff could collect voluntary repatriation data from all agencies to provide a consolidated report, but there were no specific plans or time frames for this.

Some NAGPRA Items Have Not Been Repatriated Due to a Lack of Tribal Requests, Tribal Disputes, and Availability of Reburial Sites

A total of 7,401 human remains and 61,198 associated funerary objects published in a notice of inventory completion had not been repatriated as of September 30, 2009. Repatriations did not occur for a variety of reasons.

The most common reason that repatriations did not occur is that the culturally affiliated Indian tribe(s) or Native Hawaiian organization(s) did not make a request for the return of the human remains and associated funerary objects, according to agency NAGPRA program officials and our survey results. For example, Forest Service NAGPRA staff told us that the most significant challenge to repatriations has been the lack of requests from culturally affiliated entities. They noted that tribes are often not prepared to deal with repatriation for a variety of reasons. In some cases, Forest Service, NPS, and tribal officials told us that tribes lack cultural protocols to deal with NAGPRA, and specific cultural protocols and new ceremonies need to be developed before a request or transfer of human remains and objects can be made. Responses to our survey of 12 agencies to obtain the repatriation status of human remains and associated funerary objects included in 147 notices of inventory completion show that the lack of a request from culturally-affiliated Indian tribes and Native Hawaiian organizations has prevented repatriations of human remains in 25 percent of the cases.

Another reason repatriations did not occur is because, in some cases, multiple competing repatriation requests were received, and the federal agency could not clearly determine which requesting party is the most appropriate. Section 7(e) of NAGPRA provides that in these situations the federal agency may retain the item until the requesting parties reach agreement on its disposition or the dispute is resolved under NAGPRA's provisions or in court.[63] For example, in a case involving human remains that represent approximately 1,400 individuals removed from the Tonto National Forest in Arizona, there is a disagreement among some of the culturally affiliated tribes over the place and manner of the final disposition of the human remains. According to the Forest Service, because this involves differing cultural views among culturally affiliated tribes, it is leaving the matter to the tribes to resolve. As a result, the repatriation cannot proceed until the disagreement is resolved.

Table 10. Reburial Policies for Eight Key Federal Agencies

Agency	Reburial policy	Source of policy	Effective date
BIA	BIA does not have a policy because the federal government holds the land in trust for the benefit of the tribal or individual Indian landowners, who make decisions about reburial on their lands. BIA reported it does not play an active part in these decisions other than to ensure that all landowners are in agreement with the reburial and that an appropriate environmental review is done, if necessary.	No written policy	Not applicable
BLM	Current guidance allows for NAGPRA materials encountered during the course of disturbance activities to be reburied as close as possible to the site. The guidance also states that reburial of NAGPRA items repatriated from BLM collections may be made on the public lands. This is a discretionary authority and reburial proposals are evaluated on a case-by-case basis.	BLM Instruction Memorandum No. 2007-002	Oct. 11, 2006
BOR	BOR does not allow burials on BOR facilities, lands, or water bodies.	43 C.F.R. § 423.28	Dec. 11, 2008
Corps of Engineers	A 2000 act allows the Secretary of the Army to identify and set aside areas at civil works projects for the reburial of Native American human remains, at federal expense, when the remains were discovered on project land initially.	Pub. L. No. 106-541, § 208 (2000), *codified at* 33 U.S.C. § 2338	Dec. 11, 2000
Forest Service	The Forest Service policy is to support, where appropriate, requests from Indian tribes or lineal descendants for reburial of human remains and objects on Forest Service lands. The Forest Service will provide an explanation to the affected Indian tribe or lineal descendent for any request that is denied.	Pub. L. No. 110-246, Subtitle B, § 8103 (2008), *codified at* 25 U.S.C. § 3053; and Forest Service Manual Interim Directive 1560-2009-1	June 18, 2008 (Law) and June 30, 2009 (Interim Directive)
FWS	There is no specific policy regarding reburials, but FWS said that its Compatibility Policy on the uses of a national wildlife refuge will allow reburials on a case-by-case basis.	FWS Compatibility Policy	Nov. 17, 2000
NPS	Reburial of Native American human remains in the same park unit from which they were removed may be permitted under current NPS policy.	Management Policies 2006, 5.3.4 and 6.3.8	Aug. 31, 2006

Table 10. (Continued)

Agency	Reburial policy	Source of policy	Effective date
TVA	TVA reported that it has no written policy on reburial of NAGPRA items on TVA land but it has entered into discussions with Indian tribes on the issue. TVA also noted that is has allowed the reburial of newly discovered or intentionally excavated NAGPRA items (section 3 of NAGPRA) to be reburied on federal land that it manages.	No written policy	Not applicable

Source: Documents from and interviews with each agency.

Table 11. Policies or Practices for Funding Tribal Repatriation and Reburial Expenses by Eight Federal Agencies for Their Historical Collections

Agency	Funding available?	Allowed purposes	Written policy, if any
BIA	Yes	• Case-by-case basis	No written policy
BLM	Yes	• Preparation and packaging of items being repatriated • Transportation of items being repatriated.	Multiple BLM instruction memoranda and handbooks
BOR	Yes	• BOR policy allows compensation of lineal descendants, tribes, and organizations for activities, such as consultation, that occur prior to repatriation.	Guidelines for Payment of Consultation Fees Relating to Native American Graves Protection and Repatriation Act, Aug. 7, 1995
Corps of Engineers	Yes	• Food and water in very limited situations. • Reimbursement of travel expenses when invited by the federal government to retrieve items or attend reburial ceremony. • Determination and preparation of burial site. • Access roads, grave markers, and security measures. • Preparation of remains.	Director of Civil Works Memorandum endorsed July 7, 2009, Northwestern Division Policy on "Costs Associated with Repatriation and Reburial"
Forest Service	Yes	• In all regions, except Region 3, the Forest Supervisors have the discretionary authority to cover tribal expenses for repatriations. In Region 3 the Regional Forester has the authority.	Forest Service Handbook 1509.13 - American Indian and Alaska Native Relations Handbook. Chapter 10 - Consultation With Tribes, Mar. 3, 2004
FWS	Yes	• Although there is no funding set aside for repatriation expenses, it may be available on a case-by-case basis by refuge managers. No formal policy or allowed purposes available.	None
NPS	Yes	• Tribal repatriation expenses, including consultation costs, covered whenever possible and as appropriate.	No written policy
TVA	No	• To date, TVA has not funded tribal expenses specifically for repatriations because they have not yet repatriated any items under NAGPRA.	None

Source: Documents from and interviews with officials from each agency.

The availability of an acceptable burial site is also an important reason why some repatriations were not completed promptly. This has been challenging, in part, due to the federal agencies' reburial policies on their lands, which have varied over time. Most of the key federal agencies that manage land where NAGPRA items were found currently have policies that allow the reburial of the remains and objects on the land they manage (see table 10). BOR does not allow reburial on land that it manages. Tribes have cited the lack of reburial sites as a challenge to repatriation.

The lack of financial resources may also prevent or delay repatriations. Repatriations may involve a variety of expenses, including preparing a reburial site, transporting the items from their present location to the reburial site, access roads, grave markers and security measures, preparation of remains, and travel expenses of tribal officials involved with the reburial. For example, officials from the Confederated Tribes of the Umatilla Reservation said that funding for repatriation work is their largest challenge. They said that one of the few sources of relief is National NAGPRA grants, but that these grants are difficult to get. The Caddo Nation historic preservation staff also told us that their office relies on federal grants to carry out NAGPRA repatriation work and said more funding is needed. In their 2008 report on NAGPRA implementation, the Makah Indian tribe and the National Association of Tribal Historic Preservation Officers recommended Congress provide more funding at the federal and tribal levels. They found that many Indian tribes or Native Hawaiian organizations do not have resources for training or repatriation activities. As previously mentioned, the Review Committee has also recommended additional funding for the grant program. The National NAGPRA program has awarded an average of $53,893 annually in repatriation grants to Indian tribes and Native Hawaiian organizations. On average about six tribes per year receive these grants to help with expenses associated with repatriating NAGPRA items from museums. Repatriation grants are not available to tribes for repatriations from federal agencies, according to National NAGPRA staff.

The key federal agencies that we reviewed had different policies on the extent to which they would fund repatriation expenses and reburial of items from their historical collections (see table 11). For example, the Corps' policy includes a specific list of allowed expenditures, while BIA and FWS have no formal policy but will fund some expenses on a case-by-case basis. BOR will fund only tribal activities, such as consultation, that occur prior to repatriation.

Federal Agencies Have Published 78 Notices of Intent to Repatriate Covering 34,234 Objects

As of the end of fiscal year 2009, federal agencies had published 78 notices of intent to repatriate in the *Federal Register* covering 34,234 objects—unassociated funerary objects, sacred objects, or objects of cultural patrimony (see table 12). An agency official said that almost all of these repatriations will proceed because, in accordance with NAGPRA, the notices are based on the summaries, the agency already had consulted and culturally affiliated the items, and that an Indian tribe or Native Hawaiian organization had made a repatriation claim prior to the publication of the notice of intent to repatriate. In some cases, where multiple groups are affiliated with the items, the groups must reach consensus on who will receive the items before the repatriation can proceed.

CONCLUSIONS

After passage of the act, many federal agencies faced a monumental task in trying to identify all of their NAGPRA items and culturally affiliating them, to the extent possible, within the statutory deadlines. The difficulty of the task was compounded at some agencies by overall poor management and oversight of their museum collections over the years. NAGPRA compliance was generally assigned to cultural resources staff as a collateral duty, and trying to resolve the status of an item that the agency may have had for over 100 years was frequently a low priority when weighed against more immediate deadlines. While the act authorizes the Secretary of the Interior to assess civil penalties against museums for noncompliance, no enforcement mechanism exists to ensure federal agency compliance except through litigation by private parties. Despite the fact that key federal agencies have now had almost 20 years to comply with the act, they still have not fully complied. Furthermore, it is difficult for policymakers to determine how much work the federal agencies have left to achieve full compliance because the agencies generally do not have an estimate of the remaining work nor their needs for staff and resources to complete their NAGPRA activities for their historical collections.

Table 12. Objects Included in Notices of Intent to Repatriate as of September 30, 2009

Agency	Number of notices of intent to repatriate	Unassociated funerary objects	Sacred objects	Objects of cultural patrimony	Total number of objects
Department of the Interior					
BIA	6	24,200	3	0	24,203
NPS	26	3,352	2,470	2	5,824
BLM	3	408	0	0	408
FWS	9	4	0	94	98
BOR	1	74	0	0	74
Indian Arts and Crafts Board	1	0	0	0	0
Subtotal	**46**	**28,038**	**2,473**	**96**	**30,607**
Department of Defense					
Corps of Engineers	6	339	0	0	339
U.S. Army	1	8	0	0	8
Subtotal	**7**	**347**	**0**	**0**	**347**
Forest Service	19	1,793	201	620	2,614
Department of Energy	4	343	296	0	639
Department of Justice	2	26	1	0	27
Total	**78**	**30,547**	**2,971**	**716**	**34,234**

Source: National NAGPRA database.

Note: TVA and other federal agencies have not published any notices of intent to repatriate for summary items—unassociated funerary objects, sacred objects, and objects of cultural patrimony—as of September 30, 2009.

In the cases where the federal agencies have completed inventories with culturally affiliated human remains and associated funerary items, much of the compliance work has already been accomplished. However, for a variety of reasons, over the years, the publication of notices of inventory completion for some of these items in the *Federal Register* did not occur. Until agencies publish notices of inventory completion for the remaining culturally affiliated human remains and associated funerary objects in the *Federal Register*, they cannot be repatriated.

NAGPRA's enactment and National NAGPRA's original development of the list of Indian tribes for the purpose of carrying out NAGPRA coincided with an ongoing debate within Interior about the status of ANCSA corporations. However, Interior's Solicitor has since clarified the status of the ANCSA corporations, and they are no longer on BIA's list of federally recognized tribes. Accordingly, the rationale for National NAGPRA continuing to include them as Indian tribes for the purpose of carrying out NAGPRA is unclear.

Because repatriation involves addressing both the interests of Native Americans who want the remains of their ancestors and their cultural and sacred objects returned to them and the scientific and research interests of museums, it is important that all sides continue to be fully engaged in the process and it is important that the Review Committee and National NAGPRA be viewed as objective, balanced, and fair. In setting up the Review Committee with three members nominated from each side, the act tried to balance the interests of Native Americans and museums. However, actions by National NAGPRA have fueled concerns about not only its but also the Review Committee's objectivity and transparency, especially through the inappropriate interference in the nomination process and failing to ensure that all the nominations considered for appointment meet the act's requirements.

In addition, data on repatriations are not centrally tracked and reported or readily available to affected Indian tribes and Native Hawaiian organizations. As a result, neither National NAGPRA nor the Review Committee can report this information in their annual reports to Congress. Without this information, policymakers cannot assess the overall effectiveness of the act. Furthermore, not making this information readily accessible to Indian tribes and Native Hawaiian organizations is an impediment to repatriation because a list of published items not yet repatriated would allow tribes to easily identify items that have been affiliated to them and allow them to request more information and, in turn, perhaps request repatriation.

RECOMMENDATIONS FOR EXECUTIVE ACTION

We are making the following five recommendations to improve NAGPRA implementation:

To enhance federal agency NAGPRA compliance, we recommend that the Secretaries of Agriculture, Defense, and the Interior, and the Chief Executive Officer of the Tennessee Valley Authority direct their cultural resource management programs to develop and provide to Congress

- a needs assessment listing specific actions, resources, and time needed to complete the inventories and summaries required by NAGPRA sections 5 and 6 for their historical collections; and
- a timetable for the expeditious publication in the *Federal Register* of notices of inventory completion for all remaining Native American human remains and associated funerary objects that have been culturally affiliated in inventories.

To clarify which entities are eligible under NAGPRA, we recommend that National NAGPRA, in conjunction with Interior's Office of the Solicitor, reassess whether ANCSA corporations should be considered as eligible entities for the purposes of carrying out NAGPRA given the Solicitor's opinion and BIA policy concerning the status of ANCSA corporations.

To improve the confidence in the Review Committee and its support among NAGPRA practitioners, we recommend the Secretary of the Interior direct National NAGPRA to strictly adhere to the nomination process prescribed in the act and, working with Interior's Office of the Solicitor as appropriate, ensure that all Review Committee nominations are properly screened to confirm that the nominees and nominating entities meet statutory requirements.

To provide policymakers with information to assess the overall effectiveness of the act and to provide Indian tribes and Native Hawaiian organizations readily accessible information on items that are available for repatriation, we recommend that the Secretaries of Agriculture, Defense, the Interior, and the Chief Executive Officer of the Tennessee Valley Authority direct their cultural resource management programs to report their repatriation data to National NAGPRA on a regular basis, but no less than annually, for each notice of inventory completion they have or will publish. Furthermore, National NAGPRA should make this information readily available to Indian tribes and Native Hawaiian organizations and the Review Committee should publish the information in its annual report to Congress.

APPENDIX I: OBJECTIVES, SCOPE, AND METHODOLOGY

This appendix details the methods we used to examine the implementation of the Native American Graves Protection and Repatriation Act (NAGPRA). We were asked to determine:

(1) the extent to which federal agencies have complied with NAGPRA's requirements for their historical collections;
(2) the activities taken by the Review Committee to fulfill its role under NAGPRA and what challenges, if any, it faces;
(3) the actions taken by National NAGPRA to fulfill its responsibilities under NAGPRA; and
(4) the extent to which federal agencies reported repatriating Native American human remains and objects.

We examined NAGPRA implementation in detail for eight federal agencies with significant historical collections: the Department of the Interior's Bureau of Indian Affairs (BIA), Bureau of Land Management (BLM), Bureau of Reclamation (BOR), U.S. Fish and

Wildlife Service (FWS), and the National Park Service (NPS); the U.S. Army Corps of Engineers (Corps); the Department of Agriculture's U.S. Forest Service; and the Tennessee Valley Authority (TVA). We reviewed NAGPRA and its implementing regulations in 43 C.F.R. Part 10 and the final rule on the disposition of culturally unidentified human remains published recently in the *Federal Register*.[64] For each agency we reviewed records on NAGPRA compliance, such as inventories, summaries, *Federal Register* notices, consultations, and agreements with Indian tribes or Native Hawaiian organizations, collection records and repatriation forms or letters, other correspondence, agency databases, if any, and the National NAGPRA database and paper files. To check the reliability of the data on published notices in the National NAGPRA database (officially called "NAGPRA 20"), we compiled this data into one table and compared it to actual notices of inventory completion and notices of intent to repatriate published in the *Federal Register*. Of the 419 notices contained in the table we created using NAGPRA 20 data, we found a small number of data entry errors that we corrected. This data provides the basis for overall statistics on the program and the universe of notices for which we needed to seek repatriation data because not all of the agencies involved tracked and reported it.

Considering that NAGPRA implementation happens at field locations around the country as well as at headquarters, we planned visits to some of these locations. We compiled a list of agency field locations with significant NAGPRA collections and activities. Based on these lists, we selected a judgmental sample of six areas for site visits that would allow us to visit as many of the key agencies as possible. Table 13 identifies the geographic areas and the levels of agency officials we met with in each location as well as tribal and museum officials.

In total we met with the national-level NAGPRA coordination staffs for each of the eight key agencies in our review, as well as staff with NAGPRA responsibilities at either regional, state, district, local, or field levels for the key agencies, as applicable. Because we selected a judgmental sample of locations to visit, the information we obtained during these visits may not be generalized to all federal agencies and jurisdictions across the country. However, because we selected a variety of locations, the information we obtained at these locations provided us with a good perspective on the actual NAGPRA implementation efforts by federal agencies.

During our review we interviewed officials from Indian tribes, tribal organizations, museums, and scientific organizations as well as current and former Review Committee members. During our interviews with these officials we asked questions regarding one or more of our objectives. During our review we maintained an open door policy and we accommodated any Indian tribe, museum, organization, or Review Committee member that wanted to meet with us or provide information in writing. As a result, our methodology was supplemented by meetings with additional Indian tribes, museums, and Review Committee members that approached us on an ad hoc basis. While we had specific discussion topics for each of these interviews related to one or more of our four objectives, we did not impose a limit on the topics that could be discussed. The interviews and visits for this review included:

Table 13. Types of Federal, Tribal, and Museum Officials That GAO Met with During Site Visits

Site visit location	Agencywide NAGPRA coordinator	Regional, district, or state-level staff	Local or field office staff	Tribal cultural resource management staff	Multi-tribe listening sessions	Museum officials
St. Louis, MO and Springfield, IL	Corps	Corps	None			✓
Knoxville, TN	TVA	None	None			✓
Albuquerque and Pecos, NM	Forest Service	Forest Service	Forest Service and NPS	✓	✓	
Denver area and Loveland, CO	NPS and BOR	BOR, BLM, and FWS	BOR			
Phoenix and Tucson, AZ	None	BIA, BLM, and NPS	Forest Service and BOR	✓	✓	✓
Portland, OR area and Centralia, WA	None	Corps, Forest Service, BLM, NPS, and FWS	Forest Service and NPS	✓	✓	

Source: GAO summary of site visit locations and meetings.

- We interviewed officials from Indian tribes and tribal organizations either in conjunction with on our site visits, in Washington, D.C., or by telephone, including, the Caddo Nation of Oklahoma, the Four Southern Tribes (Gila River Indian Community of the Gila River Indian Reservation, Arizona; Salt River Pima-Maricopa Indian Community of the Salt River Reservation, Arizona; Ak-Chin Indian Community of the Maricopa (Ak Chin) Indian Reservation, Arizona; and Tohono O'odham Nation of Arizona), the Navajo Nation of Arizona, New Mexico and Utah; the Santa Clara Pueblo of New Mexico; Big Pine Band of Owens Valley Paiute Shoshone Indians of the Big Pine Reservation, California; Pyramid Lake Paiute Tribe of the Pyramid Lake Reservation, Nevada; Seneca Nation of New York; Confederated Tribes of the Umatilla Reservation, Oregon; and the Western Apache NAGPRA Working Group (San Carlos Apache Tribe of the San Carlos Reservation, Arizona; Tonto Apache Tribe of Arizona, White Mountain Apache Tribe of the Fort Apache Reservation, Arizona; and the Yavapai-Apache Nation of the Camp Verde Indian Reservation, Arizona); the Affiliated Tribes of Northwest Indians; the Inter Tribal Council of Arizona, Inc.; the Morning Star Institute; the Native Association of Tribal Historic Preservation Officers; and the Native American Rights Fund.
- We visited nonfederal entities (museums) serving as repositories for federal archeological collections in Illinois (Illinois State Museum), Tennessee (Frank H. McClung Museum at the University of Tennessee), and Arizona (Arizona State Museum at the University of Arizona in Tucson, Arizona). In addition, we interviewed other officials from museums and scientific organizations either in conjunction with our site visits, in Washington, D.C., or by telephone, including the American Museum of Natural History in New York, New York; the Field Museum in Chicago, Illinois; the Phoebe A. Hearst Museum of Anthropology at the University of California in Berkeley, California; the Peabody Museum of Archaeology and Ethnology at Harvard University in Cambridge, Massachusetts; the Heard Museum in Phoenix, Arizona; the American Association of Physical Anthropologists; and the Society for American Archeology. Since the focus of our report was on federal agencies' implementation of NAGPRA, these interviews provided background information and we did not attempt to interview a representative sample of museum officials.
- We selected nine current and past members of the Review Committee for interviews through a network analysis based on four factors: (1) the entity that nominated them, (2) the length of their tenure on the Committee, (3) the period during which they served, and (4) whether they chaired the Committee. One of the selected members declined to be interviewed. We interviewed two additional members during the course of our review.

Also related to all four of our objectives, we reviewed our prior reports on agency archeological resource preservation, relevant Interior Inspector General reports, academic sources, and the 2008 report by the Makah Indian tribe and the National Association of Tribal Historic Preservation Officers on NAGPRA implementation. We also attended the Arizona State University conference "Repatriation at Twenty" in January 2010.

For our first objective, to determine the extent to which federal agencies have complied with their NAGPRA requirements for their historical collections, we obtained data from the

NAGPRA 20 database on the federal agencies' notices of inventories and summaries as published in the *Federal Register* notices through the end of fiscal year 2009. The database contained the dates that National NAGPRA received inventories and summaries from federal agencies and museums. To assess whether summaries and inventories were generally prepared on time by agencies we did the following. We determined that because the NAGPRA database did not contain the date that the documents were prepared, it was only partially useful for determining compliance with the statutory deadlines. Therefore, if the summaries and inventories were received by National NAGPRA before and near the statutory deadline, we determined that the documents had been completed in compliance with the act. We also reviewed agency files and interviewed agency officials in the eight key agencies involved in our review for information on timeliness. We used all of these sources to assess whether summaries and inventories were generally prepared on time by agencies.

We analyzed the NAGPRA 20 database for reliability and verified all of the database information on notices of inventory completion, notices of intent to repatriate, and corrections of this information contained in the database. In addition, we assessed the reliability of relevant fields in the tables for summaries and inventories in the database by electronically testing for obvious errors in accuracy and completeness, reviewing information about the data and the system that produced them, and interviewing National NAGPRA officials knowledgeable about the data. When we found logical inconsistencies in the data, we clarified these with National NAGPRA officials before conducting our analyses. We determined that the data were sufficiently reliable for the purposes of using several fields related to when agencies submitted inventories and summaries. However, we found the database to be unreliable for purposes of tracking culturally unidentifiable human remains and objects because the items entered into the culturally unidentifiable portion of the NAGPRA 20 database are not deleted when they are affiliated. Rather, in some cases, a notation is made in the notes field. We analyzed text recorded in the notes fields of the inventory data to assess whether human remains and objects listed as culturally unidentifiable had been culturally affiliated.

In addition to Inspector General, and other reports, we considered relevant reports identified in literature searches or recommended by NAGPRA experts, including a study by a National NAGPRA intern, the Corps' Mandatory Center for Expertise for the Curation and Management of Archeological Collections, several academic journal articles and other materials concerning the curation of archeological collections, NAGPRA implementation, and cultural resource management.

To track agency compliance with NAGPRA, we reviewed each agency's records at headquarters and the field, such as inventories, summaries, *Federal Register* notices, and other documents. On our site visits, we interviewed national, regional, state, and local agency staff about their implementation of NAGPRA, in particular about the procedures they followed to identify their historical NAGPRA collections, to determine their level of confidence with their identification of NAGPRA items in their archeological collections. Our analysis is based both on the testimonial evidence and documents from agencies supplemented by Inspector General reports. In addition, we interviewed selected tribal and museum officials for their views on these efforts.

In order to identify cases in which human remains and associated funerary objects that were culturally affiliated in agency inventories, but not yet published in *Federal Register* notices, we examined information from three sources: (1) the June 2008 report by the Makah

Indian tribe and the National Association of Tribal Historic Preservation Officers, (2) a report on the topic by a National NAGPRA intern, and (3) inventory data from NPS's "NAGPRA 20" database. We could not rely on National NAGPRA data alone because it was incomplete. We created a list of federal agency units mentioned in two or three of these reports, and then examined records at National NAGPRA offices, including the original inventories and published notices of inventory completion, to determine which units had in fact not published the relevant notices. In order to reduce the risk of undercounting, we examined the full agency-submitted inventories for each of the agency units listed in our examples. Through our analysis, we discovered that some agency units were listed erroneously in previous reports because of typing errors, or because the affiliated human remains had actually been correctly published in notices of intended disposition.[65]

To address our second objective to determine the actions taken by the Review Committee to fulfill its role under NAGPRA and the challenges it faces, we analyzed the Committee's annual reports to Congress, meeting minutes, and reports by National NAGPRA. We reviewed documentation outlining Review Committee policies and procedures including Review Committee charters. We reviewed the Federal Advisory Committee Act and regulations, and our prior reports on the topic to understand the Review Committee's role as a federal advisory committee.[66] We interviewed current and former Review Committee members and National NAGPRA officials to learn more about the Review Committee's activities and the extent and quality of the support provided by National NAGPRA. We attended two Review Committee meetings (Seattle, Washington, in May 2009, and Sarasota, Florida, in October 2009) and observed an online training course on the role of the Review Committee in February 2010.

To understand primary functions of the Review Committee—recommendations in cases of (1) requests for dispositions of culturally unidentifiable human remains and in (2) disputes—we reviewed files maintained by National NAGPRA on behalf of the Review Committee.

We reviewed *Federal Register* notices describing the Review Committee's findings of fact and recommendations with regard to these disputes and requests for disposition of culturally unidentifiable human remains. We interviewed officials with Interior's Office of the Solicitor and National NAGPRA about the role of the Review Committee on behalf of the Department of the Interior. With respect to dispositions, we examined letters from the designated federal officer informing interested parties of the Committee's recommendations to determine the extent of the department's independent review of and concurrence with the recommendations. Based on the sources above, we determined that for dispositions, the Review Committee issued distinct recommendations regarding particular culturally unidentifiable human remains in 61 cases. National NAGPRA reports that the Committee considered 66 requests related to culturally unidentifiable human remains as of September 30, 2009. National NAGPRA listed some of these requests with additional subparts because the Committee considered the facts of the request at more than one meeting. In one case, the Committee issued distinct recommendations for each of two subparts, so we counted that request as two cases. We reviewed all the requests and subparts and determined that the Committee issued distinct recommendations 67 times. To focus our analysis on requests related to the disposition of particular culturally unidentifiable human remains we excluded 6 requests from our analysis. In 2 of these, the Committee recommended approval of a protocol, and no particular culturally unidentifiable human remains were involved. In 3 of these, the

Committee deferred issuing a recommendation, and 1 request involved only objects (no human remains). Thus, we analyzed 61 cases where the Review Committee made distinct recommendations regarding the disposition of particular culturally unidentifiable human remains. We determined the status of Review Committee recommendations in disposition cases, and disputes by contacting officials with the involved museums and federal agencies, and reviewing documents they provided.

We identified challenges that the Review Committee faces and the perceptions of the Review Committee through interviews of current and former Review Committee members, officials from museum and scientific organizations, Indian tribes, and tribal organizations.

To address our third objective to determine the actions National NAGPRA has taken to facilitate federal agency implementation of NAGPRA, we reviewed the act and its implementing regulations for the duties assigned to National NAGPRA, as delegated to it by the Secretary of the Interior. We interviewed National NAGPRA staff, including the Program Manager and staff responsible for publishing notices, administering the Review Committee, running the grants program, and developing and maintaining National NAGPRA's databases. To learn more about Interior's decision to include Alaska Native corporations in the definition of Indian tribe, as provided for in the regulations, we interviewed staff from Interior's Office of the Solicitor, reviewed Review Committee meeting minutes and transcripts, and analyzed National NAGPRA's "List of Indian tribes for the purposes of carrying out NAGPRA and Native Hawaiian organizations that have appeared in notices." With regard to National NAGPRA's actions regarding the nomination process we reviewed files on the 14 times nominations were solicited for Review Committee openings since NAGPRA was enacted.[67]

We reviewed NPS budget justifications for the NAGPRA program as well as National NAGPRA annual reports. We reviewed a table developed by National NAGPRA that provided information on 79 draft notices withdrawn by museums (55) and federal agencies (24). We used this information, along with supporting documents, to determine the status of the 24 draft notices withdrawn by federal agencies. We obtained and reviewed data on the grants program and interviewed three grants panelists to understand the grants process. We determined that the grants data was sufficiently reliable to provide a table with key grants data over time by Indian tribe and museum, including numbers of applications submitted and awarded and the funding requested and awarded. We attended two online training courses (i.e., webinars) presented by National NAGPRA—one on notices provided in January 2010 and one on the Review Committee provided in February 2010—and discussed students' training evaluations with National NAGPRA staff to learn more about the training program. In addition, we attended the NAGPRA Basics day-long training sessions before the Review Committee's meeting in Seattle, Washington, (May 2009) and Sarasota, Florida, (October 2009). We reviewed information contained on the National NAGPRA Web site, including the various databases provided.

For our fourth objective to determine the extent to which federal agencies have reported repatriating Native American human remains and objects for notices of inventory completion published in the *Federal Register*, we obtained data from the three agencies that track their repatriations—the Corps, the Forest Service, and NPS. For the other five key federal agencies and others publishing NAGPRA notices of inventory completion, we determined that there were no readily available sources of data on their repatriations. We have examined the reliability of the data from the three agencies that reported on repatriations and the data from

National NAGPRA database. We interviewed agency staff that compiled the data on their methods and checks for accuracy to assess reliability of the data.

We deployed a survey asking contacts in four key agencies and eight other agencies with published notices that did not collect data about whether the number of human remains or associated funerary objects included in each notice of inventory completion had actually been repatriated through fiscal year 2009, and if not, why not. We did not survey TVA because they had not published any notices of inventory completion through fiscal year 2009. We sent initial notification emails to test e-mail addresses. We also notified agency contacts by e-mail on how to access the survey and asked for responses within 2 weeks. After the survey had been available for 2 weeks, we reminded respondents by e-mail to complete surveys, and followed the e-mail with personal phone calls beginning a few days later. Through these efforts we obtained a 99 percent response rate. Respondents filled in surveys on 145 of 147 published notices of inventory completion. Because this survey was not based on a sample, there were no sampling errors. However, the practical difficulties of conducting any survey may introduce errors, commonly referred to as non-sampling errors. For example, difficulties in how a particular question is interpreted, in the sources of information that are available to respondents, or in how the data were entered into a database or were analyzed can introduce unwanted variability into the survey results. We took steps in the development of the questionnaire, the data collection, and the data analysis to minimize these non-sampling errors. For instance, a survey specialist designed the questionnaire in collaboration with GAO staff that have subject-matter expertise. Further, the draft questionnaire was pretested with a number of agency officials to ensure that the questions were relevant, clearly stated, and easy to comprehend. When the data were analyzed, a second, independent analyst checked all computer programs.

We also sought information on the challenges to repatriation of human remains or objects through interviews and documents from agency officials, and from representatives of Indian tribes and Native Hawaiian organizations. In addition, we asked agency officials for their policies on reburial of human remains and objects on their lands and the extent to which the agency would assist tribes with the expenses of repatriation—as both were identified as factors affecting the ability of native groups to accept repatriations and rebury remains and objects. We sought data on the extent of National NAGPRA grants to tribes for the purposes of repatriation.

We conducted this performance audit from July 2009 to July 2010 in accordance with generally accepted government auditing standards. Those standards require that we plan and perform the audit to obtain sufficient, appropriate evidence to provide a reasonable basis for our findings and conclusions based on our audit objectives. We believe that the evidence obtained provides a reasonable basis for our findings and conclusions based on our audit objectives.

Appendix II: List of 28 New and Restored Indian Tribes since NAGPRA Was Enacted

The regulation on future applicability, which became effective on April 20, 2007, in part, established deadlines for federal agencies and museums to prepare summaries and inventories for new tribes added to BIA's official list of federally recognized tribes.[68] Specifically, agencies and museums have 6 months to prepare a summary and 2 years to prepare an inventory after the new tribe's placement on the BIA list, or after the effective date of the future applicability rule, whichever is later.

In November 2001, we reported on BIA's process for recognizing new tribes.[69] At that time, we identified 47 newly recognized tribes and 37 restored tribes, for a total of 84 newly recognized or restored tribes since 1960. While our November 2001 report contained detailed information on the 47 newly recognized tribes in a table on pages 25 to 26, it did not contain similar information on the 37 restored tribes. We provided detailed information on the 37 restored tribes in a table on pages 13 to 14 of an October 2006 report.[70] In the October 2006 report, we also updated the cumulative number of newly recognized and restored tribes. While no additional tribes were restored between our November 2001 report and our October 2006 report, the Delaware Tribe of Indians of Oklahoma—a newly recognized tribe—was removed from BIA's official list of federally recognized tribes during that time period and the Cowlitz Indian Tribe in the state of Washington was added as a newly recognized tribe. By deleting one tribe and adding another, in our October 2006 report, the total number of newly recognized or restored tribes remained at 84—47 newly recognized tribes and 37 restored tribes.

Since our October 2006 report, the Delaware Tribe of Indians of Oklahoma has been added back on the list, the Mashpee Wampanoag Tribe in the state of Massachusetts has been newly recognized, and the Wilton Rancheria in California has been restored. These actions bring the total of new or restored tribes since 1960 to 87—49 newly recognized tribes and 38 restored tribes—as of BIA's last official list of federally recognized tribes published on August 11, 2009.[71]

Twenty-eight of the 87 new or restored tribes have been recognized or restored since NAGPRA was enacted on November 16, 1990 (see table 14).

Federal agencies and museums were required to prepare summaries and inventories for the 25 tribes that were recognized or restored after NAGPRA's enactment and before the effective date of the future applicability rule by October 20, 2007, and April 20, 2009, respectively. For the three most recent newly recognized or restored tribes—the Mashpee Wampanoag Tribe, the Delaware Tribe of Indians, and the Wilton Rancheria—the deadline for summaries was 6 months after the tribe was included in BIA's list of federally recognized tribes and for inventories is 2 years after the tribe's inclusion in the BIA list. The Mashpee Wampanog Tribe was first included in the BIA list published on April 4, 2008; the Delaware Tribe and the Wilton Rancheria were first included in the August 11, 2009, list.[72]

Table 14. List of 28 New and Restored Indian Tribes Since NAGPRA Was Enacted

Tribe	Newly recognized or restored	Date recognized or restored	How the tribe was recognized or restored
Guidiville Rancheria of California	Restored	Sept. 6, 1991	Federal court restoration, *Scotts Valley Band of Pomo Indians of the Sugar Bowl Rancheria v. United States*, No. C-86-3660-WWS (N.D. Cal. 1991)[a]
Lytton Rancheria of California	Restored	Sept. 6, 1991	Federal court restoration, *Scotts Valley* [a]
Scotts Valley Band of Pomo Indians of California	Restored	Sept. 6, 1991	Federal court restoration, *Scotts Valley* [a]
Aroostook Band of Micmac Indians of Maine	Newly recognized	Nov. 26, 1991	Congressional recognition, Pub. L. No. 102-171, 105 Stat. 1143 (1991)
Mechoopda Indian Tribe of Chico Rancheria, California	Restored	Apr. 17, 1992	Federal court restoration, *Scotts Valley* [b]
Catawba Indian Nation	Restored	Oct. 27, 1993	Congressional restoration, Pub. L. No. 103-116, 107 Stat. 1118 (1993)
Ione Band of Miwok Indians of California	Newly recognized	Mar. 22, 1994	Decision by Interior's Assistant Secretary-Indian Affairs
Mohegan Indian Tribe of Connecticut	Newly recognized	May 14, 1994	Administrative recognition under 25 C.F.R. pt. 83
Pokagon Band of Potawatomi Indians, Michigan and Indiana	Newly recognized	Sept. 21, 1994	Congressional recognition, Pub. L. No. 103-323, 108 Stat. 2152 (1994)
Little River Band of Ottawa Indians, Michigan	Newly recognized	Sept. 21, 1994	Congressional recognition, Pub. L. No. 103-324, 108 Stat. 2156 (1994)
Little Traverse Bay Bands of Odawa Indians, Michigan	Newly recognized	Sept. 21, 1994	Congressional recognition, Pub. L. No. 103-324, 108 Stat. 2156 (1994)
United Auburn Indian Community of the Auburn Rancheria of California	Restored	Oct. 31, 1994	Congressional restoration, Pub. L. No. 103-434, 108 Stat. 4533 (1994)

Table 14. (Continued)

Tribe	Newly recognized or restored	Date recognized or restored	How the tribe was recognized or restored
Central Council of the Tlingit & Haida Indian Tribes	Newly recognized	Nov. 2, 1994	Congressional recognition, Pub. L. No. 103-454, 108 Stat. 4792 (1994)
Paskenta Band of Nomlaki Indians of California	Restored	Nov. 2, 1994	Congressional restoration, Pub. L. No. 103-454, 108 Stat. 4793 (1994)
Jena Band of Choctaw Indians, Louisiana	Newly recognized	Aug. 29, 1995	Administrative recognition under 25 C.F.R. pt. 83
Huron Potawatomi, Inc., Michigan	Newly recognized	Mar. 17, 1996	Administrative recognition under 25 C.F.R. pt. 83
Samish Indian Tribe, Washington	Newly recognized	Apr. 26, 1996	Administrative recognition under 25 C.F.R. pt. 83
Match-e-be-nash-she-wish Band of Potawatomi Indians of Michigan	Newly recognized	Aug. 23, 1999	Administrative recognition under 25 C.F.R. pt. 83
Snoqualmie Tribe, Washington	Newly recognized	Oct. 6, 1999	Administrative recognition under 25 C.F.R. pt. 83
Shawnee Tribe, Oklahoma	Newly recognized	Dec. 27, 2000	Congressional recognition, Pub. L. No. 106-568, 114 Stat. 2913 (2000)
Federated Indians of Graton Rancheria, California	Restored	Dec. 27, 2000	Congressional restoration, Pub. L. No. 106-568, 114 Stat. 2939 (2000)
Lower Lake Rancheria, California	Newly recognized	Dec. 29, 2000	Decision by Interior's Assistant Secretary-Indian Affairs (reaffirmation of recognition)
King Salmon Tribe	Newly recognized	Dec. 29, 2000	Decision by Interior's Assistant Secretary-Indian Affairs (reaffirmation of recognition)
Sun'aq Tribe of Kodiak	Newly recognized	Dec. 29, 2000	Decision by Interior's Assistant Secretary-Indian Affairs (reaffirmation of recognition)
Cowlitz Indian Tribe, Washington	Newly recognized	Jan. 4, 2002	Administrative recognition under 25 C.F.R. pt. 83

Table 14. (Continued)

Tribe	Newly recognized or restored	Date recognized or restored	How the tribe was recognized or restored
Mashpee Wampanoag Tribe, Massachusetts	Newly recognized	May 23, 2007	Administrative recognition under 25 C.F.R. pt. 83
Delaware Tribe of Indians, Oklahoma	Newly recognized	May 27, 2009	Direct government-to-government relations were reestablished with the Delaware Tribe of Indians through its reorganization under the Oklahoma Indian Welfare Act. The reorganization of its tribal government, separate from that of the Cherokee Nation, Oklahoma, was pursuant to a Memorandum of Agreement between the two tribes.[c]
Wilton Rancheria, California	Restored	June 8, 2009	Federal court restoration, *Wilton Miwok Rancheria and Dorothy Andrews v. Salazar*, No. C-07-02681 (JF) (PVT), and *Me-Wuk Indian Community of the Wilton Rancheria v. Salazar*, No. C-07-05706 (JF) (N.D. Cal. 2009)[d]

Source: GAO-02-49, GAO-07-23R, and the *Federal Register*.

Note: On June 18, 2010, BIA published its final determination to acknowledge the Shinnecock Indian Nation. 75 Fed. Reg. 34760 (June 18, 2010). Two interested parties requested reconsideration of the final determination by the Interior Board of Indian Appeals so the determination is not yet effective.

[a] 57 Fed. Reg. 5214 (Feb. 12, 1992).

[b] 57 Fed. Reg. 19133 (May 4, 1992).

[c] In 1996, BIA published a notice (1) retracting the 1979 determination that the Department would engage in government-to-government relations with the Delaware Tribe only through the Cherokee Nation and (2) recognizing the Delaware Tribe. These actions were overturned in court. *See* Cherokee Nation of Oklahoma v. Norton, 389 F.3d 1074 (10th Cir. 2004), *cert. denied* 126 S. Ct. 333 (2005). As a result, in 2005, the Delaware Tribe of Indians was removed from the BIA's list of federally recognized tribes published in the *Federal Register*. *See* 70 Fed. Reg. 71194 (Nov. 25, 2005).

[d] 74 Fed. Reg. 33468 (July 13, 2009). The district court's jurisdiction to enter into the stipulated agreement restoring the tribe is the subject of a current appeal to the 9th Circuit. If the 9th Circuit Court of Appeals finds that the district court lacked jurisdiction, the stipulated agreement and restoration is void.

Appendix III: National NAGPRA's Lack of Authority to Ensure Federal Agency Compliance with NAGPRA

National NAGPRA is charged with assisting federal agencies and others with the NAGPRA process. NAGPRA and its implementing regulations do not provide National NAGPRA or any other federal entity with tools to encourage or ensure that federal agencies within or outside of the Department of the Interior comply with the act. The civil penalties established in section 9 of NAGPRA do not apply to federal agencies; only to museums. Absent such tools, there are limited options for holding agencies that are not in compliance with the act accountable. In addition, the mechanism that NAGPRA specifically provides to ensure federal agency compliance—lawsuits by nonfederal parties, such as Indian tribes, against federal agencies—is rarely used.

In contrast to its role vis-à-vis federal agency compliance, National NAGPRA does have authority to encourage and ensure museum compliance.[73] Through fiscal year 2009, 248 counts of alleged failure to comply with NAGPRA had been made against 43 museums. The number of allegations has increased substantially in recent years. In fiscal years 2008 and 2009 alone, 141 counts were alleged. National NAGPRA, in coordination with the NPS Law Enforcement Program, has investigated 126 of the 248 counts and has found over three-quarters of those investigated—108—to be unsubstantiated. At the end of fiscal year 2009, there was a significant backlog of 122 counts to be investigated. These investigations have resulted in penalties totaling $38,490 levied against six museums through fiscal year 2009. The first notice of failure to comply was served on a museum in 2006 and, according to National NAGPRA officials, has resulted in museums taking compliance more seriously and also in the increase in allegations.

There has been some discussion over where to house National NAGPRA or whether to create a new compliance oversight office all together. As discussed in the background section of this chapter, amid conflict of interest concerns, the Secretary separated the functions of National NAGPRA into Park NAGPRA, to handle NPS compliance, and National NAGPRA, to facilitate NAGPRA implementation governmentwide. After this separation, National and Park NAGPRA were housed in different places within NPS and reported up a separate chain of command. Some believe there is still a conflict of interest in having National NAGPRA housed within NPS, as it is also an agency that must comply with the act. They have suggested it be removed from NPS, eliminating any conflict issues, and elevated in stature by, for example, placing it within the Office of the Secretary of the Interior. The June 2008 report by the Makah Indian tribe and the National Association of Tribal Historic Preservation Officers suggested an even greater elevation, recommending the establishment of an Inter-Agency NAGPRA Implementation Council within the executive branch—possibly within the Office of Management and Budget—that would assure federal agency compliance, among other things. This continues to be an issue of some debate.

APPENDIX IV: INFORMATION ON THE RECENT REGULATION ADDRESSING DISPOSITION OF CULTURALLY UNIDENTIFIABLE HUMAN REMAINS

Section 8(c)(5) of NAGPRA made the Review Committee responsible for recommending specific actions for developing a process for the disposition of culturally unidentifiable human remains in the possession or control of museums and federal agencies. The Review Committee published its first draft of recommendations regarding the disposition of culturally unidentifiable human remains and associated funerary objects for public comment in June 1995. In response to comments, the Committee published a revised draft for public comment in August 1996. Subsequently, the Committee published draft principles of agreement regarding the disposition of culturally unidentifiable human remains in 1999. The Committee published its final recommendations in June 2000. (See table 8 in the body of the report for the citations for these actions.) In addition, the Review Committee submitted comments to the Secretary in 2000, 2003, and 2008.

In October 2007, Interior published a proposed rule for public comment regarding the disposition of culturally unidentifiable human remains. The proposed rule generated over 100 comments from various interested parties, such as Indian tribes, museums, and museum or scientific organizations. Many have noted that the proposed rule departed from the Review Committee's final 2000 recommendations. While some commenters—both tribes and museums—were generally supportive of the proposed rule and welcomed its publication, some commenters also raised concerns with the proposed rule that resulted in Interior making extensive revisions to the rule before issuing a final rule on March 15, 2010. For example, several commenters were concerned by the proposed rule's requirement for museums and federal agencies to consult with and offer to transfer control of culturally unidentifiable human remains under certain circumstances to the Indian tribe or Native Hawaiian organization with a cultural relationship to the region from which the human remains were removed. The final rule does not contain this requirement.

Given the rulemaking's long history and the volume of comments Interior received on the proposed rule, this appendix describes certain provisions of the final rule, presents certain comments Interior received on the proposed rule that are available on www.regulations.gov, and provides Interior's response to the comments. This appendix does not and is not intended to serve as a summary of all the comments Interior received on the proposed rule; the preamble to the final rule discusses all of the comments.

Statutory Authority

Several museums and scientific organizations' comments argued that Interior lacked authority to promulgate this rule for two reasons. First, they argued that section (8)(c)(5) is a clear instruction for the Review Committee to make recommendations to Congress for possible future legislative action, but does not authorize Interior to take any regulatory action itself. They note that the committee report accompanying the version of the bill debated on the House floor stated that the House Committee on Interior and Insular Affairs looks forward to the Review Committee's recommendations on the process for disposition of culturally unidentifiable human remains.[74] Second, museums and scientific organizations argued that NAGPRA clearly limited repatriation to human remains that could be culturally affiliated because the act balanced the interests of Indian tribes and Native Hawaiians with those of museums and scientists. In their view, the rule impermissibly expands the scope of the act.

Indian tribes either did not comment on Interior's statutory authority or stated that they believed the rule was authorized. One tribe noted that 25 U.S.C. § 9 authorizes the President to prescribe such regulations as he may think fit for carrying into effect the various provisions of any act relating to Indian affairs and that Congress has routinely delegated broad authority to the Executive Branch to manage Indian affairs. Based on these other laws and NAGPRA's language and structure, this tribe argued that the culturally unidentifiable rule is authorized as long as the rule was consistent with and not precluded by the plain language of the act. Furthermore, the tribe stated that the culturally unidentifiable rule was plainly designed to carry out the act, reasonably related to the act's purposes, and not precluded by the act.

Interior contends that section 13 of NAGPRA, which authorizes Interior to promulgate regulations implementing the act, provides the statutory authority for the rule. The preamble to the final rule explains that section (8)(c)(5) of the act made the Review Committee responsible for recommending specific actions for developing a process for disposition of culturally unidentifiable human remains because Congress anticipated that not all items could be geographically or culturally affiliated with an Indian tribe or Native Hawaiian organization. Therefore, Interior interpreted the intent of Congress as authorizing the Secretary of the Interior to promulgate regulations governing the disposition of culturally unidentifiable human remains after considering the Review Committee's recommendations.

Interior has noted that an earlier version of the bill that became NAGPRA directed the Review Committee to provide its recommendations regarding the disposition of culturally unidentifiable human remains to the Secretary and Congress. However, the language regarding the Secretary and Congress was subsequently stricken from the bill. Interior has interpreted this sequence of changes and the act's requirement that the Secretary consult with the Review Committee in the development of regulations as authorizing Interior to promulgate regulations governing the disposition of culturally unidentifiable human remains after considering the Review Committee's recommendations on the matter. Moreover, Interior has stated that even if Congress did not expressly delegate authority or responsibility to implement a particular provision or fill a particular gap in the act, it can still be apparent from an agency's generally conferred authority and other statutory directives that Congress would expect the agency to be able to speak with the force of law when the agency addresses ambiguities in the statute or fills a gap in the enacted law.

In addition, Interior notes that 25 U.S.C. § 9 authorizes the Secretary to make such regulations as he may think fit for carrying into effect the various provisions of any act relating to Indian Affairs. Interior argues that "because NAGPRA is Indian law, the Secretary may promulgate any regulations needed to implement it under the broad authority to supervise and manage Indian affairs given by Congress."[75]

Consultation

The final rule, among other things, requires museums and federal agencies to consult with (1) an Indian tribe(s) or Native Hawaiian organization(s) that makes a disposition request for culturally unidentifiable human remains and (2) with federally recognized Indian tribes and Native Hawaiian organizations from whose tribal or aboriginal lands the remains were removed before offering to transfer control of the culturally unidentifiable human remains.[76] Some museums questioned the imposition of this extra burden of consultation because National NAGPRA's online database of culturally unidentifiable human remains contains sufficient information for Indian tribes and Native Hawaiian organizations to submit requests. Interior has said that this provision restates the consultation required under section 5 of the act and 43 C.F.R. § 10.9, which requires museums and federal agencies to consult with Indian tribes from whose tribal lands the human remains and associated funerary objects originated, that are or are likely to be culturally affiliated to the remains and objects, and from whose aboriginal lands the humans and objects originated while preparing their inventories. Therefore, Interior has said that museums and federal agencies that consulted with Indian tribes and Native Hawaiian organizations about the culturally unidentifiable human remains while compiling their inventories are not required by this new rule to consult again unless a disposition request is made.

Right of Possession and Transfer of Control

If the museum or federal agency cannot prove that it has a right of possession, the final rule also requires them to offer to transfer control of the culturally unidentifiable human remains in accordance with the priority order listed in the regulation.[77] NAGPRA defines right of possession as "possession obtained with the voluntary consent of an individual or group that had authority of alienation."[78] Museums and federal agencies have right of possession for Native American human remains that were originally acquired, excavated, exhumed, or otherwise obtained with full knowledge and consent of the next of kin or the official governing body of the appropriate culturally affiliated Indian tribe or Native Hawaiian organization.

Museums and scientific organizations generally commented that right of possession could never be established for culturally unidentifiable human remains because neither the next of kin or an appropriate culturally affiliated Indian tribe or Native Hawaiian organization could have consented to the original acquisition. Museums argued that NAGPRA's definition of right of possession ignores state property laws that give museums legal title to human remains and items removed from private property with the consent of landowners. Because museums have legal title to these human remains and items, these groups argue that the return of culturally unidentifiable human remains would violate the Takings Clause of the Constitution.[79] Museums and scientific organizations also note that this rule would deprive the world of scientific information on the biological and cultural development of humans and would impact many museums' ability to educate the public about these issues.

Interior has noted that NAGPRA's definition of right of possession created an ownership presumption and that as a federal law it would preempt any state property law on the same subject matter under the Supremacy Clause of the Constitution.[80] Interior also observed that the regulatory requirement to offer to transfer control of culturally unidentifiable human remains did not apply in circumstances where a court of competent jurisdiction has determined that the repatriation of the human remains in the possession or control of a museum would result in a taking of property without just compensation within the meaning of the Fifth Amendment.

In addition to the right of possession issue, some museums and scientific organizations also assert that the final rule requires museums and federal agencies to offer to transfer control of culturally unidentifiable human remains absent any request or claim from an Indian tribe or Native Hawaiian organization. These museums and scientific organizations state that this requirement is inconsistent with NAGPRA and greatly exceeds the statute's scope because the act's requirement to repatriate culturally affiliated human remains and objects is triggered only upon a request being made. According to Interior, the requirement to offer to transfer control is not triggered until an Indian tribe or Native Hawaiian organization listed in the priority order makes a disposition request. Absent such a request, Interior said that museums and federal agencies are not required to offer to transfer control of culturally unidentifiable human remains, however, Interior noted that 43 C.F.R. § 10.11(b)(ii) allows museums and federal agencies to initiate the repatriation process without a request, especially if they identify the tribes that occupied the land from which the remains originated.

Non-federally Recognized Tribes

If none of the Indian tribes or Native Hawaiian organizations in the priority order agrees to accept control, the final rule allows museums and federal agencies to transfer control of the culturally unidentifiable human remains to other Indian tribes or Native Hawaiian organizations or to non-federally recognized Indian tribes, if the Secretary of the Interior recommends the transfer.[81] In their comments, some tribes objected to this provision because it makes the transfer of control voluntary and at the discretion of the museum or federal agency. These tribes wanted the rule to require museums and federal agencies to transfer control to non-federally recognized tribes from whose tribal or aboriginal lands the remains were removed.

At least one Indian tribe, however, only wanted the rule to permit repatriation of culturally unidentifiable human remains to federally recognized Indian tribes. Museum and scientific organizations echoed this comment by questioning Interior's authority in requiring museums to obtain the Secretary's prior recommendation when the Secretary lacked authority over non-federally recognized Indian tribes or noting the difficulty museums and federal agencies would have in identifying which non-federally recognized tribes had a legitimate claim.

Interior responded by noting that it followed the lead of Congress in expanding the possible recipients of culturally unidentifiable human remains to include non-federally recognized tribes both in assuring that the remains went to the Indian group that had the closest cultural connection to the remains, even if that group is not federally recognized, and in maintaining the priority position of the government-to-government relationship, by not making disposition to non-federally recognized tribes mandatory. In addition, Interior acknowledged that mandating the return of culturally unidentifiable human remains to non-federally recognized Indian tribes would be contrary to the terms of NAGPRA and the government-to-government relationship between the United States and federally recognized tribes, but that nothing in the act prohibited the voluntary transfer of human remains to non-federally recognized tribes with appropriate safeguards for the rights of federally recognized tribes. Interior has said that the Secretary will continue the current practice of asking the Review Committee for a recommendation on disposition requests from non-federally recognized Indian tribes.

Associated Funerary Objects

The final rule allows museums and federal agencies to transfer control of funerary objects associated with culturally unidentifiable human remains and recommends that such transfers occur if not precluded by federal or state law.[82] Several museums and scientific organizations objected to this provision because it lacked a statutory basis and stated that this "recommendation" inappropriately pressured museums and agencies to divest themselves of objects in their collection that do not have any demonstrated cultural affiliation with NAGPRA claimants.

Tribes requested that the final rule require museum's and federal agencies to transfer control of the associated funerary objects belonging to culturally unidentifiable human remains. Tribes argued that funerary objects represent offerings intended as gifts and spiritual offerings to the deceased and are understood to be the property of the deceased. For Indian tribes, separation of the human remains from the funerary objects is a grievous spiritual injury to the deceased and grievous emotional injury to Native Americans. One tribe said that requiring museums and federal agencies to transfer control of associated funerary objects reflects the canons of construction for Indian laws—that the law be liberally construed in favor of Indians and all ambiguities resolved in favor of the Indians. Tribes also argued that some museums would never return the associated funerary objects unless required to do so.

Section (8)(c)(5) of the act, which is the only provision in the act that refers to or uses the term culturally unidentifiable, makes the NAGPRA Review Committee responsible for recommending specific actions for developing a process for disposition of culturally unidentifiable human remains but does not mention associated funerary objects. Interior has said that it did not consider it appropriate to make the provision to transfer culturally unidentifiable associated funerary objects mandatory because of the statute's silence, common law regarding human remains and associated funerary objects, and the right of possession and takings issues that a mandatory disposition of associated funerary objects would raise which are not clearly resolved in the statute or legislative history.

Appendix V: Status of Review Committee Recommendations Made in 12 Disputes

Year	Federal agency or museum	Indian tribe, group, or Native Hawaiian organization that brought the dispute	Review Committee finding[a]	Review Committee recommendations	Status of Review Committee's recommendations
1993	P.A. Hearst Museum UCLA-Berkeley	Hui Malama I Na Kupuna O Hawai'i Nei	A relationship of shared group identity can be reasonably traced between present day Native Hawaiian organizations and the human remains.	Museum should revise determination of cultural affiliation for human remains and notify Native Hawaiian organizations directly and by *Federal Register* notice that the human remains are available for repatriation.	*Partially implemented.* Museum published a *Federal Register* notice and repatriated the human remains. We did not determine whether the museum changed the cultural affiliation determination.
1993	P.A. Hearst Museum UCLA-Berkeley	Hui Malama I Na Kupuna O Hawai'i Nei	The Committee was unable to determine that the preponderance of the evidence indicates that there is a relationship of shared group identity that can be reasonably traced between present day Native Hawaiian organizations and the human remains.	Museum should transfer the human remains to a museum in Hawaii for future consideration of cultural affiliation and care.	*Fully implemented.* Museum transferred the human remains to the Bishop Museum. Subsequently, the Bishop Museum determined there was a shared group identity and subsequently repatriated the remains.
1997	City of Providence, RI	Hui Malama I Na Kupuna O Hawai'i Nei, and the state of Hawaii's Office Of Hawaiian Affairs	The object is a sacred object and a relationship of shared group identity can be reasonably traced between the Office of Hawaiian Affairs and Hui Malama I Na Kupuna O Hawai'i Nei and the Native	Museum should reconsider its determination of the object's classification. The object should be considered a sacred object. Museum should repatriate the object to a Native Hawaiian organization.	*Status unknown.* The museum did not publish a *Federal Register* notice and we did not determine whether the museum reconsidered its determination of the object's classification or whether the museum repatriated the object. Dispute resulted

(Continued)

Year	Federal agency or museum	Indian tribe, group, or Native Hawaiian organization that brought the dispute	Review Committee finding[a]	Review Committee recommendations	Status of Review Committee's recommendations
			Hawaiians who created and used it.		in litigation.
1999	NPS's Chaco Culture National Historical Park	Hopi Tribe of Arizona	Tribes were not given adequate opportunity to consult on a one-to-one basis and make concerns known outside of a public forum. Agency applied a looser criterion of cultural relationship to geographical place as a basis for determining cultural affiliation than it should have. Agency needs to do more to evaluate and weigh evidence pertaining to cultural affiliation.	Agency should withdraw its published notice and reassess its determination of cultural affiliation. Agency should not use collective consultation in lieu of individual tribal consultation when requested by an Indian tribe.	*Not implemented*. Agency declined to withdraw its published notice and reassess its determination of cultural affiliation.[b]
2001	BLM's Nevada State Office	Paiute-Shoshone Tribe of the Fallon Reservation and Colony, Nevada	State Office has not given fair and objective consideration and assessment of all the available information and evidence in the dispute. The preponderance of the evidence indicates a relationship of shared group identity that can be	Agency should repatriate human remains and associated funerary objects.	*Not implemented*. Agency has not repatriated the human remains. We did not determine whether agency repatriated the objects. Dispute resulted in litigation.

(Continued)

Year	Federal agency or museum	Indian tribe, group, or Native Hawaiian organization that brought the dispute	Review Committee finding[a]	Review Committee recommendations	Status of Review Committee's recommendations
			reasonably traced between the Paiute-Shoshone Tribe of the Fallon Reservation and Colony, Nevada, and the human remains and associated funerary objects from Spirit Cave in Nevada.		
2002	Denver Art Museum	Western Apache NAGPRA Working Group	The information and statements submitted and presented by the Museum and the Working Group is sufficient to establish by a preponderanc e of the evidence that the items are both sacred objects and objects of cultural patrimony. Further, they are culturally affiliated with the constituent tribes of the Working Group.	Museum should consider the oral testimony provided by the Working Group, consult anthropological literature, re-evaluate the determination for repatriation, and inform the Committee of the museum's findings within 90 days.	*Not implemented*. Museum published a notice of intent to repatriate in the *Federal Register* describing the items as sacred objects to which the museum holds the right of possession. Although an official from the Western Apache Working Group reported that the museum followed the letter of the recommendation by considering the Group's oral testimony and consulting anthropological literature, the museum did not follow the spirit of the recommendations which was, according to the official, to reclassify the object.

(Continued)

Year	Federal agency or museum	Indian tribe, group, or Native Hawaiian organization that brought the dispute	Review Committee finding[a]	Review Committee recommendations	Status of Review Committee's recommendations
2003	Bishop Museum	Royal Hawaiian Academy of Traditional Arts	Museum's repatriation process for the items was flawed and is incomplete. The place and manner of the return of the items was not consistent with NAGPRA. Museum is responsible for the completion of the repatriation process for the items.	Museum should recall the loan of the items to Hui Malama I Na Kupuna O Hawai'i Nei, make the items available to all consulting parties, and renew the consultation process for repatriation.	*Not implemented*. According to an official with the Royal Hawaiian Academy of Traditional Arts, Hui Malama I Na Kupuna O Hawai'i Nei denied the Bishop Museum's request for the items. Dispute led to litigation.[c] Funerary objects were removed from cave and are in possession of the Bishop Museum.
2005	Bishop Museum	Hui Malama I Na Kupuna O Hawai'i Nei	The Review Committee declines to come to a finding about whether the objects are objects of cultural patrimony. Further, the Committee believes that the current location of the objects is appropriate.	Museum and Hui Malama o Mo'omomi should work together to revise memorandum of agreement to require consent of Hui Malama o Mo'omomi prior to the removal of the objects from the Island of Molokai.	*Status unknown*. Items are still under the control of the Bishop Museum.
2005	Bishop Museum	Hui Malama I Na Kupuna O Hawai'i Nei	Museum failed to overcome the inference that the museum did not have the right of posession to the object. Museums and federal agencies must repatriate cultural items within 90 days of receipt of	Museum should continue process of consultation to determine appropriate claimant(s) for unassociated funerary objects. Once repatriation has taken place, the transaction must be documented in a way consistent with Hawaii state law.	*Status unknown*. Items are still under the control of the Bishop Museum.

(Continued)

Year	Federal agency or museum	Indian tribe, group, or Native Hawaiian organization that brought the dispute	Review Committee finding[a]	Review Committee recommendations	Status of Review Committee's recommendations
			a written request for repatriation that satisfies NAGPRA requirements.		
2005	NPS's Hawaii Volcanoes National Park	Hui Malama I Na Kupuna O Hawai'i Nei	Agency has been very slow in going through the NAGPRA process. The number of potential claimants for the items has grown over time. Agency has not sufficiently investigated right of possession. Agency should expand the involvement of Native Hawaiian participation and testimony.	Agency should initiate consultation with all claimants and interested parties, investigate the right of possession issue, and take steps to complete repatriation by 2005.	*Partially implemented.* According to an agency official, the agency has conducted consultation and has considered the right of possession issue. Further the agency has issued a notice of intent to repatriate, but repatriation has not taken place because claimants disagree on disposition and agency cannot determine the most appropriate claimant.
2006	Field Museum	White Mountain Apache Tribe of the Fort Apache Reservation, Arizona	The items are consistent with the definition of object of cultural patrimony. Museum has not presented evidence sufficient to overcome the inference that the museum does not have a right of possession to the items.	Museum should consider the oral testimony and written evidence provided by the White Mountain Apache Tribe and change its determination of the items to recognize their status as objects of cultural patrimony. Museum should acknowledge that it lacks right of possession to the items.	*Not implemented.* Museum did not change its determination of the items and did not state that it lacked right of possession.

(Continued)

Year	Federal agency or museum	Indian tribe, group, or Native Hawaiian organization that brought the dispute	Review Committee finding[a]	Review Committee recommendations	Status of Review Committee's recommendations
2008	New York State Museum	Onondaga Nation of New York	The preponderance of the evidence shows a relationship of shared group identity between the Onondaga Nation (and the greater Haudenosaunee Confederacy, of which the Nation is a member-nation) and the human remains.	Museum should expeditiously repatriate human remains to the Onondaga Nation. Further, museum should reevaluate the cultural affiliation of all Native American human remains in its possession or under its control that had been determined to be culturally unidentifiable using the preponderance of the evidence to determine cultural affiliation.	*Partially implemented.* Museum repatriated the human remains. A museum official said that it has been and continues to be a policy of the museum to use a preponderance of all evidence as the standard for deciding cultural affiliation. However, it is unclear whether the museum has reevaluated the cultural affiliation of all of its culturally unidentifiable Native American human remains.

Source: GAO analysis based on discussions with federal agency, museum, Native American, and National NAGPRA officials; and *Federal Register* notices.

Note: This appendix contains the status of Review Committee recommendations on 12 disputes brought before the Review Committee as of September 30, 2009. As part of our review, we did not assess whether agencies or museums reassessed or re-evaluated cultural affiliations for NAGPRA items when the Review Committee recommended they do so. For our analysis, we relied on National NAGPRA information provided to the Review Committee on the status of disputes, *Federal Register* notices stating the Review Committee's recommendations and findings of fact for each dispute and any notices that resulted from the dispute.

[a] Findings in this column relate directly to the Review Committee's recommendations and are not inclusive of all the Review Committee's findings for these disputes.

[b] In this dispute, National NAGPRA data indicates that the items have been repatriated.

[c] In the legal settlement, among other things, the court directed that (1) the 83 items to be removed from the cave; (2) the Bishop Museum be given possession of the items; and (3) the Bishop Museum restart consultation and repatriation.

APPENDIX VI: OTHER ACTIVITIES CONDUCTED BY NATIONAL NAGPRA

In addition to promulgating regulations and providing administrative support to the Review Committee, National NAGPRA has conducted a number of activities to carry out the responsibilities assigned by NAGPRA to the Secretary of the Interior. This appendix summarizes these other activities.

Inventories, Summaries, and *Federal Register* Notices

National NAGPRA has received federal agency and museum inventories and summaries and published notices in the *Federal Register*, as NAGPRA's implementing regulations require. According to its Fiscal Year 2009 Annual Report, from fiscal years 1992 through 2009, National NAGPRA received inventories from 1,317 federal agencies and museums and summaries from 1,551 federal agencies and museums and has entered some of this information into a database. Along with the inventories, federal agencies and museums also submit draft notices of inventory completion and draft notices of intent to repatriate, which National NAGPRA prepares for publication. National NAGPRA's Annual Report also states that, during this same period, it published 1,295 notices of inventory completion and 477 notices of intent to repatriate in the *Federal Register* for federal agencies and museums.

National NAGPRA has increased the number of notices it has published in the *Federal Register* in recent years. Specifically, the number of notices published in the *Federal Register* increased to 180 in fiscal year 2008 and to 200 in fiscal year 2009 compared to about 100 per fiscal year in 2003 through 2007. Furthermore, according to the National NAGPRA Program Manager, notice publications have increased with fewer staff—there has been only one staff person dedicated to publishing notices from 2005 through 2009 while there have been multiple staff assigned to this task in previous years. In our interviews with federal agency officials and Review Committee members, a number of them complimented National NAGPRA on its increased efficiency in publishing notices.

In addition to recent increases in the number of notices published, National NAGPRA has reduced a backlog of notices that were awaiting publication. In 2004, the year the current National NAGPRA Program Manager started in her position, there were about 300 draft notices awaiting publication, some of which had been submitted close to a decade earlier. These notices needed some action by the originator before they could proceed to publication. Prior National NAGPRA management had an "on-hold" category for such notices and had taken them out of the publication process, in a sense leaving them in limbo. In 2005, National NAGPRA eliminated the "on-hold" status and set out to clear this backlog by contacting the originating entity of each notice and requesting that they contact National NAGPRA to resolve it. National NAGPRA's correspondence further stated that notices would be considered withdrawn if the originating entity did not respond within a specified time frame. Through fiscal year 2009, over 220 had been published, 21 were awaiting publication, and 79 were withdrawn—24 by federal agencies (see table 15). Notices were withdrawn by agencies and museums for a variety of reasons, including:

Table 15. Draft *Federal Register* Notices Withdrawn by Federal Agencies and their Status as of June 2010

Federal agency	Human remains in the draft notices[a]	Date draft notice received for publication processing	Date draft notice removed from publication processing	Status as of June 2010
National Park Service (NPS)				
San Juan Island National Historic Park	unknown	Nov. 16, 1995	June 3, 2008	Items covered in a published notice
Tumacacori National Historic Park	24	Nov. 16, 1995	Nov. 27, 2007	Items covered in a published notice
Dinosaur National Monument	8	Nov. 16, 1995	Apr. 4, 2006	Revised determination to culturally unidentifiable
Hawaii Volcanoes National Park	1	Nov. 16, 1995	July 5, 2006	Other [b]
Canyon de Chelly National Monument	193	Nov. 16, 1995	Nov. 30, 2007	No new notice submitted for publication[c]
El Morro National Monument	17	Nov. 16, 1995	Nov. 27, 2007	No new notice submitted for publication[c]
Glen Canyon National Recreation Area	about 10	Nov. 16, 1995	Nov. 27, 2007	No new notice submitted for publication[c]
Grand Canyon National Park	28	Nov. 16, 1995	Nov. 30, 2007	Requested disposition of culturally unidentifiable remains at October 2009 Review Committee meeting
Hovenweep National Monument	4	Nov. 16, 1995	Nov. 27, 2007	Items covered in a published notice
Lake Mead National Recreation Area	33	Nov. 6, 1995	Nov. 30, 2007	No new notice submitted for publication[c]
Mesa Verde National Park	unknown	Nov. 16, 1995	Jan. 27, 2006	Items covered in a published notice
Montezuma Castle National Monument	11	Nov. 16, 1995	Nov. 30, 2007	No new notice submitted for publication[c]
Petrified Forest National Park	7	Nov. 16, 1995	Nov. 27, 2007	No new notice submitted for publication[c]
Tuzigoot National Monument	about 412	Nov. 16, 1995	Nov. 30, 2007	No new notice submitted for publication[c]
Walnut Canyon National Monument	34	Nov. 16, 1995	Nov. 27, 2007	No new notice submitted for publication[c]
Wupatki National Monument	60	Nov. 16, 1995	Nov. 27, 2007	No new notice submitted for publication[c]
Bureau of Reclamation (BOR)				
Mid-Pacific Region	36	Oct. 1, 1998	Feb. 1, 2008	BOR not in control
Mid-Pacific Region	9	Aug. 31, 1999	Feb. 1, 2008	No new notice submitted for publication

Table 15. (Continued)

Federal agency	Human remains in the draft notices[a]	Date draft notice received for publication processing	Date draft notice removed from publication processing	Status as of June 2010
Mid-Pacific Region	4	June 30, 2000	Feb. 1, 2008	No new notice submitted for publication
Mid-Pacific Region	1	Nov. 20, 1995	Nov. 21, 2008	BOR not in control
U.S. Army				
Aberdeen Proving Ground	5	Feb. 17, 1999	Sept. 2, 2008	Revised determination to culturally unidentifiable
Waianae Army Recreation Center	unknown	Oct. 26, 1999	Aug. 3, 2006	Other [d]
BIA	not applicable	Dec. 6, 2001	June 19, 2007	Items covered in a published notice
Forest Service's Siuslaw National Forest	1	Mar. 21, 2001	Feb. 20, 2008	New notice submitted is pending publication

Source: National NAGPRA.

Note: All of the notices were notices of inventory completion except for the BIA notice which was a notice of intent to repatriate.

[a] Human remains were counted using the "minimum number of individuals" method.

[b] According to a National NAGPRA official, the human remains listed in the draft notice of inventory completion were actually incorporated into an unassociated funerary object. The official said that, as such, they are not a "human remains" under NAGPRA, but rather an unassociated funerary object. Because of this, the draft notice should have been for a notice of intent to repatriate. However, no claim had been made and, therefore, the Hawaii Volcanoes National Park removed it from the publication process. In commenting on a draft of this chapter, NPS stated that the original inventory was submitted in error and that this unassociated funerary object was subsequently published in a notice of intent to repatriate

[c] In commenting on a draft of this chapter, NPS stated that although NPS has not submitted a new notice for publication, the park unit has received NAGPRA project funds, hired interns, and/or utilized park funds in support of tribal consultation, updating the inventory, and finalizing and publishing the notice of inventory completion.

[d] According to a National NAGPRA official, the human remains were part of an ongoing interment that began prior to NAGPRA enactment. The Waianae Army Recreation Center subsequently reinterred the human remains according to an agreement that had been reached prior to NAGPRA and in the same place as the other remains.

- the items had already been included in a published notice;
- the agency or museum had revised the cultural determination to culturally unidentifiable; and
- the agency or museum was actually not in control of the items.

The withdrawal of these notices has been controversial and was the subject of discussion at a congressional hearing in October 2009.

National NAGPRA's Grants Program

National NAGPRA has administered a grants program to assist Indian tribes, Native Hawaiian organizations, and museums in conducting consultations and repatriations. Since the inception of the grants program through fiscal year 2009, National NAGPRA has received 1,341 grant applications from tribes, Native Hawaiian organizations, and museums and awarded 628 grants totaling about $33 million. Of the total awarded, $22.4 million, or about 68 percent, has gone to tribes and Native Hawaiian organizations and $10.5 million, or about 32 percent, has gone to museums (see table 16). Further, 513 grants worth about $31.8 million have been awarded for consultation grants and 115 grants worth about $1.2 million have been awarded for repatriation grants.

The grants program has been controversial in part due to confusion over how much funding was actually available for grants. NPS has allocated a portion of the NAGPRA grants budget request line item to cover a portion of National NAGPRA's operating expenses (another portion has been provided by NPS's Cultural Resources Program), but did not indicate this in its budget justifications until fiscal year 2011. Two investigations by Interior's Office of Inspector General on the alleged improper use of NAGPRA funds found a lack of clarity over the use of the grants budget request line item. Specifically, the Inspector General responded to allegations that (1) NPS had illegally diverted millions in grant funding for purposes not covered by NAGPRA and (2) the National NAGPRA Program Manager had improperly reprogrammed grant funds for administrative purposes. Both investigations found no wrongdoing, stating that NPS and National NAGPRA had discretion to use the funds as it did. NPS's fiscal year 2011 budget justification has addressed this issue by moving the operating expenses out of the grants budget request and into the NPS Cultural Resources Program budget request, thus separating the funding for grants and operating expenses. Table 17 shows the enacted line item for grants and NPS's use of it for grants and operating expenses from fiscal years 1994 through 2009.

Table 16. NAGPRA Grant Applications Submitted by and Awarded to Tribes and Native Hawaiian Organizations and Museums, Fiscal Years 1994 through 2009

	Tribes and Native Hawaiian organizations				Museums			
Fiscal year	Number of applications submitted	Amount requested	Number of applications awarded	Amount awarded	Number of applications submitted	Amount requested	Number of applications awarded	Amount awarded
1994	103	$5,917,848	15	$986,200	113	$6,698,044	25	$1,116,800
1995	62	3,769,680	24	1,387,925	56	2,408,169	19	854,075
1996	53	3,416,799	20	1,150,985	33	1,530,039	19	946,905
1997	54	3,148,112	27	1,425,600	20	1,055,915	10	550,650
1998	62	3,552,820	29	1,562,700	23	1,025,062	16	775,720
1999	57	3,296,265	32	1,648,220	22	2,251,416	11	687,780
2000	84	4,814,432	31	1,629,170	28	1,276,775	14	622,830
2001	53	3,048,378	33	1,802,180	20	1,042,261	13	635,820
2002	57	3,460,873	31	1,708,268	16	961,775	9	537,552
2003	60	3,681,184	31	1,690,502	12	668,730	9	497,806
2004	41	2,369,685	29	1,535,659	17	1,037,649	11	646,341
2005	41	2,404,899	20	918,560	17	1,060,299	8	471,669
2006	53	3,074,228	29	1,500,965	16	750,172	10	393,893
2007	36	2,092,697	23	1,312,868	16	815,239	12	548,825
2008	29	1,694,314	20	1,091,687	12	557,579	11	488,164
2009	47	2,630,918	24	1,092,787	28	1,709,913	13	753,809
Total	**892**	**$52,373,131**	**418**	**$22,444,276**	**449**	**$24,849,037**	**210**	**$10,528,639**

Source: National NAGPRA.

Table 17. Enacted NAGPRA Grants Funding, Amount Used for Grants, and Their Difference, Fiscal Years 1994 through 2009

(Dollars in thousands)			
Fiscal year	**Enacted NAGPRA grant budget request line item in NPS's annual budget justification**[a]	**Amount NPS used for grants**	**Difference**
1994	$2,300[b]	$2,103	$197
1995	2,296[b]	2,242	54
1996	2,296[c]	2,098	198
1997	2,296[c]	1,976	320
1998	2,496[c]	2,338	158
1999	2,496[c]	2,336	160
2000	2,472[c]	2,252	220
2001	2,467	2,438	29
2002	2,467	2,246	221
2003	2,451	2,188	263
2004	2,437	2,182	255
2005	2,403	1,390	1,013[d]
2006	2,368	1,895	473
2007	2,368	1,862	506
2008	2,331	1,580	751[e]
2009	2,331	1,847	484

Source: NPS Budget Justifications and National NAGPRA.

Note: According to National NAGPRA's Annual Reports for fiscal years 2005 through 2009, NPS provided funds annually for National NAGPRA operating expenses from its Cultural Resources Program budget ranging from $162,000 to $350,000. Also, in fiscal year 2009, NPS Law Enforcement provided an additional $45,000 for enforcement support and training.

[a] In addition to the grant budget request line item, NPS's annual budget justification includes a separate budget request line item for grant administration that has ranged from about $150,000 to about $190,000 annually.

[b] This figure is the amount enacted to date provided in the budget justification.

[c] This figure is the estimate provided in the budget justification.

[d] In fiscal year 2005, Interior used $667,800 of NAGPRA funding to pay Department of Justice legal fees in its defense for Bonnichsen v. United States, also known as the "Kennewick Man" case.

[e] This amount includes $300,000 that NPS had originally allocated to grants but instead used for a cooperative agreement for the development of video and training and associated technical support. According to National NAGPRA's Fiscal Year 2008 Annual Report and the National NAGPRA Program Manager, the funding was shifted away from grants because the grants recommended by the NAGPRA grants panel for funding were less than the amount available and because of a strong recommendation from the NAGPRA grants panel to use the funds to build tribal and museum grant writing capacity. In addition, according to a grants panelist and the National NAGPRA Program Manager, a number of applications in 2008 were of relatively low quality.

National NAGPRA Databases

National NAGPRA has made progress in making data available to tribes, museums, federal agencies, and the general public. It currently maintains six online searchable databases, such as a Native American consultation database and databases for published notices, and has plans to develop a summaries database. According to the National NAGPRA Program Manger, National NAGPRA had developed only one database as of 2005. While these databases are providing more information to NAGPRA practitioners, some federal agencies and museums have complained about the databases containing incorrect information. The National NAGPRA Program Manager told us that she is aware of this issue and is working to correct the problems. The program manager explained that part of this problem stems from earlier efforts to expedite the publication of notices, but without reconciling data. Specifically, NPS staff as well as contract employees hired in 2000 to publish notices did not reconcile the numbers of human remains and objects listed in the notices with those listed in inventories and summaries, and this left data inaccuracies. For example, an agency or museum might have listed human remains as culturally unidentifiable in an inventory, but later affiliated and repatriated those remains and not informed National NAGPRA so they could update their database. By not reconciling this information, data in the culturally unidentifiable database would be incorrect.

National NAGPRA Training and Educational Materials

National NAGPRA has provided training to and developed educational materials for Indian tribes, museums, and federal agencies to improve NAGPRA implementation. Course titles include Determining Cultural Affiliation and Writing and Managing a Successful Grant. A NAGPRA Basics course is typically offered the day before the beginning of each Review Committee meeting. These courses are taught by National NAGPRA staff as well as contractors and are offered in various locations across the country, as posted on National NAGPRA's Web site. Also, starting in June 2009, National NAGPRA began offering "webinars," which are interactive online courses. Participants follow the course online as well as via telephone and can ask questions either orally or by submitting them on the Web site. In fiscal year 2009, National NAGPRA and its contractors provided 15 courses to 612 participants. According to a National NAGPRA official, feedback obtained on these courses has generally been positive and has been used to improve training. For example, based on feedback that its NAGPRA Basics course was too simplistic for some and too complex for others, National NAGPRA now plans to offer two basics courses—one for newcomers and one for more experienced NAGPRA practitioners.

In terms of educational materials, National NAGPRA is developing a series of videos to create a training series on NAGPRA-related issues. National NAGPRA has conducted about 50 interviews with tribal, museum, and federal agency officials and Review Committee members to create a historic archive of resources on consultation, notices, and repatriation, among other things. Also, in 2009, National NAGPRA published a brochure on the history of the grants program that included data as well as stories about specific grants and what they accomplished.[83]

Despite National NAGPRA's training efforts, we found a general lack of knowledge about NAGPRA requirements among federal agencies. For example, TVA completed inventories prior to consulting with potentially affiliated Indian tribes; whereas NAGPRA requires that consultation be conducted prior to completing inventories.[84] Further, Corps and FWS officials stated that, in some instances, their agencies had only begun developing notices of inventory completion after receiving a repatriation request from an Indian tribe for remains or associated funerary objects that had been culturally affiliated in the agency's inventory; whereas NAGPRA requires publication of these notices regardless of whether a repatriation request has been received.[85]

APPENDIX VII: COMMENTS FROM THE DEPARTMENT OF AGRICULTURE

USDA United States Department of Agriculture | Forest Service | Washington Office | 1400 Independence Avenue, SW Washington, DC 20250

File Code: 2300/1420
Date: JUL 15 2010

Ms. Anu K. Mittal
Director, Natural Resources and Environment
Government Accountability Office
441 G. Street, NW
Washington, DC 20548

Dear Ms. Mittal:

We appreciate the opportunity to review and comment on the draft Government Accountability Office (GAO) report, GAO-10-768, "Native American Graves Protection and Repatriation Act: After Almost 20 Years, Key Federal Agencies Still Have Not Fully Complied with the Act." In general, the Forest Service agrees with the findings, conclusions and recommendations in the report.

We appreciate and note careful consideration given by the GAO auditors to all of our suggestions on technical corrections and clarifications of facts. As a result, we do not need to burden this response with those matters.

We appreciate your recognition in your report that the Forest Service is one of the agencies that did the most extensive work to identify NAGPRA items.

We find the proposed executive actions to be reasonable, and our agency anticipates fully implementing those proposed executive actions.

If you have any questions, please contact Donna M. Carmical, Chief Financial Officer, at 202-205-1321 or dcarmical@fs.fed.us.

Sincerely,

Thomas L. Tidwell

THOMAS L. TIDWELL
Chief

cc: Michael Kaczor, Sandy T Coleman, Frank E Wozniak, Kathleen A Clemens

APPENDIX VIII: COMMENTS FROM THE DEPARTMENT OF THE INTERIOR

United States Department of the Interior

OFFICE OF THE SECRETARY

Washington, DC 20240

TAKE PRIDE IN AMERICA

JUL 20 2010

Ms. Anu K. Mittal
Director, Natural Resources and Environment
U.S. Government Accountability Office
441 G Street, N.W.
Washington, D.C. 20548

Dear Ms. Mittal:

Thank you for providing the Department of the Interior the opportunity to review and comment on the draft Government Accountability Office Report entitled, *NATIVE AMERICAN GRAVES PROTECTION AND REPATRIATION ACT: After Almost 20 Years, Key Federal Agencies Still Have Not Fully Complied with the Act* (GAO-10-768).

The Department appreciates the diligent work of the Government Accountability Office (GAO) team that prepared the report and collected a large amount of data. We believe GAO has produced an informative summation of the complex issues associated with the Native American Graves Protection and Repatriation Act Program (NAGPRA).

The Department generally concurs with the recommendations. Please find enclosed the actions that have already been taken and that are underway to address GAO's recommendations. Also enclosed are bureau-specific comments and technical comments that should be considered for the final report.

It is important to recognize the substantial progress of the Federal agencies within Interior to step up NAGPRA compliance activities including progress in training and consultation with tribes and Native Hawaiian organizations. A full analysis of compliance with the Act should include the past and current programs, as well as processes and policies that an agency has in place for responding to the Acts requirements.

As the GAO states, the Federal agencies acknowledge that they still have more work to do. We are committed to fully complying with NAGPRA. Because of the complexities of the activities required by the Act, our progress towards compliance with NAGPRA will be a focused and on-going effort. The varied and interrelated complexities of NAGPRA—completion of inventories and summaries, consultation with tribes and Native Hawaiian organizations, determination of affiliation, analysis of claims to identify the most appropriate claimant, handling items newly discovered in collections or other museums, consultation and dealing with inadvertent discoveries, etc., require an on-going process for Federal land managers.

For additional information, please contact the NAGPRA Program Director, Sherry Hutt, at (202)354-1479.

Sincerely,

Rhea Suh
Assistant Secretary
Policy, Management and Budget

Enclosure

Government Accountability Office Draft Report
NATIVE AMERICAN GRAVES PROTECTION AND REPATRIATION ACT: After Almost 20 Years, Key Federal Agencies Still Have Not Fully Complied with the Act
(GAO-10-768)

Status of Recommendations:

Recommendation 1: Direct the cultural resource management programs to develop and provide Congress a needs assessment listing specific actions, resources, and time needed to complete the inventories and summaries required by NAGPRA sections 5 and 6 for their historical collections.

Response: This is underway in most of the bureaus within Interior. Interior is committed to completing this process. However, one of the greatest challenges in completing summaries and inventories of all NAGPRA items is locating collections and acquiring information from repositories. Federal collections are curated in public museums, universities, and other repositories at the direction of the Antiquities Act of 1906 and the Archaeological Resources Protection Act of 1979 (ARPA). Museums are also in possession of collections from public lands that were not collected under permit or were moved from the repository originally designated in the permit, and therefore not traceable through the federal permit records. These instances illustrate the importance of repositories notifying agencies upon discovery of Federal collections in their possession.

The NAGPRA needs assessment components that necessitate coordination with non-federal repositories curating DOI museum collections must be integrated with the DOI corrective action plan. The corrective action plan was developed in response to the findings in the Office of the Inspector General's (OIG) report entitled, *Department of the Interior Museum Collections: Accountability and Preservation* (C-IN-MOA-0010-2008).

In addition to the requisite resources, the needs assessment should recognize that the completion of NAGPRA summaries and inventories of all Native American human remains, funerary objects, sacred objects, and objects of cultural patrimony in DOI control will only be possible with the cooperation and assistance of repositories that possess DOI collections and with effective, responsive consultation with Indian tribes and Native Hawaiian organizations.

Recommendation 2: Direct the cultural resource management programs to develop and provide Congress a timetable for expeditious publication in the Federal Register of notices of inventory completion for all remaining Native American human remains and associated funerary objects that have been culturally affiliated in inventories.

Response: Interior bureaus are at varied levels of completion based on the respective size of their collections. As the lack of sufficient resources is a challenge, Interior will develop a timetable that considers this challenge in completing the needs assessment and in meeting any timetable.

Recommendation 3: To clarify the list of Indian tribes eligible under NAGPRA, the National NAGPRA in conjunction with Interior's Office of the Solicitor, reassess whether ANCSA corporations should be considered as eligible entities for the purposes of carrying out NAGPRA given the Solicitor's opinion and BIA policy concerning the status of ANCSA corporations.

Response: The ANCSA corporations were put on the National NAGPRA Program list of tribes for consultation in April 2010, and they were removed in May 2010.

Recommendation 4: To improve the confidence in the Review Committee and its support among NAGPRA practitioners, National NAGPRA should strictly adhere to the nomination process prescribed in the act and, working with Interior's Office of the Solicitor as appropriate, ensure that all Review Committee nominations are properly screened to confirm that the nominees and nominating entities meet statutory requirements.

Response: The Review Committee nomination procedures were revised in 2008 to ensure full transparency. Interior will ask the Solicitor's Office to review these procedures.

Recommendation 5: To provide policymakers with information to assess the overall effectiveness of NAGPRA and provide Indian tribes and Native Hawaiian organizations readily accessible information on items available for repatriation, the GAO recommends that the Secretaries of Agriculture, Defense, and the Interior, and the Chief Executive Officer to the Tennessee Valley Authority direct their cultural resource management programs to report their repatriation data to National NAGPRA on a regular basis, but no less than annually, for each notice of inventory completion they have published or plan to publish.

Response: After review and acceptance of an annual reporting template from National NAGPRA, DOI bureaus will work toward completing an annual report beginning in 2011. National NAGPRA will then compile an annual summary report of agency data.

APPENDIX IX: COMMENTS FROM THE TENNESSEE VALLEY AUTHORITY

TVA

Tennessee Valley Authority, 400 W. Summit Hill Drive, Knoxville, Tennessee 37902

Anda A. Ray
Senior Vice President
Environment and Technology

July 15, 2010

Ms. Anu K. Mittal
Director, Natural Resources and Environment
U.S. Government Accountability Office
441 G Street Northwest
Washington, DC 20548

Dear Ms. Mittal:

We appreciate the opportunity to provide comments on draft report (GAO-10-768), prepared by the General Accountability Office, entitled, Native American Graves Protection and Repatriation Act: After Almost 20 Years, Key Federal Agencies Still Have Not Fully Complied with the Act. Our substantive and technical comments on this draft report are provided in the enclosure to this letter.

The Tennessee Valley Authority (TVA) agrees with the conclusions and recommendations of the draft report, subject to a few reservations noted in the enclosed comments. The assessment of needs to complete the inventories and summaries required under sections 5 and 6 of the Native American Graves Protection and Repatriation Act (NAGPRA), and the development of a timetable for the publication of notices for inventory completion would help the agency in its efforts to establish the cultural affiliation of the NAGPRA items in TVA's collection. Determining the cultural affiliations will, in turn, facilitate the repatriation of these items. We have listed below some of TVA's accomplishments in moving towards the goal of repatriating the NAGPRA items in its collection.

- While work still remains in establishing cultural affiliations, TVA has high confidence in the identification of a vast majority of the NAGPRA items in its collections at museums in Alabama, Kentucky, and Tennessee.
- TVA hosted a Tribal Consultation Workshop in May 2002, at which the contents of TVA's NAGPRA collections were discussed with representatives of federally recognized tribes with interest in the Southeastern United States.
- TVA hosted a second Tribal Consultation Workshop in May 2007 to further consult with tribes regarding the contents of the NAGPRA collection; the tribal representatives were provided a compact disc of the preliminary NAGPRA inventory.
- TVA contributed funds for the creation of a digital base of the NAGPRA items curated in the University of Tennessee's McClung Museum.
- TVA created a database of NAGPRA items from written records supplied by the Alabama Museum of Natural History at the University of Alabama.

Ms. Anu K. Mittal
Page 2
July 15, 2010

- TVA staff traveled to North Carolina and Oklahoma during FY 2005 to conduct face-to-face meetings with representatives of nine federally recognized tribes.
- TVA staff traveled to Alabama, Louisiana, Missouri, Mississippi, Oklahoma, and Texas during FY 2006 to conduct face-to-face meetings with representatives of 11 federally recognized tribes.
- TVA assigned an employee in 2005 to serve part-time as the Native American Liaison; subsequently, a full time position of Native American Liaison was created in May 2009.
- In April 2009, TVA created a new position of senior specialist whose primary function is NAGPRA coordination.
- TVA has conducted multiple dispositions (post-1990) of Native American human remains that were either inadvertent discoveries or the result of intentional excavations.
- For FY 2010, as of June 2010, TVA has spent approximately $55,000 on NAGPRA compliance.
- Prior to the enactment of NAGPRA, TVA repatriated 137 sets of human remains from its Tellico project.

We respectfully request that the GAO modify the draft report to accommodate TVA's comments as outlined herein or include this letter (and enclosure) in the appendix of the final report.

If there are questions, please contact Wayne R. Gildroy, Assistant General Counsel, at (865) 632-7361.

Sincerely,

Anda A. Ray

Anda A. Ray

Enclosure

End Notes

[1] Pub. L. No. 101-601, 104 Stat. 3048-58 (1990), *codified at* 25 U.S.C. §§ 3001-3013. The implementing regulations for the act are at 43 C.F.R. pt. 10. The items covered by NAGPRA are defined in table 1.

[2] NAGPRA has a separate provision for Native American items newly excavated or discovered on federal or tribal lands after the date of enactment, referred to as new or inadvertent discoveries and intentional excavations. New or inadvertent discoveries and intentional excavations are covered in section 3 of the act (25 U.S.C. § 3002) and the identification and repatriation of NAGPRA items within collections that existed on or before the date of enactment, referred to as historical collections, are covered in sections 5, 6, and 7 (25 U.S.C. §§ 3003-3005). In accordance with NAGPRA's implementing regulations, section 5, 6, and 7 also apply to collections federal agencies and museums acquire, from sources other than federal or tribal land, after NAGPRA's enactment. This chapter focuses on historical collections.

[3] "Native American" means of, or relating to, a tribe, people, or culture that is indigenous to the United States. 25 U.S.C. § 3001(9).

[4] "Indian tribe" means any tribe, band, nation, or other organized group or community of Indians, including any Alaska Native village (as defined in, or established pursuant to, the Alaska Native Claims Settlement Act) which is recognized as eligible for the special programs and services provided by the United States to Indians because of their status as Indians. 25 U.S.C. § 3001(7). "Native Hawaiian organization" means any organization which (1) serves and represents the interests of Native Hawaiians, (2) has as a primary and stated

purpose the provision of services to Native Hawaiians, and (3) has expertise in Native Hawaiian affairs, and shall include the Office of Hawaiian Affairs and Hui Malama I Na Kupuna O Hawai'i Nei. 25 U.S.C. § 3001(11).

[5] NAGPRA requires repatriation to lineal descendants under certain circumstances, for example when a direct lineal descendant of an individual who owned a sacred object requests repatriation. In this chapter, we refer to repatriation of culturally affiliated human remains and objects to Indian tribes and Native Hawaiian organizations but intend that reference to include lineal descendants when applicable.

[6] Makah Indian Tribe and the National Association of Tribal Historic Preservation Officers, *Federal Agency Implementation of the Native American Graves Protection and Repatriation Act* (Washington, D.C.: June 30, 2008).

[7] As of September 30, 2009, there were 20 living current and former Review Committee members; 3 former members are deceased.

[8] The federal government has come into possession of collections, and Native American collections in particular, through other means. For example, in the late 1880s, the Surgeon General issued a directive for military personnel in the field to gather the skulls of Native Americans killed in battle for the purposes of scientific study. The remains were first stored and studied at the Army Medical Museum, then later became part of the Smithsonian Institution's collections.

[9] A repository is a facility such as a museum, archeological center, laboratory or storage facility that is managed by a university, college, museum, or other educational or scientific institution, a federal, state, or local government agency, or Indian tribe that can provide professional, systematic, and accountable curatorial services on a long-term basis. 36 C.F.R. § 79.4(j).

[10] According to TVA officials, its NAGPRA items are confined to the collections in Alabama, Kentucky, and Tennessee.

[11] The Smithsonian Institution's repatriation requirements were established in 1989 and amended in 1996. *See* National Museum of the American Indian Act, Pub. L. No. 101-185, §§ 11-17, 103 Stat. 1336, 1343-7 (1989); Pub. L. No. 104-278, §§ 3-5, 110 Stat. 3355-7 (1996) (codified as amended at 20 U.S.C. §§ 80q-9 to -15).

[12] "Possession" means having physical custody of human remains, funerary objects, sacred objects, or objects of cultural patrimony with a sufficient legal interest to lawfully treat the objects as part of its collection for purposes of these regulations (43 C.F.R. § 10.2(a)(3)(i)); and "control" means having a legal interest in human remains, funerary objects, sacred objects, or objects of cultural patrimony sufficient to lawfully permit the federal agency or museum to treat the objects as part of its collection for purposes of these regulations whether or not the human remains, funerary objects, sacred objects, or objects of cultural patrimony are in the physical custody of the federal agency or museum (43 C.F.R. § 10.2(a)(3)(ii)). Often collections controlled by federal agencies are in the possession of a nonfederal repository.

[13] 25 U.S.C. § 3001(4) (federal agency); and 25 U.S.C. § 3001(8) (museum).

[14] The Antiquities Act of 1906 authorized the Secretaries of the Interior, Agriculture, and Army to issue permits for the examination of ruins, excavation of archeological sites, and the gathering of objects of antiquity on lands under their jurisdiction. Pub. L. No. 59-209, 34 Stat. 225 (1906), *codified at* 16 U.S.C. §§ 431-433. These three departments adopted joint regulations that authorized the Secretaries to issue the permits after receiving a recommendation on the permit application from the Smithsonian Institution. The Archaeological Resources Protection Act of 1979 replaced the Antiquities Act of 1906. Pub. L. No. 96-95, 93 Stat. 721 (1979), *codified at* 16 U.S.C. §§ 470aa-mm. In 1981, when the Archaeological Resources Protection Act process came into effect, NPS issued permits for all government agencies, and some agencies eventually began issuing permits themselves.

[15] Federal regulations regarding how agencies should oversee and manage these collections removed from federal lands but preserved in public museums were not promulgated until September 1990, 2 months before NAGPRA was enacted. 55 Fed. Reg. 37616 (Sept. 12, 1990).

[16] U.S. Department of the Interior, Office of the Inspector General, *Department of the Interior – Museum Collections: Accountability and Preservation*, Report No. C-IN-MOA-0010-2008 (Washington, D.C.: Dec. 16, 2009).

[17] 25 U.S.C. § 3001(2).

[18] NAGPRA's implementing regulations direct federal agencies and museums to retain possession of culturally unidentifiable human remains pending promulgation of 43 C.F.R. § 10.11 (the regulation to govern the disposition of culturally unidentifiable human remains) unless legally required to do otherwise, or recommended to do otherwise by the Secretary of the Interior. Recommendations regarding the disposition of culturally unidentifiable human remains may be requested prior to final promulgation of 43 C.F.R. § 10.11. 43 C.F.R. § 10.9(e)(6). The regulation to govern the disposition of culturally unidentifiable human remains, 43 C.F.R. § 10.11, was promulgated on March 15, 2010, and became effective on May 14, 2010. 75 Fed. Reg. 12378 (Mar. 15, 2010). Appendix IV further discusses this regulation.

[19] 43 C.F.R. § 10.8(f).

[20] 43 C.F.R. § 10.10(f)(1).

[21] 25 U.S.C. § 3006.

[22] Pub. L. No. 101-601, § 8(c)(3) (1990), *codified at* 25 U.S.C. § 3006(c)(3).

[23] Pub. L. No. 101-601, § 8(c)(4) (1990), *codified at* 25 U.S.C. § 3006(c)(4). The Review Committee's authority under sections 8(c)(3) and section 8(c)(4) is separate and distinct from the Review Committee's authority to hear and make recommendations regarding the disposition of culturally unidentifiable human remains. We refer to these findings, recommendations, and facilitating the resolution of disputes that do not involve culturally unidentifiable human remains simply as "disputes" in this chapter.

[24] Pub. L. No. 92-463, 86 Stat. 770 (1972) (classified at 5 U.S.C. app. 2); 41 C.F.R. pt. 102-3.

[25] Federal conflict-of-interest statutes (18 U.S.C. § 201), including the principal criminal financial conflict-of-interest statute (18 U.S.C. § 208), apply to regular and, in large part, special government employees.

[26] 58 Fed. Reg. 31122 (May 28, 1993) (proposed rule); and 60 Fed. Reg. 62134 (Dec. 4, 1995) (final rule). The final rule was effective on January 3, 1996.

[27] Although its location within NPS has changed over time, and it has been called different things over time, for simplicity in our report we will refer to the office that has carried out the Secretary of the Interior's national responsibilities under NAGPRA since 1990 as National NAGPRA.

[28] Although consultation grants are technically referred to as consultation/documentation grants, for the purposes of this chapter, we will refer to them as consultation grants.

[29] Pub. L. No. 92-203, 85 Stat. 688 (1971), *codified as amended at* 43 U.S.C. §§ 1601-1629h. ANCSA directed the establishment of 12 for-profit regional corporations—1 for each geographic region in Alaska comprised of Natives having a common heritage and sharing common interests—and over 200 village corporations. It also allowed nonresident Alaska Natives to elect to establish a 13th regional corporation. In addition, ANCSA section 14(h)(2) allowed groups that did not qualify to form an Alaska Native village corporation to form Alaska Native "group" corporations and ANCSA section 14(h)(3) allowed Alaska Natives living in Sitka, Kenai, Juneau, and Kodiak to establish "urban" corporations.

[30] H.R. Rep. No. 103-781 at 2-3 (1994).

[31] For additional information on BIA's administrative process for granting federal recognition see GAO, *Indian Issues: Improvements Needed in Tribal Recognition Process*, GAO-02-49 (Washington, D.C.: Nov. 2, 2001). Also see enclosure II of GAO, *Indian Issues: BLM's Program for Issuing Individual Indian Allotments on Public Lands Is No Longer Viable*, GAO-07-23R (Washington, D.C.: Oct. 20, 2006), for information on new and restored tribes.

[32] The Federally Recognized Indian Tribe List Act of 1994, Pub. L. No. 103-454, Title I (1994), recognizes that the Secretary of the Interior is charged with keeping a list of all federally recognized tribes that should be accurate and regularly updated since it is used by the various departments and agencies of the United States to determine the eligibility of certain groups to receive services from the United States and that the list should reflect all of the federally recognized Indian tribes in the United States that are eligible for the special programs and services provided by the United States because of their status as Indians. Additionally, in response to the omission of the Central Council of Tlingit and Haida Indian Tribes of Alaska from BIA's 1993 list, Congress passed the Tlingit and Haida Status Clarification Act to reaffirm and acknowledge that the Council is a federally recognized tribe. Pub. L. No. 103-454, Title II (1994). The Council has been included in subsequent BIA lists of federally recognized tribes.

[33] 74 Fed. Reg. 40218 (Aug. 11, 2009).

[34] Op. Sol. Int. M-36975 (Jan. 11, 1993).

[35] Curation is the process of managing and preserving a collection according to professional museum and archival practices.

[36] GAO, *Are Agencies Doing Enough or Too Much for Archaeological Preservation? Guidance Needed*, CED-81-61 (Washington, D.C.: Apr. 22, 1981).

[37] U.S. Department of the Interior, Office of the Inspector General, *Department of the Interior – Museum Collections: Accountability and Preservation*, Report No. C-IN-MOA-0010-2008 (Washington, D.C.: Dec. 16, 2009).

[38] 25 U.S.C. § 3004.

[39] Six months after the November 16, 1995, deadline for the completion of inventories was May 16, 1996.

[40] 60 Fed. Reg. 62134 (Dec. 4, 1995). National NAGPRA did issue guidance prior to the promulgation of the regulation, including summary and inventory templates to agencies, but agencies stated that they were not always received by the appropriate agency staff.

[41] *See* 25 U.S.C. § 3003(c).

[42] Federal agency officials told us that they generally place a higher priority on compliance with NAGPRA section 3 (new or inadvertent discoveries and intentional excavations) versus sections 5 and 6 (historical collections) for a variety of factors. First, unlike historical collections, section 3 does not allow human remains and objects to be classified as culturally unidentifiable, and it provides a priority order for determining ownership, control, and transfer of custody. Second, while substantial research may be required to determine the locations in which historical collections were originally excavated or found, agencies already have this information for new or inadvertent and intentional discoveries. Third, if discoveries are made during the course of major projects, such as construction, the project must be temporarily halted to comply with NAGPRA.

[43] Pub. L. No. 89-665, 80 Stat. 915 (1966), *codified as amended at* 16 U.S.C. §§ 470 to 470x-6.

[44] Pub. L. No. 91-190, 83 Stat. 852 (1970), *codified at* 42 U.S.C. §§ 4321, 4331-4335.

[45] In this case, originally filed in 1996 and commonly known as the Kennewick Man case, recreational spectators found human skeletal remains outside of Kennewick, Washington, on land managed by the Corps. Four federally recognized tribes and one non-federally recognized tribe claimed the remains were of an ancestor. The court ruled that the statutory text was written in the present tense ("of, or relating to, a tribe, people, or culture that is indigenous") and thus unambiguously required that human remains bear some relationship to a presently existing tribe, people, or culture to be considered Native American. Bonnichsen v. United States, 367 F.3d 864 (9th Cir. 2004). The remains are currently held at the Burke Museum at the University of Washington.

[46] For additional information on our analysis of disposition requests for culturally unidentifiable human remains, see appendix I.

[47] 75 Fed. Reg. 12378 (Mar. 15, 2010).

[48] In June 2000, the Review Committee published its principles of agreement in the *Federal Register* after it had already made recommendations on 15 disposition requests involving culturally unidentifiable human remains. 65 Fed. Reg. 36462 (June 8, 2000).

[49] 43 C.F.R. § 10.9(e)(6).

[50] In these two instances, Interior did not concur with the Review Committee's determination that the human remains were more likely than not Native American.

[51] GAO, *Federal Advisory Committee Act: Issues Related to the Independence and Balance of Advisory Committees*, GAO-08-611T (Washington, D.C.: Apr. 2, 2008).

[52] U.S. Department of the Interior, NPS, National NAGPRA Program, *Federal Agency NAGPRA Statistics* (Washington, D.C.: Oct. 31, 2006).

[53] NAGPRA requires that the Review Committee maintain a list of culturally unidentifiable human remains. 25 U.S.C. § 3006(c)(5). The Review Committee tasked National NAGPRA with this responsibility and the office maintains an online searchable database.

[54] Since NAGPRA's enactment, National NAGPRA has published 10 nomination solicitations for Review Committee members in the *Federal Register*; the first in August 1991 and the most recent in March 2010. National NAGPRA has also administered the nomination process for the consensus member. This does not require a solicitation in the *Federal Register* as the list of nominees is developed and consented upon by the other Review Committee members.

[55] Op. Sol. Int. M-36975 (Jan. 11, 1993).

[56] Because the BIA list is limited to entities found to be Indian tribes, as that term is defined and used in 25 C.F.R. Part 83, it does not include a number of non-tribal Native entities in Alaska that contract with or receive services from BIA pursuant to specific statutory authority, including ANCSA village and regional corporations and various tribal organizations.

[57] 67 Fed. Reg. 18033 (Apr. 12, 2002).

[58] 68 Fed. Reg. 33964 (June 6, 2003).

[59] 71 Fed. Reg. 47512 (Aug. 17, 2006).

[60] In addition to publishing solicitations in the *Federal Register* for nominations to the Review Committee, National NAGPRA has, at times, also conducted other activities aimed at a broad audience to solicit nominations. For example, National NAGPRA has sent mailings to all Indian tribes eligible under NAGPRA to solicit nominations. We have no concerns with this process because it is broad-based and inclusive and allows for greater participation in the process.

[61] Federal agencies define repatriation as the transfer of control (legal title). Repatriation does not necessarily include the transfer of physical possession of the human remains and/or objects, as long the place and manner of repatriation is determined in consultation with the Indian tribe or Native Hawaiian organization making the repatriation request.

[62] Forest Service officials stated that it and some other federal agencies have periodically presented aggregate repatriation data at Review Committee meetings. The information presented to the Review Committee would also be available to National NAGPRA.

[63] 25 U.S.C. § 3005(e).

[64] 75 Fed. Reg. 12378 (Mar. 15, 2010).

[65] Notices of intended disposition are published in certain newspapers by the federal agencies responsible for NAGPRA items that were intentionally excavated or inadvertently discovered on federal lands after NAGPRA's enactment. Unlike notices of inventory completion and notices of intent to repatriate, they are not published in the *Federal Register*.

[66] GAO, *Federal Advisory Committees: Additional Guidance Could Help Agencies Better Ensure Independence and Balance*, GAO-04-328 (Washington, D.C.: Apr. 16, 2004); and GAO, *Federal Advisory Committee Act: Issues Related to the Independence and Balance of Advisory Committees*, GAO-08-611T (Washington, D.C.: Apr. 2, 2008).

[67] Of the 14 nominations, 10 were published in the *Federal Register* because National NAGPRA was seeking to fill positions that required the nomination by an Indian tribe, a Native Hawaiian organization, or a traditional Native American religious leader, or national museum or scientific organization. Because the remaining four positions were filled by the Secretary appointing an individual from a list developed and approved by the other Review Committee members, a *Federal Register* notice was not required.

[68] 43 C.F.R. § 10.13(c)(1).

[69] GAO, *Indian Issues: Improvements Needed in Tribal Recognition Process*, GAO-02-49 (Washington, D.C.: Nov. 2, 2001).

[70] GAO, *Indian Issues: BLM's Program for Issuing Individual Indian Allotments on Public Lands Is No Longer Viable*, GAO-07-23R (Washington, D.C.: Oct. 20, 2006).

[71] 74 Fed. Reg. 40218 (Aug. 11, 2009). On June 18, 2010, BIA published its final determination to acknowledge the Shinnecock Indian Nation. 75 Fed. Reg. 34760 (June 18, 2010). Two interested parties requested reconsideration of the final determination by the Interior Board of Indian Appeals so the determination is not yet effective.

[72] 73 Fed. Reg. 18553 (Apr. 4, 2008); and 74 Fed. Reg. 40218 (Aug. 11, 2009).

[73] 25 U.S.C. § 3007.

[74] H.R. Rep. 101-877, at 16 (1990).

[75] 75 Fed. Reg. 12378, 12398 (Mar. 15, 2010) (citations omitted).

[76] 43 C.F.R. § 10.11(b)(1), (2).

[77] 43 C.F.R. § 10.11(c)(1).

[78] 25 U.S.C. § 3001(13).

[79] U.S. Const., amend. V.

[80] U.S. Const., Art. VI, cl. 2.

[81] 43 C.F.R. § 10.11(c)(2).

[82] 43 C.F.R. § 10.11(c)(4).

[83] U.S. Department of the Interior, National Park Service, *Journeys to Repatriation: 15 Years of NAGPRA Grants, 1994-2008* (Washington, D.C.: August 2009).

[84] 25 U.S.C. § 3003(b)(1)(A).

[85] NAGPRA requires agencies to notify Indian tribes and Native Hawaiian organizations that have been culturally affiliated with human remains and/or associated funerary objects within 6 months after the completion of the inventory. 25 U.S.C. § 3003(d)(1). A copy of the notice must be provided to National NAGPRA for publication in the *Federal Register* (a notice of inventory completion). 25 U.S.C. § 3003(d)(3).

In: Native American Graves and Repatriation
Editor: Kathy J. Bergmann

ISBN: 978-1-61122-410-8

Chapter 2

NATIVE AMERICAN GRAVES PROTECTION AND REPATRIATION REVIEW COMMITTEE REPORT TO THE CONGRESS FOR 2008

United States Department of the Interior

INTRODUCTION

Passage of the Native American Graves Protection and Repatriation Act of 1990 (NAGPRA) marked a watershed in the long and often troubled relationship between Native Americans and many of this country's educational institutions, museums, and public agencies. NAGPRA provides for the disposition of Native American cultural items human remains, funerary objects, sacred objects, and objects of cultural patrimony removed from Federal or tribal lands to lineal descendants or Indian tribes or Native Hawaiian organizations based on geographic or cultural affiliation. NAGPRA also prohibits trafficking of Native American cultural items. Lastly, NAGPRA provides for the repatriation of Native American cultural items in museum and Federal agency collections to lineal descendants or culturally affiliated Indian tribes or Native Hawaiian organizations.

NAGPRA directs the Secretary of the Interior to establish and maintain the Native American Graves Protection and Repatriation Review Committee to monitor and review the summary, inventory, and repatriation requirements of the Act. The Review Committee operates in accordance with the Federal Advisory Committee Act and a charter issued by the Secretary of the Interior. The Review Committee's actions and findings are advisory, although they may be admissible in court proceedings.

This chapter is prepared and submitted to Congress, as required by NAGPRA, to identify progress made and barriers encountered in implementing the summary, inventory, and repatriation requirements of the Act.

Review Committee Activities

This chapter summarizes the Review Committee's activities for calendar year 2008. The Review Committee convened three times during the reporting period: January 8 via teleconference; May 15-16 in De Pere, WI; and October 11-12 in San Diego, CA.

All of the seven members continued to serve on the Review Committee during calendar year 2008. Members appointed from nominations received from national museum organizations and scientific organizations were Dan Monroe, Vincas Steponaitis and Alan Goodman. Members appointed from nominations received from Indian tribes, Native Hawaiian organizations, or traditional religious leaders were Donna Augustine, Willie Jones and Rosita Worl. The seventh member, appointed from a list of persons developed and consented to by all of the other members of the Review Committee, was Colin Kippen.

The Review Committee's activities are prescribed by the Review Committee's charter and the Act. During calendar year 2008 the Review Committee

- Monitored the inventory and identification process conducted by museums and Federal agencies.
- Made recommendations regarding the disposition of culturally unidentifiable human remains from Arizona, Colorado, Kentucky, Michigan, Nebraska, Tennessee, Washington, and West Virginia. For further information regarding recommendations of the Review Committee on these dispositions we direct the reader to: www.nps.gov/history/NAGPRA/Review/Summary_Requests_RC_1994-2008.pdf
- Consulted with representatives of the Secretary of the Interior regarding proposed regulations for the disposition of unclaimed cultural items (43 CFR 10.7). At the October meeting in De Pere, WI the Review Committee was provided with transcripts of the consultations regarding these proposed regulations. The transcripts were extensive, and the Review Committee requested a manageable executive summary from the National NAGPRA office. In the May 2009 meeting held in Seattle, WA the Review Committee was given the executive summary on a compact disc with the underlying documents, along with a two-page report from the drafting committee of the proposed regulations. Further work related to these proposed regulations was deferred by the Review Committee to the October 2009 meeting in Sarasota, FL, and will be reported on in the 2009 report to Congress.
- Consulted with Indian tribes, Native Hawaiian organizations, museums, and Federal agencies on inventory, identification, and repatriation activities.

Progress Made

Most museums and Federal agencies appear to have carried out the provisions of NAGPRA in good faith.

Section 5 of the Act requires all museums and Federal agencies that have possession or control over Native American human remains and associated funerary objects to compile inventories of such items in consultation with Indian tribes and Native Hawaiian organizations. As of December 31, 2008, inventories had been completed by 1,257 institutions (including both museums and Federal agencies).

Section 6 of the Act requires all museums and Federal agencies that have possession or control over collections that may contain unassociated funerary objects, sacred objects, or objects of cultural patrimony to complete summaries of such collections. As of December 31, 2008, summaries had been completed by 1,065 institutions (including both museums and Federal agencies).

Section 7 of the Act requires all museums and Federal agencies to repatriate human remains, funerary objects, sacred objects, and objects of cultural patrimony upon the request of known lineal descendants or culturally affiliated Indian tribes or Native Hawaiian organizations. While the number of actual repatriations is not monitored, notices published in the Federal Register provide a measure of museums and Federal agencies that have agreed to repatriate cultural items. As of December 31, 2008, museums and Federal agencies had published 1,147 notices of inventory completion accounting for the remains of 36,531 individuals and 771,014 associated funerary objects. Museums and Federal agencies had also published 425 notices of intent to repatriate accounting for 3,771 sacred objects, 381 objects of cultural patrimony, 806 cultural items that fit both the sacred and cultural patrimony categories, and 215 unspecified cultural items.

Select museums and Federal agencies have consulted with tribes and Native Hawaiian organizations and conducted the necessary research to affiliate Native American and associated funerary objects that had previously been determined to be culturally unidentified individuals (CUI). Thus far, 2,321 human remains have been affiliated from those on the CUI database.

Barriers Encountered

While the Review Committee is pleased with the progress noted above, we also wish to call attention to the barriers encountered with NAGPRA. Review of the progress of NAGPRA reveals that 118,400 Native American human remains and 828,641 associated funerary objects have been labeled and indicate that over 60% of human remains held by museums and Federal agencies have not been assigned a reasonable cultural affiliation. While some individuals may be labeled culturally unidentifiable because of lack of information, these numbers might be drastically reduced if, as required by NAGPRA legislation, more consultation were carried out. Further research and consultation is required to bring all museums and Federal agencies into compliance with the law, and thus to dramatically decrease the number of human remains on the CUI database and fulfill the intent of the law.

The Review Committee views this issue very seriously and is considering steps that can be made to ensure museums, Federal agencies, and tribes have the resources and opportunities to increase consultation. To this end, the Review Committee is very concerned about the costs of compliance. These costs include documentation, consultation, travel, and the transfer of cultural items. Most of these costs are borne by museums, Federal agencies, and tribes. The National NAGPRA Program administers a competitive grant program to assist in funding some of these activities. In FY 2009, requests totaling $4.2 million were received, and grants totaling $1.8 million were awarded. With the advent of the culturally unidentifiable (CUI) database placing information in the inventories on-line and accessible to tribes, it is anticipated that there will be a resurgence of consultation activity on a large scale. We feel this indicates a positive step toward full compliance, and note the extreme importance of providing funds for tribes and institutions to complete this work. The future success of the program rests solidly in such actions.

The number of human remains that could be repatriated may increase dramatically if tribes, museums and Federal agencies had more extensive funding to complete consultation and research of the remains on the culturally unidentifiable database. We have already begun to see the positive effects of the online database, as evidenced in the number of requests for Review Committee recommendations for disposition of the remains, and the number of positive recommendations. There is a serious need for further funding of the grant program to allow the law to work most effectively as it was intended.

Nearly 19 years after NAGPRA s passage, three key sections of the implementing regulations are still pending. Currently, a proposed rule for disposition of culturally unidentifiable human remains (43 CFR 10.11) has been published and public comment has been received. The January 8, 2008 Review Committee meeting was for the sole purpose of entering comment on the proposed rule. At that time the Review Committee unanimously passed a resolution recommending that the Assistant Secretary publish a new proposed rule for public comment before a final rule is enacted. The National NAGPRA Program reported to the Review Committee at the May 2008 meeting in De Pere, WI that the Assistant Secretary felt the 90-day comment period was sufficient, and the comments went into draft and review at the Department of the Interior for the remainder of 2008. With the change of administration in 2009, the rule is currently in review a second time. The Review Committee eagerly awaits the implementation of this rule as it is of critical importance for tribes and affects a large number of collections still remaining in control of museums and Federal agencies.

In 2008 there was no progress on the rule for the disposition of unclaimed human remains, funerary objects, sacred objects, or objects of cultural patrimony (43 CFR 10.7). In addition, in 2008, no action was taken on 43 CFR 10.15(b), failure to claim where no repatriation or disposition has occurred, as it is too early to determine what the remainder population will be once 10.7 and 10.11 are in place. This will become clearer and needs to be addressed after completion of rule 10.7 and 10.11.

The Review Committee believes it is of utmost importance that these rules be completed and implemented as soon as possible, and continues its efforts to ensure that this goal is achieved.

The Review Committee continues to be concerned that overall Federal agency compliance with NAGPRA has been uneven, difficult to measure, and lacking in transparency despite the huge role Federal agencies play in implementing the terms of the Act. This lack of accurate information about the status of Federal agency compliance makes it difficult to know whether these Federal agencies are meeting their responsibilities to the stakeholders under the Act and impedes the oversight functions envisioned for the Review Committee when the Act was created. This lack of data also makes it impossible to meaningfully evaluate whether the requisite constitutionally mandated government-to-government relationship between Federal agencies and Indian tribes is occurring through the consultation provisions contained within the Act and its related administrative rules. The Review Committee has three times requested a GAO study of Federal agency compliance, and such a study has been instigated by the GAO at the request of the Senate Indian Affairs Committee and the House Committee on Natural Resources. We are pleased to have this study in progress and anticipate results in 2010.

Also with regard to Federal agency and museum compliance, the Review Committee is very concerned with the actions and final outcomes of disputes that come before the Review Committee. It is our hope that these disputes are settled in a timely manner, but we currently are limited in our ability to track the final outcome of these cases. We would like to know which disputes have been resolved, how many resulted in reburial, and how many went on further to litigation in court.

In 2008 only one dispute came before the Review Committee. The dispute was between the Onondaga Nation and the New York State Museum and related to the cultural affiliation of 180 individuals removed from the Engelbert site. The Review Committee heard the dispute at its October meeting in San Diego, and ruled in favor of the Onondaga Nation. The meeting minutes related to this dispute can be found online at: http://www.nps.gov/ history/nagpra/ REVIEW/ meetings/RCMIN038.pdf. The findings and recommendations of the Review Committee related to this case have been published in the Federal Register, and are also available online at: http://www.nps.gov/nagpra/ REVIEW/ RCNOTICES/RCF13.htm

By talking with the legal counsel of the Onondaga Nation, the Review Committee has learned of the positive final outcome of this dispute. In September 2009, the remains were repatriated and then reburied by the Onondaga Nation. However, this repatriation did NOT include the associated funerary objects from the burials, which are held at another institution (SUNY Binghamton). The Onondaga Nation requested repatriation of all associated funerary objects, but is still in discussion with SUNY Binghamton about this claim. Neither the Onondaga Nation nor the New York State Museum applied for a NAGPRA repatriation grant to fund the repatriation.

The Review Committee will continue to attempt to track the outcome of disputes that come before the Review Committee. It would be very problematic to find that, after all the effort and labor put into bringing disputes before the Review Committee, there is a consistent lack of positive outcomes. We feel it is critical to understand how the dispute and finding of fact processes are working, as this will aspect of NAGPRA compliance.

The Review Committee is encouraged by the organized manner in which civil penalties investigations are proceeding since publication of the final rule on civil penalties (43 CFR 10.12). We are pleased that the backlog of cases in need of investigation, substantiation, and disposition was reduced in 2008, yet we note that 23 new cases have been submitted, leaving 60 cases yet to be investigated involving 26 museums. The present investigator has done a commendable job at reducing the backlog of cases, but he is currently assigned at the rate of only 10 hours per week. The Review Committee believes that this investigator should be assigned full-time to NAGPRA cases while not decreasing existing funding for enforcement of the Archaeological Resources Protection Act (ARPA).

The ability to rebury as close to the original interment site as possible is an issue of great importance to many Native Americans. Since many of the human remains subject to NAGPRA originate from burials on Federal lands, agencies' reburial policies often determine whether a repatriation can be fully satisfactory. Unfortunately, there is no uniform Federal policy on reburial. The Review Committee recommends that a uniform reburial policy on Federal lands be developed in consultation between Federal agencies and Indian tribes and Native Hawaiian organizations, and adopted.

As a key piece of human-rights legislation, NAGPRA has played an essential role in empowering Native American communities to recover culturally important items from Federal agencies and museums. In so doing it has helped to right past wrongs, and has also fostered new, more productive relationships between Native communities and these agencies and museums. NAGPRA has led to many successes, but its future success depends on continued support from Congress, particularly in overcoming some of the barriers identified above.

RECOMMENDATIONS

Authorized by the Native American Graves Protection and Repatriation Act [25 U.S.C. 3006], the Native American Graves Protection and Repatriation Review Committee has served since 1992 to monitor and review implementation of the Act. At its October 30-31, 2009 meeting, the Review Committee made the following recommendations:

1. **Costs to Comply with NAGPRA.** The Review Committee recommends that Congress appropriate the following amounts for FY 2009 to ensure continued implementation of the Act:
   - At least $4.1 million in grants to Indian tribes, Native Hawaiian organizations, and museums;
   - The amount requested by the administration that is targeted for each Federal agency's compliance efforts.

   The Review Committee also recommends that the President request the same amounts listed above in the FY 2011 budget proposal. With the recent promulgation of 43 CFR 10.13 (ongoing compliance due dates) and the pending promulgation of 43 CFR 10.7(lands) and 43 CFR 10.11(CUI), we expect consultation activity to increase in coming years, which will regenerate an increasing volume of NAGPRA grant requests.
2. **Open Hearings to Determine Progress Made and Barriers Encountered by Tribes and Federal Agencies and Museums.** The Review Committee acknowledges that there are barriers encountered by tribes, museums, and Federal agencies with regard to NAGPRA. We are aware of some of these (as outlined above), but we feel that it is most productive to hear from these groups themselves about the barriers es, museums and Federal agencies who have beenthey ve encountered. Trib actively involved in the on-the-ground workings of NAGPRA are the ones best equipped to offer details of how the law is working, the progress made, and the barriers encountered. For this reason, the Review Committee recommends that Congress hold open hearings related to NAGPRA in which representatives who represent a wide range of the communities involved in NAGPRA are invited to testify and share their views and experiences. This will provide an invaluable resource that can guide any future improvements to NAGPRA.
3. **Meeting with Museum and Federal Agencies with large CUI Inventories.** As a way to better understand the problems encountered by museums and Federal agencies with large holdings of CUIs, the Review Committee recommends meeting

with such agencies and tribes that are possible descendants at one of its next meetings.

4. **Development of Reburial Policy.** The Review Committee recommends that a uniform reburial policy on Federal lands be developed in consultation between Federal agencies and Indian tribes and Native Hawaiian organizations, and adopted.
5. **Definition of Native American.** The Review Committee recommends strongly that Congress amend the definition of "Native American" at 25 U.S.C. 3001 (9) by adding the words "or was" so that it reads: "'Native American' means of, or relating to, a tribe, people, or culture that is or was indigenous to the United States."

The Review Committee respectfully submits these recommendations with the full and unanimous support of all members.

Native American Graves Protection and Repatriation Review Committee Members

Donna Augustine (traditional religious leader)
Term: 2006-2010
Nominated by: Aroostook Band of Micmac Indians of Maine, Houlton Band of Maliseet Indians of Maine, Passamaquoddy Tribe of Maine, and Penobscot Tribe of Main

Alan Goodman
Term: 2007-2011
Nominated by: American Anthropological Association

Willie Jones (traditional religious leader)
Term: 2004-2008
Nominated by: Lummi Tribe of the Lummi Reservation, Washington

Colin Kippen
Term: 2005-2009
Nominated by: Concurrence of other Review Committee members

Dan Monroe
Term: 1992-1997
Nominated by: American Association of Museums, Museum Trustee Association
Term: 2004-2008
Nominated by: American Association of Museums

Vincas Steponaitis
Term: 2004-2008
Nominated by: Society for American Archaeology

Rosita Worl
Term: 2001-2006
Nominated by: Huna Heritage Foundation on behalf of Huna Totem Corporation
Term: 2007-2009
Nominated by: Huna Heritage Foundation on behalf of Huna Totem Corporation
Chair: 2004-end of term 2009

CHARTER: NATIVE AMERICAN GRAVES PROTECTION AND REPATRIATION REVIEW COMMITTEE

A. OFFICIAL DESIGNATION.
The official designation of the Committee is the Native American Graves Protection and Repatriation Review Committee (Committee).

B. PURPOSE.
The purpose of the Committee is to monitor and review the implementation of the inventory and identification processes and repatriation activities required under sections 5, 6 and 7 of Public Law 101-601.

C. DUTIES AND RESPONSIBILITIES.
The duties of the Committee are solely advisory. Specifically, the Committee will be responsible for:

1. Monitoring and reviewing the implementation of the inventory and identification processes and repatriation activities required under sections 5, 6, and 7 of Public Law 101-601 to ensure a fair and objective consideration and assessment of all available relevant information and evidence;
2. Reviewing and making findings relating to the identity or cultural affiliation of human remains, funerary objects, sacred objects, and objects of cultural patrimony, or the repatriation of such items, upon the request of any affected party;
3. Facilitating the resolution of any disputes among Indian tribes, Native Hawaiian organizations, or lineal descendants, and Federal agencies or museums relating to the repatriation of human remains, funerary objects, sacred objects, and objects of cultural patrimony, including convening the parties to the dispute, if deemed desirable;
4. Compiling an inventory of culturally unidentifiable human remains that are in the possession or control of each Federal agency and museum and recommending specific actions for disposition of such human remains;
5. Consulting with Indian tribes, Native Hawaiian organizations, and museums on matters pertaining to the work of the Committee affecting such tribes or organizations;
6. Consulting with the Secretary in the development of regulations to carry out Public Law 101-601;
7. Performing such other related functions as the Secretary may assign to the Committee;

8. Making recommendations, if appropriate, regarding future care of human remains, funerary objects, sacred objects, and objects of cultural patrimony which are to be repatriated; and
9. Submitting an annual report to Congress on the progress and any barriers encountered in carrying out the Committee responsibilities during the year.

D. MEMBERSHIP.

1. The Committee will be composed of seven members appointed by the Secretary as follows:
   (a) Three members appointed from nominations submitted by Indian tribes, Native Hawaiian organizations, and traditional Native American religious leaders, with at least two of such persons being traditional Native American religious leaders;
   (b) Three members appointed from nominations submitted by national museum organizations and scientific organizations; and
   (c) One member appointed from nominations developed and consented to by the other members of the committee.
2. Members are appointed as Special Government Employees.
3. Terms of appointment will be for 4 years. Reappointment of current members will be for a term of 2 years. All appointments will terminate upon the termination of the Committee. Any vacancy on the Committee will be filled in the same manner in which the original appointment was made within 90 days of the occurrence of such vacancy.
4. Any member who fails to attend two successive meetings of the Committee, or who otherwise fails to substantively participate in the work of the Committee, may be removed from the Committee by the Secretary and a replacement named.
5. Members of the Committee will serve without pay, but will be reimbursed at a rate equal to the daily rate for Level IV of the Executive Schedule for each day (including travel time) for which the member is actually engaged in Committee business. While away from their homes or regular places of business in the performance of services of the Committee, members will be allowed travel expenses, including per diem in lieu of subsistence, in the same manner as persons employed intermittently in government service are allowed such expenses in accordance with Sections 5703 of Title 5 of the United States Code.
6. The Secretary will establish such rules and regulations for the Committee as are necessary. The Secretary may not appoint Federal Officers or employees to the Committee.

E. ETHICS RESPONSIBILITIES OF MEMBERS.

All members will comply with applicable ethics rules and regulations. The Department of the Interior will provide materials to those members appointed as Special Government Employees, explaining their ethical obligations and with which the members should be familiar. Consistent with the ethics requirements, members will endeavor to avoid any actions that would cause the public to question the integrity of the activities, or advice. The provisions of this paragraph do not affect any other statutory or regulatory ethical obligations to which a member may be subject.

F. ADMINISTRATION.

1. CHARTER. The Committee is subject to the provisions of the Federal Advisory Committee Act (FACA), 5 U.S.C. Appendix (1994). The Committee will take no action unless the charter filing requirements of sections 9 and 14(b) of FACA have been complied with.
2. DESIGNATED FEDERAL OFFICIAL. The Committee reports to the Secretary of the Interior, United States Department of the Interior, 1849 C Street, NW, Washington, DC 20240. The Manager, National NAGPRA program, National Park Service, or a designee will serve as the Designated Federal Official (DFO) required by section 10 of FACA to oversee the management of the Committee.
3. CHAIRPERSON. The Committee will designate one member to be Chairperson.
4. SUPPORT AND COST. Support for the Committee is provided by the U.S. Department of the Interior, National Park Service, Office of the Director. The estimated annual operating cost of the Committee is $163,000, which includes the cost of 0.5 work-years of staff support.
5. MEETINGS. The Committee will meet approximately three times a year, although it may convene more often if there is an immediate need for consultation, advice and review. All meetings of the Committee will be subject to the provisions FACA, 5 U.S.C. Appendix (1994). No Advisory Committee member, and no member of any subgroup of this Committee, shall participate in any matter in which the member has a financial interest.
6. SUBCOMMITTEES. The Committee may, in consultation with the DFO, create subcommittees from among its membership supplemented when appropriate by members of the public, provided that the role of such subcommittees will be solely to gather information or conduct research for the Committee, to analyze relevant issues and facts, or to draft proposed position papers for deliberation by the Committee. Membership on all subcommittees will be determined by the Chairperson, subject to the concurrence of the DFO. Subcommittees will meet as necessary, subject to the approval of the DFO.

G. DURATION AND DATE OF TERMINATION.

In view of the objectives, scope and purposes of the Committee, it is expected to continue into the foreseeable future. The Committee will terminate at the end of the 120-day period beginning on the day the Secretary certifies, in a report submitted to Congress, that the work of the Committee has been completed.

H. AUTHORITY.

The Native American Graves Protection and Repatriation Review Committee is established by authority of Section 8 of Public Law 101-601, November 16, 1990.

/s/ Dirk Kempthorne /November 24, 2008
Secretary of the Interior Date Signed
DATE CHARTER FILED November 24, 2008

THE NATIONAL NAGPRA PROGRAM

This chapter was prepared by the Native American Graves Protection and Repatriation Review Committee and edited and produced by the National NAGPRA Program.

The National NAGPRA Program carries out certain responsibilities for the Secretary of the Interior and Assistant Secretary for Fish and Wildlife and Parks related to implementation of NAGPRA. One of these duties is to provide administrative and staff support to the Review Committee.

Statements, views, and recommendations in this chapter are those of the Review Committee and should not be interpreted as representing the opinions of the U.S. Government.

Send inquiries about this chapter to:

David Tarler
Designated Federal Officer to the
Native American Graves Protection and Repatriation Review Committee
National NAGPRA Program
National Park Service
1201 Eye Street, NW (8th floor)
Washington, DC 20005
Tel: (202) 354-2108
Fax: (202) 371-5197

November 2009

In: Native American Graves and Repatriation
Editor: Kathy J. Bergmann
ISBN: 978-1-61122-410-8

Chapter 3

JOURNEYS TO REPATRIATION: 15 YEARS OF NAGPRA GRANTS (1994-2008)

United States Department of the Interior

"Repatriation is oftentimes a long and difficult journey, the nagpra grants program provides the resources to allow tribes, museums and other institutions to walk that journey together. The positive relationships that are fostered out of consultation allow tribes to bring closure to many of the legacy issues that remain as well as look toward the future, to a day when all human remains are treated with the respect that they so justly deserve."

— Theresa pasqual, pueblo of acoma, new mexico

GRANTS ARE PART OF THE JOURNEY

The native american graves protection and repatriation act (NAGPRA), 25 U.S.C. 3001, acknowledges tribal sovereignty and the right of Native Americans to human remains and important cultural objects affiliated with their tribe or community. Hailed as a significant landmark in human rights and Indian law, NAGPRA provides museums[1] and Federal agencies with a mechanism for resolution of claims and repatriation. Museums and Federal agencies are required to conduct a thorough assessment of their Native American collections. Cultural objects that may be sacred, objects of cultural patrimony, or unassociated funerary objects are listed in summaries and sent to potentially interested Indian tribes[2] and Native Hawaiian organizations (NHOs) to begin consultation. Interested Indian tribes or NHOs can then consult with the museum on objects of interest and make a claim for repatriation. Human remains and associated funerary objects are subject to an inventory process. Museums are required to contact Indian tribes or NHOs that may be affiliated with their collection and consult together to determine cultural affiliation. Culturally affiliated human remains and agreements to repatriate cultural items are published in the *Federal Register* and are then available to be repatriated to the appropriate Indian tribe or NHO.

NAGPRA is a process that requires a great deal of resources from museums, Indian tribes and NHOs. NAGPRA Grants assist in the costs of consultation and documentation as well as the costs of repatriation of human remains and cultural items in collections.[3]

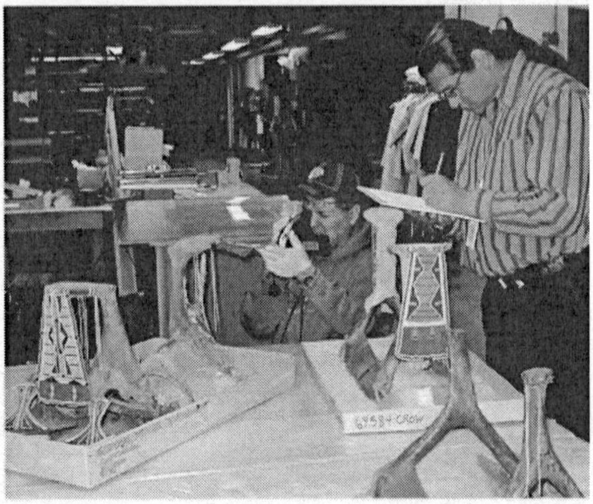

Gordon Real Bird Jr. (seated) and Jack Real Bird, Crow Tribe of Montana, photographing and taking notes on Crow saddles in the Field Museum's collections. (FY2003 Consultation/ Documentation Grant)

> In light of the important role that death and burial rites play in Native American cultures, it is all the more offensive that the civil rights of America's first citizens have been so flagrantly violated for the past century. Mr. President, the bill before us today is not about the validity of museums or the value of scientific inquiry. Rather, it is about human rights.
>
> — *Senator Daniel Inouye, Hawaii, October 26, 1990*

THE NAGPRA GRANT PROCESS

The national NAGPRA grants program annually awards approximately $2 million in grants to museums, indian tribes, and nhos to support the repatriation of native american human remains or cultural items. consultation/ documentation grants make up approximately 97% of annual grants with the remaining 3% supporting repatriation grants. Between 1994 and 2008, over $31 million dollars were awarded to 260 indian tribes, nhos and museums to support nagpra activities.[4]

The goal of the NAGPRA Grants program is to increase the number of successful repatriations through support for projects that increase the ability of tribes and museums and Federal agencies to facilitate consultations and work together through the NAGPRA process.

Consultation/Documentation Grants are competitive grants awarded annually to museums, tribes and NHOs to consult and document NAGPRA-related human remains and cultural items. Grant amounts range from $5,000 to $75,000[5] and support 18-month projects. Indian tribes and NHOs typically use grant funds for capacity building, training, data collection, database development, consultants and coalition-building activities as well as for consultations, including travel, per diem, stipends for Elders, and equipment such as cameras, scanners and digital recorders. Museums typically request funding to place their collections online, conduct further research on their collections, test for contaminants, and coordinate consultations with Indian tribes and NHOs. A single project may involve multiple Indian tribes, NHOs or museums.

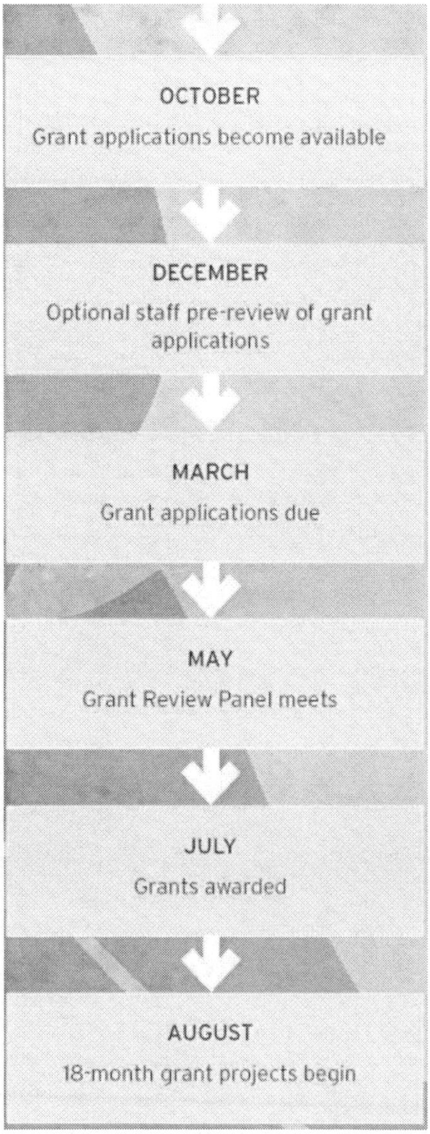

Repatriation Grants are non-competitive grants awarded to Indian tribes, NHOs and museums on a rolling basis. Grants, up to $15,000, cover costs associated with the repatriation of NAGPRA items, including: packaging and transportation of human remains or cultural objects, travel for Elders and tribal staff to the museum to conduct ceremonial activities or to coordinate packaging of the repatriated items, and staff time to coordinate repatriation activities. In addition, funding can be used for contamination issues such as the removal of contaminants or training for tribal or NHO staff on handling contaminated items.

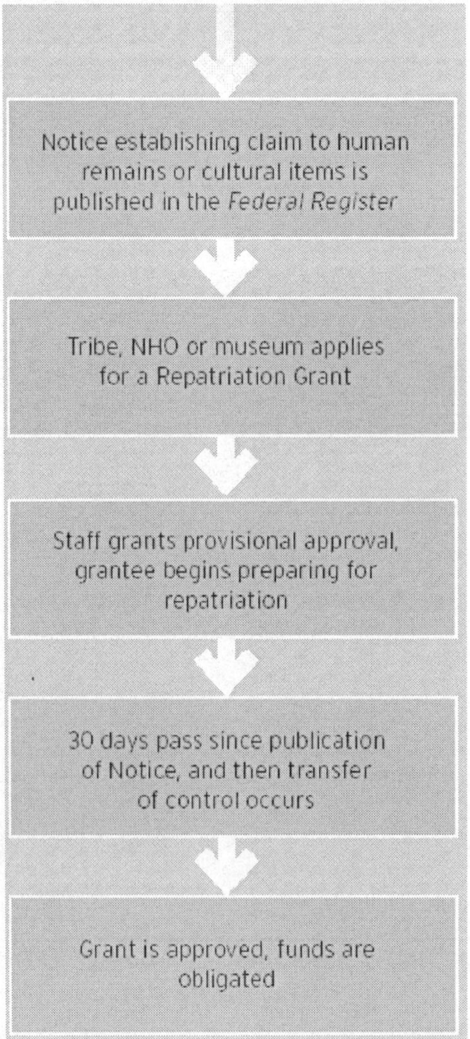

GRANTS SUPPORT COMMUNITIES

Since the inception of the NAGPRA Grants program, 260 Indian tribes, NHOs and museums in 42 states across the country have received grants to support their efforts. While the size and scope of each grant varies, the resources provided by the NAGPRA Grants program have been critical to many projects' success. The realities of conducting repatriation programs can produce challenges. Museums are often confronted with incomplete or inconsistent collections records, insufficient staff and equipment to handle requests for consultations, and inadequate resources to test for contaminants and stabilize collections. Indian tribes and NHOs face significant challenges to adequately support a NAGPRA program. Responding to summaries and requests to consult with museums that are often many miles away, working with Elders and community experts to develop documentation required for consultations, creating collections databases and repatriation policies for their tribe/NHO, and coordinating locations to both re-bury or house human remains and cultural items, has proven to be both costly and time-consuming.

And yet, as consultations are completed and repatriations occur, the effects of NAGPRA can be seen throughout the country, in museums, Indian tribes and Native Hawaiian communities. Human remains and cultural items long believed to have been lost are returned and offer priceless opportunities for healing, education and community-building. New partnerships are formed offering opportunities for information-sharing and engagement. NAGPRA grants are integral to this important community effort.

Total Amount Awarded in Grants	$ 31,163,319
Total Amount Awarded for Consultation/Documentation Grants	$30,142,926
Total Amount Awarded for Repatriation Grants	$ 1,020,393
Average Consultation Grant	$ 61,516
Average Repatriation Grant	$ 9,894
Total Number of Grants Awarded (490 for Consultation/Documentation, 102 for Repatriation)	592

NAGPRA Grants 1994–2008: Overall Statistics

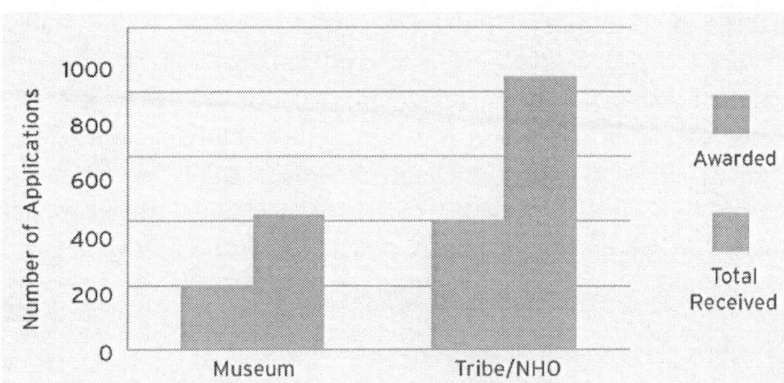

NAGPRA Grants 1994–2008: Number of Awarded Applications vs. Total Applications Received

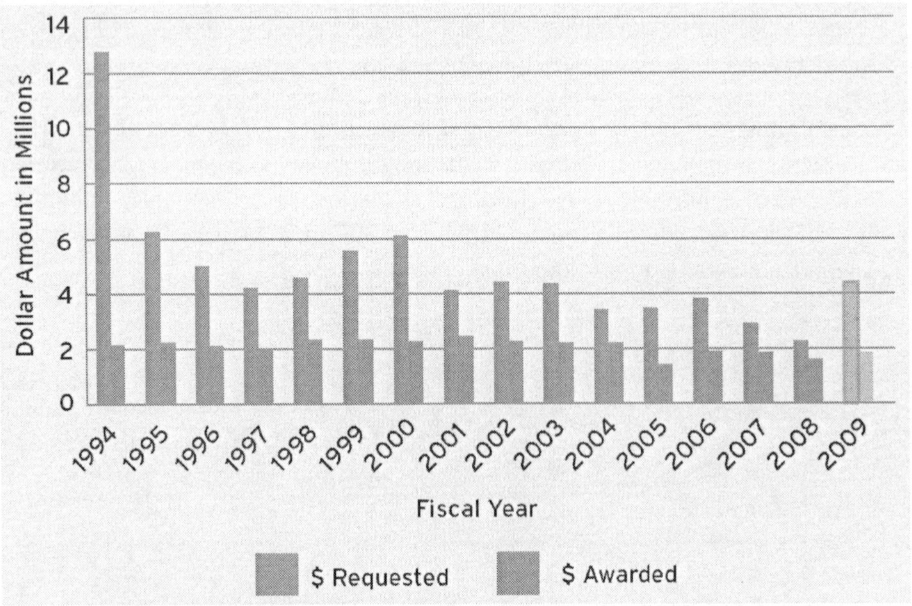

NAGPRA Grants 1994–2009: Amount Requested vs. Amount Awarded

GRANTS TELL THE STORY OF NAGPRA

In recognition of the high costs associated with the repatriation process, Congress authorized the NAGPRA grants program to support Indian tribes, NHOs and museums in their NAGPRA efforts. Over the past 15 years, NAGPRA grants have played a vital and ever-changing role in repatriation efforts. Initially, grant applications primarily requested support for compliance-related activities. Museums, Indian tribes and NHOs focused on developing internal systems and processes to manage NAGPRA activities. Over time, museums, Indian tribes and NHOs have moved beyond initial compliance to consultations and eventually repatriation activities. Today, many grants focus on creating more meaningful consultation relationships that can involve multiple museums, Indian tribes and NHOs, and often result in Notices of Inventory Completion for human remains in collections and Notices of Intent to Repatriate for cultural items claimed for repatriation. This is critical to NAGPRA, as notices establish the rights of Indian tribes and NHOs to gain control of ancestors and important objects. Other topics NAGPRA grants address include handling contaminated collections, repatriating culturally unidentifiable human remains or developing web-based technology as a tool for consultation. As the number, size and intricacy of repatriations increase,it is expected that the grants program will receive a greater number of grant requests in both categories.

Burke Museum and Central Washington University joint inter-tribal repatriation of human remains and funerary objects from the Columbia Plateau to the Confederated Tribes of the Colville Reservation, WA, Nez Perce Tribe, ID, Confederated Tribes of the Umatilla Reservation, OR, Confederated Tribes of the Warm Springs Reservation, OR, Confederated Tribes and Bands of the Yakama Nation, WA and the Wanapum Band, WA. (FY2007 Repatriation Grant)

"The Burke Museum has been awarded four Consultation/ Documentation Grants between 1994 and 2003. It has become apparent that there is a direct correlation between Consultation/Documentation Grant funding and the museum's ability to conduct meaningful consultations, publish Notices of Inventory Completion and Notices of Intent to Repatriate, and ultimately repatriate human remains and cultural items. During the most recent grant period (2003–2005) and the two years following, the Burke published 25 notices, thereby repatriating 226 individuals and over 20,000 cultural items.

It is estimated that the Burke has dedicated in excess of $1 million of its own funding in compliance of NAGPRA. The Documentation Grants have provided a critical supplement to these funds. These funds enabled the Burke to dedicate more staff time to NAGPRA, hire graduate student assistants, and most importantly, provide travel funds to allow for in- person consultation meetings. These in-depth consultations have significantly strengthened our relationships with tribes and have led to lasting relationships that will continue to go beyond NAGPRA efforts."

— *Megon Noble, NAGPRA Coordinator, Burke Museum, University of Washington, Washington*

"For me, the biggest result that we experienced as a result of our NAGPRA project was that we strengthened our ties to the Hopi and Navajo and created new connections to the Apache and Zuni Tribes."

— *Elaine Hughes, Museum of Northern Arizona, Arizona*

"It is of vital importance that sacred objects and objects of cultural patrimony of all indigenous tribes throughout the Colorado Plateau be housed and protected from all natural elements as agreed by all participating tribes. And no better place to house these important objects than the Easton Collection Center, within the confines of the Museum of Northern Arizona."

— *Tony Joe, 2009, Navajo Nation, Arizona, New Mexico & Utah*

The Easton Collection Center, Museum of Northern Arizona

Representatives from the Hopi, Navajo, Apache and Zuni tribes viewing and consulting on collections at the MNA. (FY2006 Consulation/ Documentation Grant)

THE JOURNEY STRENGTHENS RELATIONSHIPS

In 2006, the Museum of Northern Arizona (MNA) received a Consultation/ Documentation Grant to expand their consultations with the Hopi Tribe, Navajo Nation, Zuni Tribe, and the Western Apache tribes. Together with the tribes, the MNA developed a plan to implement culturally-appropriate care, handling, and housing guidelines, and created written policies and procedures for accessing sensitive tribal collections. In addition, they created the Native American Advisory Committee to work with the museum on NAGPRA issues. The Committee continued to work with the MNA on issues beyond the initial scope of the grant. Most notably, the Committee advised the MNA on the design of the new Easton Collection Center. The building's design elements embrace the worldviews of the region's Native people including an east-facing entrance to greet the sun every morning, a circular shape to invoke the cycles of life, connections to the natural world with its living roof and views of the sacred San Francisco Peaks from both inside the building and out.

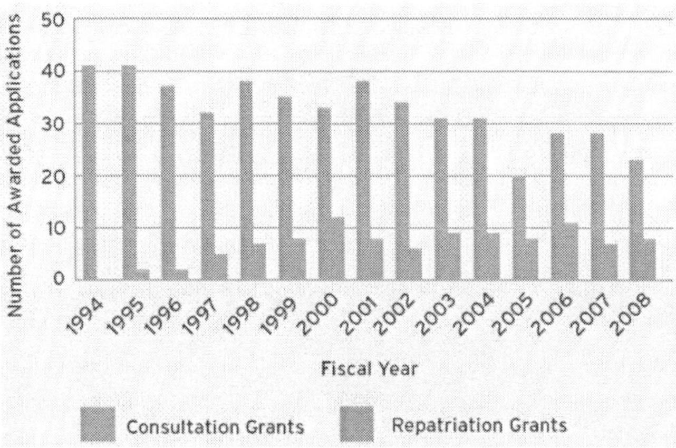

NAGPRA Grants 1994–2008: Distribution of Grants— Consultation/Documentation Grants & Repatriation Grants

Grants Benefit Museums, Indian Tribes and NHOs

The NAGPRA grants program has benefitted Indian tribes, NHOs and museums. Two-thirds of the applications received come from Indian tribes and NHOs, however, there is an even distribution in the proportion of grants awarded to museums and Indian tribes and NHOs. Although grants are awarded to a specific Indian tribe, NHO or museum, their impact often extends well beyond the grantee. Financial resources may be shared as museums will often include stipends or travel costs for participating tribes or NHOs. Likewise, tribal representatives and NHO representatives have served as resources to museums offering their knowledge about items in their collections and assisting with collections care and management. The grants program has also witnessed an increase in the number of grants supporting NAGPRA coalitions as communities come together to share information and resources, develop systems and policies for handling repatriations, and address issues of mutual concern.

Representatives from the Colorado Historical Society and the Colorado Commission of Indian Affairs. (FY2005 Consultation/Documentation Grant)

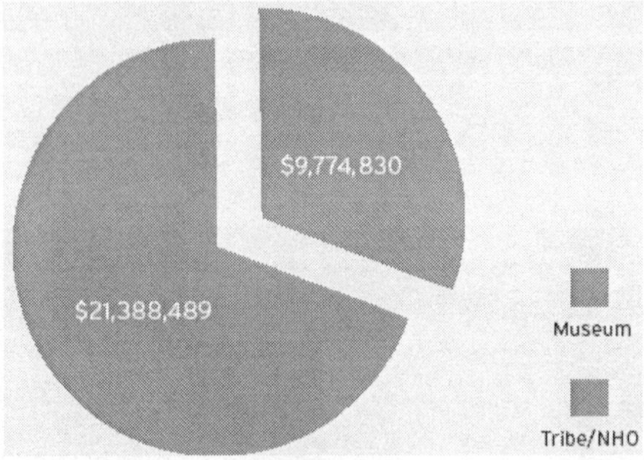

NAGPRA Grants 1994–2008: Total Amount Awarded

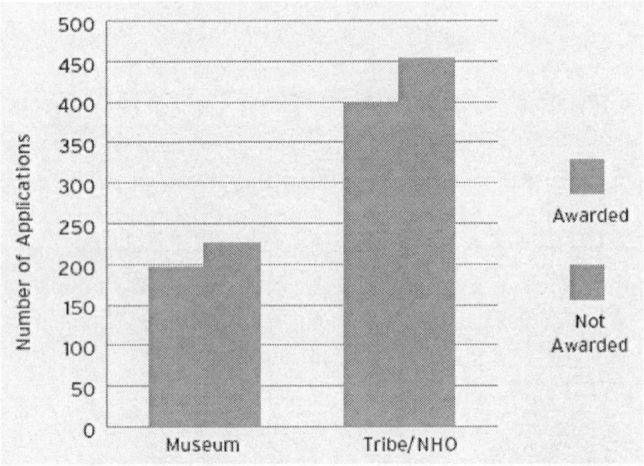

NAGPRA Grants 1994–2008: Number of Applications Awarded vs. Not Awarded

"The Colorado Historical Society, a state agency, began its NAGPRA program in 1993. Over time, we partnered with area agencies, museums and tribes to implement the law. To address the complex interplay between NAGPRA and state law, we relied on our partnership with the Colorado Commission of Indian Affairs, the Southern Ute Indian Tribe, the Ute Mountain Ute Tribe, and 45 additional tribes with ancestral ties to the state to develop a process that would facilitate tribal consultation and provide disposition for culturally unidentifiable Native American human remains and associated funerary objects found on those lands. Along the way, we forged deeply meaningful community relationships that enhanced our exhibits, provided outreach opportunities and fortified our educational programming. The end result is a trust relationship built upon transparency and hard work for all the parties, and a solution that addresses tribes' initial concerns to identify a final resting place for some of Colorado's earliest inhabitants."

— Bridget Ambler, Colorado Historical Society. *(FY2005 Consultation/ Documentation Grant)*

WALKING THE JOURNEY TOGETHER

In 2005 and 2007, the Rochester Museum & Science Center received Consultation/ Documentation grants to document over 7,000 Iroquoian (Haudenasaunee) ethnographic objects in their collections in order to facilitate consultations with Indian tribes. Haudenasaunee consultants were supported through the grant and offered valuable assistance with the collections including the development of comprehensive summaries that were used as a basis for consultation. In addition, Jamie Jacobs, a member of the Tonawanda Band of Senecas, was hired as an intern to work with the Haudenasaunee consultants on documenting and overseeing the care of the cultural items. Over the two grant periods, numerous items were documented and when appropriate, tested for contaminants. Five Indian tribes participated and over 50 people were trained on collections management issues.

> "The project was designed so the museum could know what it needed to repatriate. We can no longer be on opposing sides. We are never going to keep material that the native community says that we shouldn't be keeping."
>
> — *Bart A. Roselli, Rochester Museum & Science Center, American Indian Tribes Forum, October 31, 2007*

> "Through the collaboration of the rochester museum & science center and the tonawanda native community, i believe that the nagpra grants of 2005 and 2007 helped bring understanding to both parties. The understanding of iroquois culture and customs regarding the respect and care of sacred and ceremonial items was shared along with personal and spiritual input from the community in which the "museum relics" were born and are still living to the present day."
>
> — *Jamie Jacobs, Tonawanda Band of Seneca Indians of New York*

Jamie Jacobs using the XRF machine to test for contaminants at the Rochester Museum & Science Center, New York. (FY2007 Consultation/ Documentation Grant)

GRANTS CREATE OPPORTUNITIES

Over the past 15 years, the NAGPRA Grants program has supported efforts of museums, Indian tribes and Native Hawaiian organizations in 42 states to implement the provisions of NAGPRA. Grantees reflect the diversity of the country, ranging from small historical museums to those with substantial Native American collections, as well as Indian tribes and Native Hawaiian communities. Behind every grant is a story of healing, revival, trust-building and new opportunities for Indian tribes and Native Hawaiian organizations to work with museums and Federal agencies to forge a relationship based on mutual understanding and respect for Native American and Native Hawaiian communities, values, traditions and ancestors.

> "The repatriation of the beaver prow figure was a historical find. This one object brought significance to who we are as a people of Admiralty Island. Without NAGPRA this never would have happened. What a joy it was to see the culture of the community come to life!"
> — *Leonard John, Kootznoowoo Cultural and Education Foundation, AK. (FY1999 Consultation/Documentation Grant*)

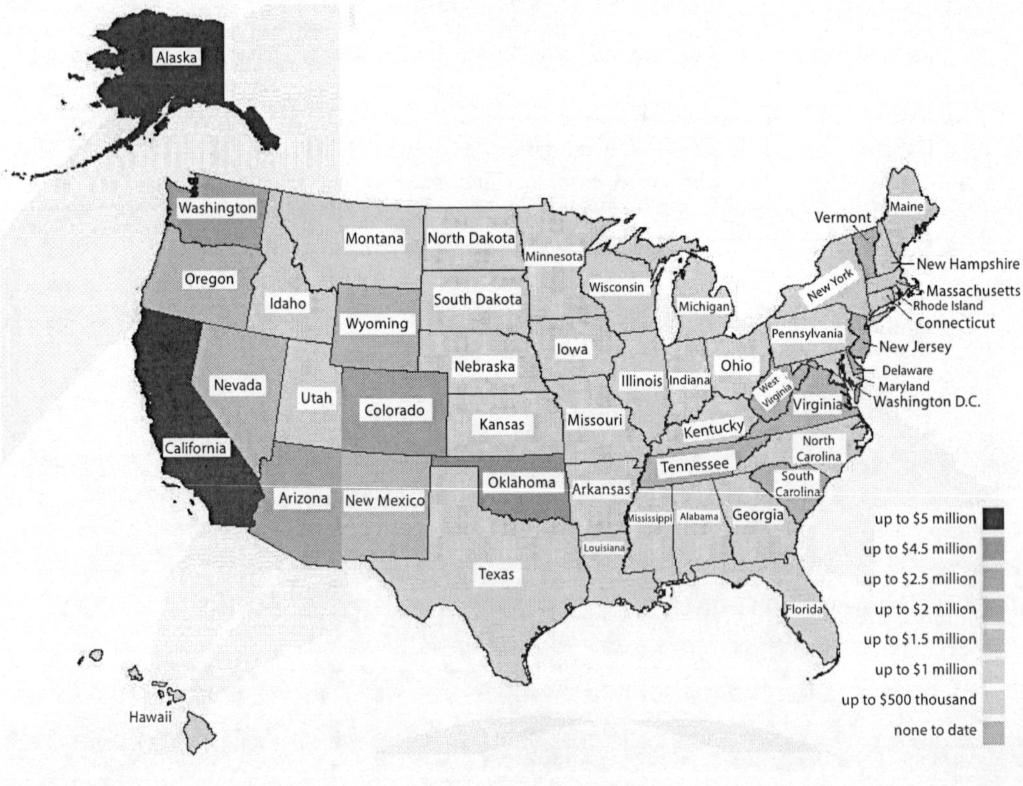

Members of Kootznoowoo Inc., Alaska during a consultation at the American Museum of Natural History, New York. (FY1999 Consultation/ Documentation Grant)

One Community's Journey

In October 2005, the Sealaska Corporation repatriated the Brown Bear Chilkat Tunic from the Phoebe Hearst Museum. The tunic was originally worn by Klukwan Kaagwaantaan Clan Leader Kudeinahaa (Mike Kadanaha) and it is believed that the tunic's spirit lives on in the item. The tunic was initially photographed during a museum visit in 2004 funded by a Consultation/Documentation Grant, and subsequently identified as part of the Klukwan Kaagwaantaan Clan at.óow (clan-owned ceremonial property) that had been missing for over 50 years. A Notice of Intent to Repatriate was published in June 2005. Sealaska Corporation wrote and received a FY2005 Repatriation Grant to allow the project director and two representatives, the Klukwan Kaagwaantaan Clan Leader (Eagle moiety) and a Raven moiety representative, to travel to the Phoebe Hearst museum to transfer possession of the garment, and then travel with the tunic to the University of Washington, Burke Museum in Seattle to have it tested for contaminants. They then travelled with the tunic to Klukwan where the tunic was welcomed home by the community.

> "I think bringing back all this (regalia) is starting to mean more to our younger generation because they didn't have anything to identify with other than our words. I think they're starting to see more and more of our old ways and (its) making them understand our culture is so important and it brings back a lot of pride and respect in who they are."
>
> — *Edwina White, Juneau Empire, "Bringing History Home: Historic Klukwan tunic repatriated to Clan." October 7, 2005*

1879

Tunic worn by Klukwan Kaagwaantaan Clan Leader Kudeinahaa at a potlatch given by Chief Shakes in Wrangel, AK.

Kaagwaataan Clan Leader Kudeinahaa in tunic, 1923.

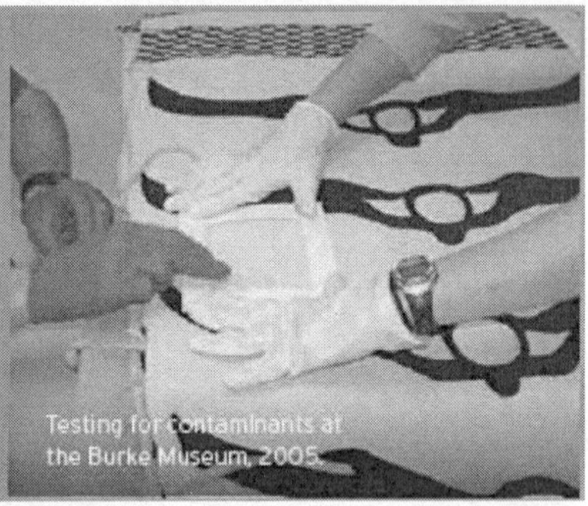

Testing for contaminants at the Burke Museum, 2005.

1923

Photograph taken of Kudeinahaa wearing the tunic. Many years later the photograph is given to Joe Hotch, the hit saati (caretaker) of the Brown Bear House, a part of the Klukwan village's Kaagwaantaan clan, by Haines historian Elizabeth Hakkinen telling him that he might need it one day.

1939

Going against Tlingit cultural property laws forbidding the sale of items such as the tunic because it is clan-owned property, the tunic is sold after Kudeinahaa's death.

1977

Daughter of the original purchaser donates tunic to the Pheobe A. Hearst Museum of Anthropology, Berkeley, CA.

2004

Tunic is photographed at the Pheobe A. Hearst Museum during a consultation visit by Sealaska Heritage Institute.

2005

Joe Hotch identifies tunic and produces photograph and other evidence to prove it belongs to his clan. Tunic returns home to the Klukwan village.

"An item like this is important to all clan houses, but it's important to the Brown Bear House because our ancestors put that together to say, 'This is what people will know you by. This is who you are. It will be important to my nephews and nieces, and it will go on down from there'."

– Joe Hotch, hit saati (caretaker) of the Brown Bear House, Kaagwaantaan Clan of Klukwan. Quoted in Chilkat Valley News, "Prized Tunic on its Way Home to Chilkat Valley" October 6, 2005

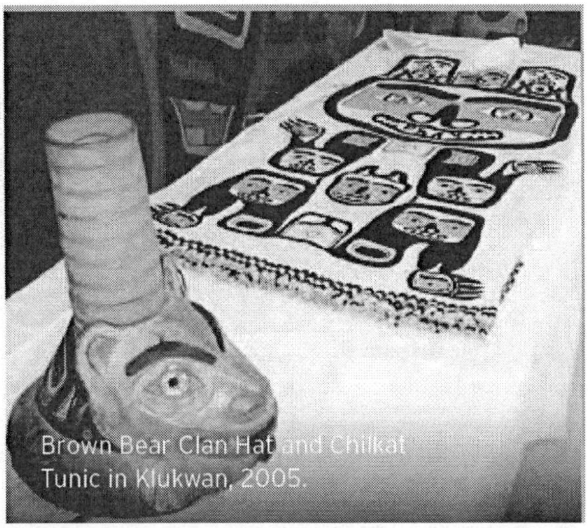
Brown Bear Clan Hat and Chilkat Tunic in Klukwan, 2005.

GRANTS MOVE NAGPRA FORWARD

The NAGPRA Grants Program has been instrumental in helping museums, Indian tribes and NHOs across the country implement the provisions of NAGPRA. Over the years, the NAGPRA Grants program has supported hundreds of projects resulting in the repatriation of tens of thousands of human remains and cultural items. NAGPRA grants provide critical resources to museums, Indian tribes and NHOs. Indeed, no other funding source that explicitly funds NAGPRA compliance is available. Despite 15 years of funding for NAGPRA, there is still much work to be done. Many Indian tribes, NHOs and museums are only beginning to develop repatriation programs. Issues not considered when the law was first passed have emerged. How can Indian tribes and NHOs manage large scale repatriations? How should museums deal with their culturally unidentifiable human remains? What is the best way to identify and deal with contamination issues? As the NAGPRA community considers these issues, museums, Indian tribes and NHOs look to the NAGPRA grants program to help fund this most important and necessary work.

"I believe that museums have a deep ethical obligation to proactively address the legacies of collecting, and the NAGPRA Grants program is a vital means of enabling museums to fulfill their duties as stewards and caretakers. From the consultations and conversations that result from dealing with NAGPRA, museums have the potential of creating new kinds of relationships with Native American communities. When tribes see that museums are genuinely committed to NAGPRA, both the spirit and the letter of the law, new friendships and partnerships can develop."

— *Chip Colwell- Chanthaphonh, Denver Museum of Nature and Science, Colorado. (FY2008 Consultation/Documentation Grant)*

"With the help of the Native American Graves Protection and Repatriation Act, and the funding of this grant, we have continued to not only reclaim and rename our past but also have asserted the identity of the Caddo as being the "Real Chiefs" governing our history and culture."

— *Bobby Gonzalez and Robert Cast, Caddo Nation of Oklahoma, A Rediscovering of Caddo Heritage, 2005. (FY2004 Consultation/Documentation Grant)*

THE JOURNEY HOME

The Little Traverse Bay Bands of Odawa Indians received a Repatriation Grant to return six funerary objects—a pipe bowl, three silver armbands, one silver cross pendant and one brass crucifix—from the Logan Museum of Anthropology in Beloit, Wisconsin, and four sets of human remains6 from the Hastings Museum of Natural and Cultural History in Hastings, Nebraska. Eric Hemenway, the tribe's Research and Repatriation Assistant and current NAGPRA Review Committee member, travelled for eight days to retrieve the human remains and cultural objects and meet the staff at both institutions. The human remains were reburied and the funerary objects are waiting to be tested for contaminants before being reburied.

October 31, 2007: Michigan

On behalf of all the tribes in Michigan, I made first contact with the Hastings Museum in Nebraska. Now, nearly two years after that phone call, going through the disposition process for culturally unidentifiable (CUI) human remains, the Federal Register process and securing a NAGPRA repatriation grant, I am ready to bring back home these old Anishnaabek.[7]

June 9, 2009: Nebraska

It feels really good to be finally picking up these old ones, it feels like all the hard work for the last two years is paying off. The curator at the Hastings Museum, Teresa Kruetzer-Hodson, has been great to work with and it's nice to finally meet her. We are doing de-accession paperwork for the museum. Now I can start heading back home.

June 10, 2009: Nebraska/Iowa Border

I am getting tired of driving. I have to stop every hour or so and stretch my legs, get the blood moving around. I miss cooking my own food, working out, and sleeping in my own bed. But my complaints are nothing in comparison to the situation of the old Anishnaabek I am bringing back home. Teresa told me, from the work they had done on the remains, the four skulls are all Indian men, from Michigan, in their early thirties. This made me really think. I am an Indian man, from Michigan, in my early thirties. I like to think, I am in the best years of my life, and it makes me sad to think these four men were in theirs when they passed. I guess I should stop thinking of myself and hurry up and get home to get these guys back in the ground.

June 11 & 12, 2009: Wisconsin

I arrived at Beloit, Wisconsin today. This is the other destination for this repatriation trip. I am retrieving burial items affiliated to my tribe. I met with Bill Green, Nicolette Meister and Michelle Burton of the Logan Museum of Anthropology to pick up the funerary objects. Of course, there is paperwork to sign, along with questions and answers. My tribe has been working with the Logan Museum for 10 years. It is so rewarding to finally repatriate these items. Even after a decade, progress can still be made if you don't give up.

June 13, 2009: Michigan

I arrived home around 3pm. I wanted to just lie on the couch and eat my favorite treat of plain yogurt, strawberries, blueberries and raspberries, but the idea of having the remains "wait around for me" got me motivated. I finished the reburial around 5pm. It was a beautiful day in the woods—sunshine, birds, not too hot. As always, after doing this, I felt like I did a good thing. I helped some other Anishnaabek. Now I could go home.

Grantees by State

Alaska

Ahtna, Inc.
Alaska State Museum
Aleutian/Pribilof Islands Association, Inc.
Alutiiq Museum & Archaeological Repository
Anvik Village
Bering Straits Foundation
Cape Fox Corporation
Central Council of the Tlingit & Haida Indian Tribes
Chickaloon Native Village
Chilkat Indian Village (Klukwan)
Chilkoot Indian Association (Haines)
Denakkanaaga, Inc.
Hoonah Indian Association
Huna Heritage Foundation
Huna Totem Corporation
Hydaburg Cooperative Association
Keepers of the Treasure
Kenaitze Indian Tribe
Kootznoowoo Inc.
Naknek Native Village
Native Village of Eyak

Native Village of Gambell
Native Village of Kiana
Native Village of Kotzebue
Native Village ofTeller
Nome Eskimo Community
Nondalton Village
Organized Village of Kake
Qawalangin Tribe of Unalaska
Sealaska Corporation
Sitka Tribe of Alaska
Tanadgusix Corporation
Univ. of Alaska Museum of the North
Village of Anaktuvak Pass
Yakutat Tlingit Tribe

ALABAMA
Univ. of Alabama Museums, Office
of Archeological Services

ARKANSAS
Arkansas Archeological Survey
Arkansas State Univ. Museum
Univ. of Arkansas System,
Arkansas Archeological Survey

ARIZONA
Arizona State Museum, Univ. of Arizona
Gila River Indian Community of the Gila River Indian Reservation
Heard Museum
Hopi Tribe of Arizona
Hualapai Indian Tribe of the Hualapai Indian Reservation
Kaibab Band of Paiute Indians of the Kaibab Indian Reservation
Museum of Northern Arizona
Salt River Pima-Maricopa Indian Community of the Salt River Reservation
White Mountain Apache Tribe of the Fort Apache Reservation
Yavapai-Apache Nation of the Camp Verde Indian Reservation
Yavapai-Prescott Tribe of the Yavapai Reservation

CALIFORNIA
Agua Caliente Band of Cahuilla Indians of the Agua Caliente Indian Reservation
Autry National Center
Barona Group of Capitan Grande
Band of Mission Indians of the
Barona Reservation
Bear River Band of the Rohnerville Rancheria
Cal. State, Fresno, Dept. of Anthropology

California Dept. of Parks and Recreation
Campo Band of Diegueno Mission Indians of the Campo Indian Reservation
Capitan Grande Band of Diegueno Mission Indians
Catalina Island Museum Society, Inc.
Chemehuevi Indian Tribe of the Chemehuevi Reservation
Death Valley Timbi-Sha Shoshone Band
Dry Creek Rancheria of Pomo Indians
Greenville Rancheria of Maidu Indians
Hoopa Valley Tribe
Karuk Tribe
Kashia Band of Pomo Indians of the Stewarts Point Rancheria
Los Angeles County Museum of Natural History
Mechoopda Indian Tribe of Chico Rancheria
Mooretown Rancheria of Maidu Indians
Phoebe A. Hearst Museum of Anthropology
Pit River Tribe
Quartz Valley Indian Community of the Quartz Valley Reservation
Rincon Band of Luiseno Mission Indians of the Rincon Reservation
Robinson Rancheria of Pomo Indians
San Diego Archaeological Center
San Diego Museum of Man
San Diego State Univ.
San Francisco State Univ., Anthropology Dept.
San Francisco State Univ., Museum Studies Program
Sherwood Valley Rancheria of Pomo Indians
Smith River Rancheria
Susanville Indian Rancheria
Table Mountain Rancheria
Torres Martinez Desert Cahuilla Indians
Tuolumne Band of Me-Wuk Indians of the Tuolumne Rancheria
Univ. of California, Los Angeles, Fowler Museum of Cultural History
Yurok Tribe of the Yurok Reservation

COLORADO

Colorado Historical Society
Colorado Springs Fine Arts Center, Taylor Museum
Denver Art Museum
Denver Museum of Nature & Science
Fort Collins Museum
Fort Lewis College
Southern Ute Indian Tribe of the Southern Ute Reservation
Univ. of Colorado Museum, Boulder
Univ. of Denver, Dept. of Anthropology/Museum of Anthropology

CONNECTICUT

Mashantucket Pequot Tribe

Mohegan Indian Tribe

FLORIDA
Miccosukee Tribe of Indians

GEORGIA
Columbus Museum of Art
Georgia Dept. of Natural Resources

HAWAII
Bernice P. Bishop Museum
Council for Native Hawaiian Advancement
Hui Malama I Na Kupuna O
Hawai'i Nei
Office of Hawaiian Affairs

IOWA
Univ. of Iowa

IDAHO
Univ. of Idaho, Alfred W. Bowers Laboratory of Anthropology

ILLINOIS
Field Museum of Natural History
Illinois State Museum

INDIANA
Indiana University, William
Hammond Mathers Museum

KANSAS
Iowa Tribe of Kansas and Nebraska
Univ. of Kansas, Museum of Anthropology

KENTUCKY
Univ. of Kentucky, William S. Webb
Museum of Anthropology

LOUISIANNA
Chitimacha Tribe
Jena Band of Choctaw Indians
Louisiana State Univ., Museum of Natural Science

MARYLAND
Maryland Historical Trust

MASSACHUSETTS
Boston Children's Museum
Peabody Essex Museum
Peabody Museum of Archaeology and Ethnology, Harvard University
Robert S. Peabody Museum of Archaeology, Phillips Academy
Springfield Science Museum
Wampanoag Tribe of Gay Head (Aquinnah)

MAINE
Houlton Band of Maliseet Indians
Maine State Museum

MICHIGAN
Detroit Institute of Arts
Grand Traverse Band of Ottawa and Chippewa Indians
Hannahville Indian Community
Keweenaw Bay Indian Community
Lac Vieux Desert Band of Lake Superior Chippewa Indians
Little River Band of Ottawa Indians
Little Traverse Bay Bands of Odawa Indians
Public Museum of Grand Rapids
Saginaw Chippewa Indian Tribe
Sault Ste. Marie Tribe of Chippewa Indians

MINNESOTA
Bois Forte Band (Nett Lake) of the Minnesota Chippewa Tribe
Grand Portage Band of the Minnesota Chippewa Tribe
Leech Lake Band of the Minnesota Chippewa Tribe
Mille Lacs Band of the Minnesota Chippewa Tribe
Minnesota Indian Affairs Council
Science Museum of Minnesota
Upper Sioux Community
White Earth Band of Minnesota Chippewa Tribe

MISSOURI
Missouri Dept. of Natural Resources

MISSISSIPPI
Mississippi State Univ., Cobb
Institute of Archaeology

MONTANA
Assiniboine and Sioux Tribes of the Fort Peck Indian Reservation
Chief Plenty Coups State Park
Confederated Salish & Kootenai Tribes of the Flathead Reservation
Northern Cheyenne Tribe

NORTH CAROLINA
Eastern Band of Cherokee Indians of North Carolina
Univ. of North Carolina at Chapel Hill

NORTH DAKOTA
Standing Rock Sioux Tribe of North & South Dakota
Three Affiliated Tribes of the Fort Berthold Reservation
Turtle Mountain Band of Chippewa Indians

NEBRASKA
Univ. of Nebraska, Lincoln
Winnebago Tribe of Nebraska

NEW HAMPSHIRE
Hood Museum of Art, Dartmouth College

NEW MEXICO
Jicarilla Apache Nation
Maxwell Museum of Anthropology,
Univ. of New Mexico
Mescalero Apache Tribe of the Mescalero Reservation
Museum of New Mexico, Museum of Indian Arts and Culture
Pueblo of Acoma
Pueblo of Jemez
Pueblo of Taos
Zuni Tribe of the Zuni Reservation

NEVADA
Duckwater Shoshone Tribe of the Duckwater Reservation
Ely Shoshone Tribe
Nevada State Museum
Paiute-Shoshone Tribe of the Fallon Reservation and Colony
Pyramid Lake Paiute Tribe of the Pyramid Lake Reservation
Shoshone-Paiute Tribes of the Duck Valley Reservation
Univ. of Nevada, Las Vegas, Dept. of Anthropology
Washoe Tribe of Nevada & California

NEW YORK
American Museum of Natural History
Brooklyn Museum of Art
New York State Museum
Rochester Museum & Science Center
Rome Historical Society
Seneca Nation of New York
St. Regis Band of Mohawk Indians
SUNY Oswego, Research Foundation

SUNY, Binghamton, Dept. of Anthropology

OHIO
Cincinnati Art Museum
Dayton Society of Natural History
Ohio Univ., Kennedy Museum of American Art

OKLAHOMA
Caddo Nation of Oklahoma
Cheyenne-Arapaho Tribes of Oklahoma
Chickasaw Nation, Oklahoma
Choctaw Nation of Oklahoma
Citizen Potawatomi Nation, Oklahoma
Comanche Nation
Delaware Nation
Delaware Tribe of Indians
Eastern Shawnee Tribe
Iowa Tribe of Oklahoma
Kaw Nation
Miami Tribe of Oklahoma
Modoc Tribe of Oklahoma
Muscogee (Creek) Nation, Oklahoma
Oklahoma Historical Society
Osage Tribe
Otoe-Missouria Tribe of Indians, Oklahoma
Ottawa Tribe of Oklahoma
Pawnee Nation of Oklahoma
Peoria Tribe of Indians of Oklahoma
Ponca Tribe of Indians of Oklahoma
Quapaw Tribe of Indians
Sac & Fox Nation, Oklahoma
Sam Noble Oklahoma Museum of Natural History, Univ. of Oklahoma
Seminole Nation of Oklahoma
Wichita and Affiliated Tribes
(Wichita, Keechi, Waco & Tawakonie)

OREGON
Burns Paiute Tribe
Confederated Tribes of the Coos, Lower Umpqua and Siuslaw Indians
Confederated Tribes of the Grand Ronde Community
Confederated Tribes of the Umatilla Reservation
Confederated Tribes of the Warm Springs Reservation
Coquille Tribe
Klamath Tribes
Oregon State Univ., Dept. of Anthropology
Oregon State Univ., Horner Collection

Southern Oregon Univ.
Univ. of Oregon Museum of Natural History

PENNSYLVANIA
Univ. of Pennsylvania Museum of Archaeology and Anthropology

RHODE ISLAND
Haffenreffer Museum of Anthropology, Brown Univ.

SOUTH DAKOTA
Cheyenne River Sioux Tribe of the Cheyenne River Reservation
Oglala Sioux Tribe of the Pine Ridge Reservation
Rosebud Sioux Tribe of the Rosebud Indian Reservation
South Dakota State Historical Society, State Archaeological Research Center

TEXAS
Panhandle-Plains Historical Museum, West Texas A&M Univ.
Texas Tech Univ., Museum
Univ. of Texas, El Paso, Centennial Museum

UTAH
Southern Utah Univ. Archeological Repository
Utah Museum of Natural History, Univ. of Utah

WASHINGTON
Central Washington Univ.
Columbia Gorge Interpretive Center Museum
Confederated Tribes and Bands of the Yakama Nation
Confederated Tribes of the Chehalis Reservation
Cowlitz Indian Tribe
Eastern Washington State
Historical Society
Jamestown S'Klallam Tribe
Lummi Tribe of the Lummi Reservation
Makah Indian Tribe of the Makah Indian Reservation
Nisqually Indian Tribe of the Nisqually Reservation
Nooksack Indian Tribe
Northwest Museum of Arts and Culture
Samish Indian Tribe
Skokomish Indian Tribe of the Skokomish Reservation
Spokane Tribe of the Spokane Reservation
Squaxin Island Tribe of the Squaxin Island Reservation
Stillaguamish Tribe
Suquamish Indian Tribe of the Port Madison Reservation
Univ. of Washington, Burke Museum

WISCONSIN
Bad River Band of the Lake Superior Tribe of Chippewa Indians
Ho-Chunk Nation of Wisconsin
Lac du Flambeau Band of Lake Superior Chippewa Indians
Menominee Indian Tribe
Milwaukee Public Museum
Oneida Tribe of Indians of Wisconsin
Stockbridge Munsee Community
Wisconsin Historical Society, Museum Division

The native american graves protection and repatriation act (NAGPRA) is a Federal law passed in 1990. NAGPRA provides a process for museums and Federal agencies to resolve control of Native American human remains and cultural items—funerary objects, sacred objects, and objects of cultural patrimony—to lineal descendants, Indian tribes and Native Hawaiian organizations.

The National NAGPRA Program assists the Secretary of the Interior with some of the Secretary's responsibilities under NAGPRA. Among its chief activities, National NAGPRA develops regulations and guidance for implementing NAGPRA; provides administrative and staff support for the Native American Graves Protection and Repatriation Review Committee; assists Indian tribes, Native Alaskan villages and corporations, Native Hawaiian organizations, museums, and Federal agencies understand the NAGPRA process; maintains Native American online databases; provides training; manages a grants program; investigates allegations of failure to comply; and makes program documents and publications available on the web.

End Notes

[1] "museum" means any institution or State or local government agency (including any institution of higher learning) that receives Federal funds and has possession of, or control over, Native American cultural items.

[2] "Indian tribe" means any tribe, band, nation, or other organized group or community of Indians, including any Alaska Native village or corporation, which is recognized as eligible for the special programs and services provided by the United States to Indians because of their status as Indians.

[3] NAGPRA grants do not cover costs of initial compliance in a summary or inventory, nor do they pertain to new discoveries on Federal or tribal lands after November 16, 1990.

[4] Some grant recipients received multiple grants over time.

[5] In FY2008, the NAGPRA Review Committee recommended an increase in Consultation/ Documentation grant award amounts from $75,000 to $90,000 due to a rise in project costs. This was implemented in FY2009.

[6] The human remains were culturally unidentifiable and the disposition was to four Michigan tribes. The Little Traverse Bay Bands of Odawa Indians agreed to travel to return the human remains to Michigan for reburial.

[7] The term Anishnaabek refers to tribes in the Great Lakes area.

In: Native American Graves and Repatriation
Editor: Kathy J. Bergmann
ISBN: 978-1-61122-410-8

Chapter 4

NATIONAL NAGPRA PROGRAM: FY09 FINAL REPORT

National Park Service, United States Department of the Interior and National NAGPRA

NAGPRA INTRODUCTION

This chapter covers activities of the National NAGPRA Program Fiscal Year 2009 (October 1, 2008 September 30, 2009). All information and statistics reported are current as of close of business, September 30, 2009. Regular reports on National Program's Website: http://www.nps.gov/history/nagpra/DOCUMENTS/INDEX.htm.

The Native American Graves Protection and Repatriation Act (NAGPRA) was enacted on November 16, 1990 to address the rights of lineal descendants, Indian tribes and Native Hawaiian organizations (NHO) to certain Native American cultural items, including human remains, funerary objects, sacred objects, and objects of cultural patrimony. The Act assigned implementation responsibilities to the Secretary of the Interior, including:

- Administering the obligations of museums and Federal agencies with regard to collections of cultural items, as follows:
    - Extending inventory deadlines for museums that demonstrate a good faith effort to comply with the law,
    - Collecting the inventories and summaries,
    - Publishing notices for museums and Federal agencies in the Federal Register,
    - Creating and maintaining a database of Culturally Unidentifiable Human Remains,
    - Making grants to assist museums, Indian tribes and NHOs in fulfilling museum responsibilities and the opportunities for Indian tribes and NHOs under the Act,
    - Assessing civil penalties on museums that fail to comply with provisions of the Act, and

- Establishing and providing staff support to the Native American Graves Protection and Repatriation Review Committee;
- Providing oversight and technical assistance in those instances where there are excavations and discoveries of cultural items on Federal and Indian lands after November 16, 1990;
- Promulgating implementing regulations;
- Providing technical assistance on the entire NAGPRA process, through:
    - Training programs,
    - Website information,
    - Reports prepared for the Review Committee, and
    - Supporting law enforcement investigation allegations of illegal trafficking in Native American human remains and cultural items.

The National NAGPRA Program serves constituents of the law which are all Federal agencies with land or collections responsibilities, museums that receive Federal funds, Native Americans, Indian tribes and NHOs, and the public.

This chapter follows the organization of the National NAGPRA Program and its responsibilities pertaining to collections, excavations/discoveries, regulations, and technical assistance given to Indian tribes and NHOs and the museums and Federal agencies that have obligations for NAGPRA compliance. Throughout the report, the term "tribe" is used, as it is in the law, to refer to federally recognized Indian tribes, Alaska Village corporations and Native Hawaiian organizations.

Summary of the National NAGPRA Program FY 2009

The following are highlights of the year and program statistics in brief.

Collections

- **Summaries received:** 1,551 total
    - 460 reporting no collection requiring a summary
- **Inventories received:** 1,317 total, from 734 institutions
    - 81 reporting no collection requiring an inventory
- **Notices of Inventory Completion:**
    - 150 published in FY 2009
    - 1,295 published in total
    - Account for 38,671 human remains and 998,731 associated funerary objects
- **Notices of Intent to Repatriate:**
    - 50 published in FY 2009
    - 477 published in total
    - Account for 144,163 unassociated funerary objects, 4,303 sacred objects, 948 objects of cultural patrimony, and 822 objects that are sacred and cultural patrimony, also 292 undesignated cultural items.

- **Notice processing:**
  - 159 received and 200 published in FY 2009
  - Aging drafts (pre-2005) 20 published in 2009, 21 remaining
- **Culturally Unidentifiable Native American Human Remains(CUI):**
  - Found in 684 inventories, from 623 institutions
  - 124,377 minimum number of individuals (MNI)
  - 4,846 total subsequently culturally affiliated to date
  - 3,363 total transferred as CUI in dispositions
  - In FY 2009: 11 Review Committee recommendations for 476 MNI
- **Grants:**
  - Requests in 2009-$4.5M (number of requests up 100% over 2008)
  - Awarded in 2009-$1.85M
  - 24 consultation/document grants awarded
  - 13 repatriation grants awarded
- **Civil Penalties:**
  - In FY 2009, investigations of 41 allegations as to 1 museum
  - In FY 2009, 11 failures to comply substantiated, 30 unsubstantiated, 5 penalties assessed
  - In total, 111 counts investigated, against 19 museums
  - In total, 12 museums have one or more substantiated failures to comply
  - Total penalties collected: $26,170, of which $19,920 was collected in FY 2009
- **Review Committee:**
  - October 11-12, 2008, San Diego, CA
  - May 23-24, 2009, Seattle, WA
  - 11 requests for disposition of 476 culturally unidentifiable individuals/451 associated funerary objects, 11 Review Committee recommendations and 11 concurrences from the Secretary of the Interior
  - 1 dispute heard in FY 2009, resulting in a notice publication
- **Excavation and Discoveries:**
  - In total, 90 Notices of Intended Disposition; 495 MNI, 4,148 AFO, 64 UFO, 4 CP*
- **NAGPRA Regulations 43 CFR 10:**
  - 10.11 Culturally Unidentifiable – final rule under consideration at the Department
  - 10.7 Unclaimed – Under development
- **Technical Assistance and Reports:**
  - Training given to 612 individuals in 15 training events, 94 training grants were awarded
  - 2,000 responses to requests for information

*MNI: Minimum number of individuals; AFO: Affiliated funerary objects; UFO: Unaffiliated funerary objects; CP: Cultural patrimony

HIGHLIGHTS OF THE YEAR FY 2009

The highlights of the year in the National NAGPRA Program and in the implementation of NAGPRA nationwide can be seen in the statistics on the prior page, but are also seen in certain events that go beyond the numbers. This section of the annual report is devoted to giving additional understanding to the National NAGPRA Program accomplishments, looking at other program activities, commenting upon issues that face NAGPRA communities, and finally, goals and projects slated for action in FY 2010.

1. National NAGPRA Program Accomplishments in Brief
   - Notices: Notice publication is a barometer of NAGPRA activity by museums and Federal agencies working with tribes and N HOs to make decisions on transfer of control of Native American human remains and cultural items. Each notice tells the story of historic collection practices and Federal agency and museum actions to consult with tribes and NHOs to resolve interests in cultural items and the disposition of human remains. There were 200 notices published in FY 2009, which indicates considerable NAGPRA efforts, an increase over FY 2008 and a 100% increase over prior years.
   - Grants: Grant requests were up 100% over the prior year and represented about \$4.5 million in requests for projects totaling \$5.2 million. Grants, which totaled \$1.85 million, were awarded for projects and repatriation expenses. An important new part of grants administration is the monitoring of grant award projects, so that all funds awarded will be used in the time allowed and will not revert to the general fund, either because projects were abandoned or the final paperwork was not completed. The goal of ensuring that all grants expiring in FY 2009 ended successfully was met in FY 2009. Training grants to tribes and museums were also awarded in this year.
   - Grants Retrospective: This year a report on 15 years of the grants program was completed for distribution in early FY 2010. "Journeys to Repatriation, 15 Years of NAGPRA Grants [1994-2008]," provides statistics on the grants program, and describes what the grants have meant to NAGPRA communities.
   - Databases: The Program report on "Native American human remains culturally affiliated in inventories, but not yet in published notices," is now on the Program website. The report disclosed some of the human remains waiting to be published in notices, but also indicated a need for further database development and entry of records received between 1996 and 2000. New emphasis was placed on the completion and release of the database of inventories of culturally affiliated human remains, to complement the CUI database, foster consultation and increase repatriation of human remains.
   - Technology development: New databases, additional capabilities of existing web products, and internal data management, all benefited from the technology contract in FY 2009 with NuAxis, further described in this chapter and completing in FY 2010.
   - Training: The number of participants receiving training was down this year from last year, reflecting less travel by the National NAGPRA team, as time was

devoted to the development of webinars and video training segments, which will increase training opportunities at much less cost to participants and increase training in far-reaching NAGPRA communities. A planning committee is working on the two-day NAGPRA at 20 event for November 15-16, 2010, to be held in Washington, DC, prior to the Review Committee meeting. Training was given with the involvement of partners: Department of Justice, FBI, Fish and Wildlife Service, Indian Arts and Crafts Board, Bureau of Indian Affairs, National Preservation Institute, NATHPO, and private contractors engaged to provide training.

- Review Committee: There were two in-person Review Committee meetings and a special committee gathering to select nominees from the Review Committee for the consensus member. The Secretary of the Interior made two Review Committee appointments this year, in a process that began with open nominations, and all nominees presented to the Department of the Interior, vetted by the White House, and with recommendations from members of Congress. The Review Committee resolved a dispute, made 11 recommendations on disposition of culturally unidentifiable human remains, and continued to play a vital role in providing a forum for public comments on NAG PRA issues. A new Designated Federal Official began the year with a new template for requesting Review Committee recommendations, which had the effect of simplifying the process for presenters and consideration by the Committee, a positive result.
- Civil penalties: Only one museum was investigated this year in a multi-count allegation, involving several Indian tribes and historic practices of several museums involved in decisions by the lead museum. Resolution of this matter will settle years of issues between the several Indian tribes and museums, avoid litigation, and further the NAG PRA process. A separate matter, scheduled for a hearing in November 2009, was resolved by a full settlement in which payment of the penalty assessment has been accomplished. The handling of civil penalty investigations continues to be focused upon resolution of cases by museum compliance, and not upon the maximization of penalties assessed.
- Regulations: The NAGPRA regulations, 43 CFR Part 10, were updated this year in compliance with the Paperwork Reduction Act, which affords the regulations full implementation through August 2012. A Federal Agency Working group is developing a draft of the reserved regulation section 10.7, guidance on disposition of unclaimed human remains and cultural items on Federal and Indian lands. In the closing days of this year, the reserved section which will provide further guidance on the disposition of culturally unidentifiable Native American human remains, 10.11, concluded its review in the Department of the Interior. Publication will abide consideration by the Office of Management and Budget.

2. Other Program Activity
    - GAO Study: The Government Accountability Office (GAO) began a study this year of Federal agency compliance with NAGPRA and the operations of the National NAGPRA Program. The GAO held initial meetings, has collected information from the National NAGPRA Program, and is meeting with Federal

agency NAGPRA coordinators in their offices around the country. This thorough study may conclude in FY 2011.

- Interns: The National NAGPRA Program has been successful in recruiting diverse interns to work with the Program on a variety of projects and reports, including Native American students. Hopefully, these recruitment efforts will result in full-time staff over time.

3. Issues Facing NAGPRA Constituents
   - Inventories: The question continually asked by the NAGPRA Review Committee has been whether all Native American human remains in collections are also listed in NAGPRA inventories. This would require an actual audit of collections, not provided for in statute as an activity of the National NAGPRA Program, but possible for the GAO.
   - Notices: The question that underlies repatriation is whether all culturally affiliated Native American human remains listed in inventories are listed in a notice of inventory completion. Completing data entry and releasing a database of culturally affiliated NAGPRA inventories is a priority for the Program. Once complete, the data will allow reports to be compiled that sort the homework to be done by museums and Federal agencies, to foster notice publication. The issue is not whether notice drafts are submitted to the National NAGPRA Program, but whether the draft is actually published as a notice, the critical precedent to repatriation. The Program does not hold, or withdraw notices.
   - Notices: In 2005, the category of "on-hold" notices was eliminated. At that time, 300 notices previously out of the publication process were put into the process. Since that time, of that group, more than 220 have been published, others were properly closed as duplicates or submitted for non-notice publication events, such as repatriation prior to the law, notices submitted that should have been a newspaper notice of new discovery on the land, or submissions by museums that did not have control or did not receive Federal funds. There is a balance of 21 open files proceeding to publication at the close of FY 2009.
   - Culturally unidentifiable Native American human remains (CU I): There are just under 40,000 Native American human remains culturally affiliated and in notices, but almost 130,000 listed as culturally unidentifiable. Study of the available data indicates that the proportions should be the reverse. Two questions should be asked: 1. Has consultation with Indian tribes and NHOs occurred that will allow information exchange and further identification? 2. Is the standard for cultural affiliation in the law being applied, or some higher standard?
   - Associated Funerary Objects: Indian tribes often ask why so many human remains have no associated funerary objects. Did the collections and study practices of the past employ such non-scientific methods that the objects and remains were separated with no record to resolve the separation?
   - Tribal NAGPRA Offices: Tribal NAGPRA offices are not funded in the same manner as Tribal Historic Preservation Offices and this often leads to a lack of capacity in tribes to deal with NAGPRA issues, including management of received inventory and summary documents, invitations for consultation, and resolving claims. The National NAGPRA Program meets part of this challenge

by assisting to rebuild tribal files of received documents, assisting tribes and museums with searching old records, which will be aided by new databases of summaries and inventories, and fostering the grants program by assisting Indian tribes and N HOs to write successful proposals. Federal agencies and museums often absorb the costs of consultation.

- Training: The need remains for more and diverse training products. This need will be met in part by efforts of the National NAGPRA Program, but the efforts of Federal agencies, museums and private companies is increasing and is welcome.
- Defining Native American in NAGPRA: There continue to be decisions on cultural affiliation and the application of NAGPRA to human remains, which are impacted by the 9th Circuit decision. Several pending NAGPRA notices have been withdrawn by the originator as the decision has been amended from "culturally affiliated" to not "Native American."

4. Goals for FY 2010
   - Databases: The National NAGPRA Program hopes to bring more of the compliance documents it holds to public access in FY 2010, in databases of summaries and of culturally affiliated inventories, as well as a database of the Notices of Disposition from Federal agency newspaper notices of new excavations and disposition decisions.
   - Aging Notices: Notices in process for years should be brought to publication in FY 2010.
   - Regulations: The section on culturally unidentifiable Native American human remains, 10.11, will hopefully reach publication this year, with technical support and training made available by the National NAGPRA Program. The section on unclaimed Native American human remains and cultural items from Federal lands, 10.7, should advance to a proposed rule. Work has begun on reviewing all of 43 CFR 10 for amendments to aide clarity.
   - As NAGPRA reaches 20 years on November 16, 2010, a NAGPRA at 20 conference is planned to address current issues and seek better means to achieve consultation, decision- making, and repatriation.
   - When the CUI rule, 10.11, is published as a final rule, consultation on Native American human remains is likely to increase, leading to amended inventories and findings of cultural affiliation. Thus, notices of inventory completion will likely increase for both culturally affiliated remains available for repatriation and culturally unidentifiable remains available for disposition. If, as the Review Committee has noted, there are museums that listed Native American human remains as culturally unidentifiable to forestall imposition of the law, then the focus will shift from designation as CUI, to amended inventories redesignating CUI to "not Native American," using the 9th Circuit standard. If this occurs, the focus of needs in NAG PRA will likely shift to a resolution of the "is or was" issue previously considered in the Senate Indian Affairs Committee.

COLLECTIONS

The sections of NAGPRA relating to collections describe the inventories, summaries, grants, notices, civil penalties and the Review Committee, which further describe administration of the law. These provisions pertain to the responsibilities of Federal agencies and museums that receive Federal funds to inventory collections of Native American human remains and associated funerary objects in consultation with potentially affiliated tribes and NHOs, and to submit an itemized list to the National NAGPRA Program. The cultural affiliation decisions of agencies and museums made in inventories of Native American human remains are reflected in Notices of Inventory Completion and those not able to be identified are listed in the inventories of Culturally Unidentifiable Human Remains, which are available on the public access database. Summaries of the remainder of the Native American collections in the possession or control of Federal agencies and museums generally describe the Native American unassociated funerary objects, sacred objects, and objects of cultural patrimony which inform consultation of museums and Federal agencies with tribes and NHOs on repatriation. Decisions to effectuate repatriation of unassociated funerary objects, sacred objects and objects of cultural patrimony are reflected in the published Notices of Intent to Repatriate.

To be in compliance with the law, museums and Federal agencies are required, in consultation with Indian tribes and NHOs, to publish notices, which reflect the cultural affiliation determinations in the inventories. Submission of a document to the National NAGPRA Program, without authorization from the originator for publication, does not fulfill compliance obligations under the law. The accommodation to originators of draft notices to place them "on-hold" was eliminated in 2005. Critical to compliance is the publication of a Notice of Inventory Completion for all of the human remains listed in the inventory as culturally affiliated to a federally recognized Indian tribe.

Regulation section 10.13, published on March 21, 2007 and effective on April 20, 2007, requires museums and Federal agencies receiving a new collection, or having collections of new Indian tribes, to prepare or update inventories within 2 years and summaries within 6 months. If the museum receives Federal funds for the first time, summaries are due in 3 years and inventories in 5 years.

Grants are available to museums and Indian tribes and NHOs to fund projects for consultation, accomplish cultural identification of items and to cover costs of repatriation. Civil penalties may be imposed upon museums found in non-compliance with the law by failing to submit inventories and summaries, consult with descendants, tribes and NHOs, and to repatriate cultural items in a timely manner. The entire NAGPRA process pertaining to collections is within the jurisdiction of the Native American Graves Protection and Repatriation Review Committee which advises the Secretary on implementation and makes recommendations toward the resolution of disputes.

The following overview of summaries, inventories and culturally unidentifiable human remains reflect an update from numbers reported in prior reports and based upon a review of the National NAGPRA Program records as of September 30, 2009.

For more information on notices, contact Jaime Laval lee, National NAGPRA Program, (Jai me_Laval l ee@contractor.nps.gov).

Summaries and Notices of Intent to Repatriate

Summaries have been received from 1,551 institutions. Additionally, 460 statements of "no summary required" have been received.

There have been 477 Notices of Intent to Repatriate published, an increase of 50 notices in FY 2009. These 477 notices account for 144,163 unassoci ated funerary objects, 4,303 sacred objects, 948 objects of cultural patrimony, 822 sacred objects that are also cultural patrimony, and 292 undesignated cultural items. The 50 new notices represent 6,712 unassociated funerary objects, 532 sacred objects, 567 objects of cultural patrimony, 16 sacred objects that are also objects of cultural patrimony, and 77 undesignated cultural items.

Inventories and Notices of Inventory Completion

Inventories have been received from 1,317 institutions. (Note: There may be duplication of reporting for collections as the law directs those museums with possession or control of collections to submit an inventory. Several museums may have collections belonging to Federal agencies, where both the museum and Federal agency submitted an inventory).

The decisions reflected in the inventories are those of the museum or Federal agency and not the National NAGPRA Program. The Program facilitates the publication of notices, which contain the decisions of the originator and which serve to establish rights of lineal descendants and tribes or N HOs to request human remains and their funerary objects. The National NAGPRA Program does not audit the collections of the reporting museum or Federal agency unit. Inventories are self-reports of the collection. The National NAGPRA Program receives amended inventories from museums and Federal agencies when an institution finds new items in its collections, changes prior determinations after further consultation with Indian tribes and NHOs, or under the continuing duty to report collections as specified in 43 CFR 10.13, future applicability of the law, receives new collections, has collections affiliated with newly recognized Indian tribes, or a museum receives initial Federal funding.

There have been 1,295 Notices of Inventory Completion published accounting for 38,671 human remains and 998,731 associated funerary objects. There were 150 notices published in FY 2009, accounting for 2,204 human remains and 227,845 associated funerary objects.

The table below reflects the status of submissions during this period:

(Note: Originators may remove a notice from publication due to error in submission or to revise at a later time after consultation with Indian tribes and N HOs. The decision is that of the originator.)

Table 1. Document Processing FY 2009

Year 2009	Beginning	Received	Removed by Originator	Published	In Processing end of FY 2009
NIC	101	117	5	150	63
NIR	18	42	1	50	9
Total:	**119**	**159**	6	**200**	**72**

Table 2. Notices Published FY1992 through FY 2009

Year	Published	M NI	AFO	UFO	SO	OCP	SO & OCP	UCI	Rec'v	Removed*
1992	2	15	12,225	0	0	0	0		3	0
1993	14	40	60,071	0	1	0	7		14	0
1994	13	1,851	275	31,681	1	1	1		19	0
1995	36	806	18,710	6	243	3	4		37	0
1996	59	2,290	116,002	32	91	17	10		198	0
1997	122	1,194	49,392	5,061	116	67	92		187	0
1998	82	5,280	31,082	2,484	14	62	165		202	0
1999	108	6,441	30,907	680	106	70	78		156	1
2000	110	2,026	21,983	3,245	552	11	28		186	5
2001	199	2,959	167,252	25,583	6	25	5		130	7
2002	143	3,157	25,301	5,903	110	3	121		109	10
2003	85	666	31,392	1,195	101	4	135		83	14
2004	103	1,528	13,924	14,294	37	9	13		63	17
2005	108	2,337	54,915	1,986	2,183	3	5		77	22
2006	100	1,373	36,017	10,303	9	6	45		96	14
2007	108	747	15,619	27,036	28	22	64	215	135	4
2008	180	3,757	85.819	7,962	173	78	33		146	56
2009	200	1,531	214,902	6,712	532	567	16	77	159	6
Total Notices:	**1,772**	**38,671**	**998,731**	**144,163**	**4,303**	**948**	**822**	**292**	**2,000**	**156**

*Draft notices removed from the process when no NAGPRA Federal Register publication was necessary. Possible reasons include: items already covered in a published notice; repository submitted original draft, but repository not in control; revised determination to culturally unidentifiable; request to remove for additional consultation, revision of inventory; or other (item covered in Notice of Intended Disposition, items not Native American, no NAG PRA jurisdiction).

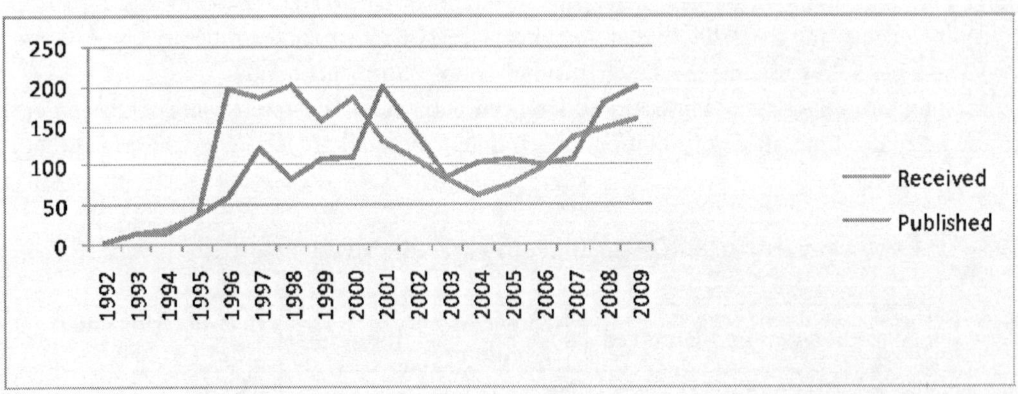

Notices by Year: Received and Published

Culturally Unidentifiable Human Remains

As part of providing administrative support for the Review Committee, the National NAGPRA Program has compiled the Review Committee's inventory of culturally unidentifiable (CUI) human remains, as required by 25 U.S.C. 3006 (c)(5). The Program has entered inventories containing determinations of culturally unidentifiable Native American human remains accounting for 124,377 individuals for whom cultural affiliation has not yet been determined and 916,432 funerary objects associated with those individuals. The number of CUI subsequently culturally affiliated to date is 4,846 and the number of CUI transferred by a disposition to a tribe is 3,363.

Pending regulations will specify a process for disposition of CUI. Meanwhile, requests for recommendations for disposition can be presented to the Review Committee, which makes recommendations to the Secretary. Notices of disposition are published upon receipt of Secretarial authorization, to allow 30 days for competing claims to be lodged prior to transfer of control. There have been 51 disposition authorizations granted by the Secretary out of 66 requests, accounting for 1,228 individuals. In this reporting period there were 11 requests for disposition recommendations, of which 11 were submitted by the Review Committee to the Secretary, accounting for 476 individuals. The Review Committee has established guidelines and a matrix for bringing a request for disposition recommendation, which can be found at www.nps.gov/history/NAGPRA

Table 3. Dispositions of Culturally Unidentifiable Native American Human Remains FY08-09

Request #		MNI/AFO
	35th Review Committee Meeting: Oct. 2007	
44	Binghamton University, NY – approved	2/0 notice pub
45	Hastings Museum of Natural History, NE	11/0
46	Michigan Technological University –approved	1/0 notice pub
47	U.S. Department of the Interior, National Park Service, Effigy Mounds National Monument, IA – approved	6/0 notice pub
48	U.S. Department of the Interior, National Park Service, Gulf Islands National Seashore, FL	13/0
	36th Review Committee Meeting: January 2008	
	No requests	
	37th Review Committee Meeting: May 2008	
40b	Colorado Historical Society – approved	Protocol
49	Hastings Museum of Natural History, NE – approved	5/0 notice pub
50	Kingman Museum – approved	4/0 notice pub
51	Mackinac State Historic Parks – approved	11/0 notice pub
52	Muskegon County Museum – approved	8/0 notice pub
53	Putnam County Commission, WV	664/0
54	Tennessee Division of Archaeology	20/0
55	U.S. Department of Agriculture, Forest Service, Daniel Boone National Forest –approved	8/0 notice pub

Table 3. (Continued)

Request #		MNI/AFO
	38th Review Committee Meeting: Oct. 2008	
56	Arizona State Museum, AZ – approved	4/1 notice pub
57	Arizona State Museum, AZ – approved	1/0 notice pub
58	Cranbrook Institute of Science, MI – approved disposition of 60 individuals. But the Secretary concurred with disposition per agreement of 39 individuals	39/58
59	Detroit Institute of Arts, MI – approved	10/0 notice pub
60	U.S. Department of the Interior, National Park Service, Fort Vancouver National Historic Site, WA – approved	11/0 notice pub
61	Kalamazoo Valley Museum, MI – approved	3/0 notice pub
	39th Review Committee Meeting: May 2009	
62	U.S. Department of the Interior, National Park Service, Great Sand Dunes National Park, CO – approved	3/0
63	U.S. Department of the Interior, National Park Service, Hovenweep National Monument, UT – approved	6/5
64	U.S. Department of the Interior, National Park Service, Pecos National Historical Park, NM – approved	153/0
65	Central Michigan University, MI – approved	144/374
66	University of Nebraska State Museum, NE – approved	2/13 groups of UFO

Grants

Requests

The sum of $1.85 million was available for grants in FY 2009. The grant application deadline for consultation/documentation grants was March 2, 2009. Repatriation grants are received on a rolling basis. A total of 79 grant applications were received: 66 consultation/documentation proposals and 13 repatriation funding requests. Of these, 48 were from Indian tribes and NHOs and 29 were from museums. The total amount of grant requests in FY 2009 was $4,535,252, over twice as much as was received in FY 2008. Grant applications for consultation/documentation projects are reviewed by an outside panel, which met on May 14-15, 2009. Each application was reviewed and ranked. Those applicants not receiving a grant received an individualized letter from the grants coordinator containing valuable feedback obtained from the panel to assist them in preparing better grant proposals in the future and in administering successful projects.

The actual number of grant applications was over double from FY 2008. The National NAGPRA Program conducted an extensive outreach campaign that included postcards, advertisements, email blasts and outreach to relevant organizations. In addition, the FY 09 Grants Review Panel noted that applications were significantly stronger than the previous year due to revisions to the application and guidelines, which helped applicants better describe their experience and project goals. Of note, a Proposal Cover Sheet was added to the application package which listed the many elements of the proposal. Applicants were required to check off each item and sign the sheet resulting in significantly more organized and understandable applications. An optional survey was added to the 2009 grant application requesting feedback regarding applicants' experience applying for grants and receiving training. Results from the surveys support our efforts to outreach Indian tribes, N HOs and museums through multiple sources as applicants found out about the Grants Program in a variety of ways.

Grants Management

Sangita Chari, Grants Coordinator and Vedet Coleman, NAGPRA Grants Administrator, continued to work together to strengthen grantee compliance. The stricter disbursement rules and stronger communication between the grant administrator and NAGPRA staff through a shared database and repeated contact with grantees has resulted in much higher rates of compliance, particularly with newer grantees. All 2004 grantees have closed out their grants, and most grants disbursed from 2004-2007 have been brought into compliance. In addition, all 2008 grantees have submitted their interim reports. For the first time, all 2009 Consultation/ Documentation grantees received training on how to manage their grant through a webinar on NAGPRA Grant Administration on September 23rd, 2009. In addition to Sangita and Vedet, Hampton Tucker, Chief of the Historic Preservation Grants Division, reviewed the grant agreement and the various administrative and financial requirements, and grantees had the opportunity to ask questions and receive feedback on how to administer their grant. Evaluations have been positive and the Program hopes to make this webinar a permanent feature.

Outreach and Training

In FY 2008, the Grants Panel requested that the National NAGPRA Program use unallocated grant funds to build the capacity of Indian tribes, NHOs and museums to administer a NAGPRA program, specifically their capacity to write successful NAGPRA grants. In response, the National NAGPRA Program partnered with the National Preservation Institute to develop NAGPRA-related seminars and provide Indian tribes, NHOs and small museums with scholarships to attend trainings that increased their knowledge regarding the legal and practical skills needed to conduct successful NAGPR programs. Two new seminars were developed, "Writing and Managing a NAGPRA Grant" and "Determining Cultural Affiliation." Scholarships were also provided to attend relevant seminars offered through the National Preservation Institute. In addition to providing scholarships to Indian tribes, N H Os and small museums to cover the cost of registration, travel grants were awarded to eligible Indian tribes and N HOs. The National Museum of the American Indian provided $15,000 to be used toward travel grants for the first training in Seattle, WA. Additional travel grants were provided through the partnership with N PI for the Chicago, IL trainings. To date, the National NAGPRA Program has conducted three trainings, one in Seattle, WA and two in Chicago, IL. Over 55 Indian tribes, N HOs and museums have been trained on writing a NAGPRA grant and 35 were trained on determining cultural affiliation. Results have been overwhelmingly positive. Additionally, four participants have used the scholarship program to attend existing N PI courses. *See Appendix for list.*

2008 marked the 15th year of the NAGPRA Grants Program. Since its inception, over $31 million have been directed to Indian tribes, NHOs and museums to support NAGPRA-related activities. To commemorate the occasion, the Grants Program produced a 16-page, full color retrospective entitled *Journeys to Repatriation: 15 Years of NA GPRA Grants (1994-2008)* showcasing both the stories and statistics behind the Grants Program. *Journeys to Repatriation* provides a comprehensive assessment of the impact of NAGPRA grants on Indian tribes, museums and communities. With the assistance of Lauren Trice, National Council for Preservation Education (NCPE) intern, the Program conducted a thorough review of the grants portfolio. In addition, the retrospective contains success stories, photographs, and quotes about the role of NAG PRA grants in the work of current and former grantees. *Journeys to Repatriation* is available in hard copy and on the NAGPRA website.

As part of the NAGPRA Training DVD series, the Grants Program finished taping for the DVD on NAGPRA Grants. The DVD outlines the NAGPRA Grants Program, provides advice on how to write a successful grant and highlights several successful grants. In addition, the DV D includes an interview with Ron Wilson, Chief Curator for the National Park Service and long-time NAGPRA Grants Panelist. Mr. Wilson discusses the NAGPRA Grants process and provides tips on what panelists look for in a successful application. The final version of the DVD will be available in FY 2010.

Table 4. Grants Awarded in FY 2009

Applicant's Name	Amount Requested
Bishop Paiute Tribe, CA	$76,516
Cal. State, Sacramento, Dept. of Anthropology, CA	$84,410
Central Council of the Tlingit & Haida Indian Tribes, AK	$89,993
Choctaw Nation of Oklahoma, OK	$89,224
Colorado Historical Society, CO	$60,075
Comanche Nation, OK	$63,191
Confederated Tribes of the Umatilla Reservation, OR	$15,860
Denver Museum of Nature & Science, CO	$51,260
Eastern Shawnee Tribe of Oklahoma, OK	$89,999
Lac du Flambeau Band of Lake Superior Chippewa Indians, WI	$89,995
Little Traverse Bay Bands of Odawa Indians, MI	$40,191
Maryland Historical Trust, MD	$15,480
Mashpee Wampanoag Tribe, MA	$90,000
Minnesota Indian Affairs Council, MN	$85,665
New York State Museum, NY	$72,925
Peoria Tribe of Indians of Oklahoma, OK	$60,483
Pioneer Historical Society of Bent County, CO	$59,087
Rochester Museum & Science Center, NY	$89,997
Sealaska Corporation, AK	$89,904
Susanville Indian Rancheria, CA	$87,170
Univ. of Washington, Burke Museum, WA	$64,455
Univ. of Wisconsin, Madison, Dept. of Anthropology, WI	$90,000
University of Colorado Museum, Boulder, CO	$58,849
White Mountain Apache Tribe of the Fort Apache Reservation, AZ	$90,000
TOTAL CONSULTATION/ DOCUMENTATION GRANTS	**$1,704,729**

Table 4. (Continued)

Name of Applicant	Amount Requested
Little Traverse Bay Bands of Odawa Indians, MI	$2,875
Sault Ste. Marie Band of Chippewa Indians, MI	$605
Central Council of Tlingit & Haida Indian Tribes of Alaska, AK	$14,295
Central Council of Tlingit & Haida Indian Tribes of Alaska, AK	$14,978
Pawnee Nation, OK	$15,000
Osage Nation, AR	$14,600
Choctaw Nation of Oklahoma, OK	$10,244
Aleutian Pribilof Islands Association, Inc., AK	$14,972
Iowa Tribe of Kansas and Nebraska, KS	$4,200
Hui Malama I Na Kupuna O Hawaii Nei, HI	$13,617
Central Council of Tlingit and Haida Indian Tribes of Alaska, AK	$14,875
Colorado Historical Society, CO	$12,565
Colorado Historical Society, CO	$9,041
TOTAL REPATRIATION GRANTS	**$141,867**

Table 5. Grants Requested and Awarded FY 1994 – FY 2009 by Tribes and Museums

TRIBES				MUSEUMS			
Year	Number of Applications Received	Amount Requested $	Amount Awarded $	Year	Number of Applications Received	Amount Requested $	Amount Awarded $
1994	106	6,091,594	1,023,200	1994	113	6,643,200	1,116,800
1995	63	3,842,289	1,387,925	1995	56	2,408,165	854,075
1996	54	3,490,414	1,150,985	1996	33	1,530,039	946,905
1997	54	3,148,112	1,425,600	1997	20	1,055,915	550,650
1998	61	3,547,254	1,557,165	1998	23	1,025,061	775,720
1999	57	3,296,264	1,648,220	1999	22	2,251,415	687,780
2000	84	4,814,432	1,629,170	2000	27	1,276,774	622,830
2001	53	3,048,377	1,802,180	2001	20	1,042,261	635,820
2002	57	3,460,873	1,708,268	2002	16	961,775	537,552
2003	60	3,708,782	1,703,194	2003	12	668,730	497,806
2004	41	2,369,685	1,535,659	2004	17	1,037,649	646,341
2005	41	2,344,891	918,560	2005	17	1,060,299	471,669
2006	52	2,999,228	1,500,965	2006	17	825,172	393,893
2007	36	2,100,960	1,247,243	2007	16	815,239	548,825
2008	29	1,691,220	1,089,554	2008	12	559,317	490,258
2009	51	2,674,813	753,809	2009	31	1,809,161	1,092,787

Civil Penalties

The civil penalties rule (43 CFR 10.12) was published as an interim rule in 1997, and as a final rule in 2003. In May 2005, through a Secretarial Order, the Secretary of the Interior gave the National NAGPRA Program the responsibility of providing staff support to the Secretary's designee on civil penalties, the Assistant Secretary for Fish and Wildlife and Parks. Since the beginning of FY 2006, the NAGPRA civil penalty coordinator, who serves in the National NAGPRA Program, and a National Park Service law enforcement officer, have been working as a team to support the Assistant Secretary. For more information on civil penalties, contact David Tarler, enforcement coordinator, National NAG PRA Program(David_Tarl er@nps.gov).

The civil penalties investigative function is housed within the National Park Service's Law Enforcement, Security and Emergency Services (LESES) branch. Civil penalty investigations are carried out by NPS law enforcement officer Bob Palmer, who currently is based at Effigy Mounds National Monument. As needed, NPS also is accommodating the National NAGPRA Program on an ongoing basis with law enforcement agents and officers across the country to assist Bob Palmer in collecting information on allegations of failure to comply.

The NAGPRA regulations set forth eight ways that a museum might fail to comply with the Act or its regulations (43 CFR 10.12 (b)(1)):

i. Sale or transfer of NAGPRA items contrary to NAGPRA.
ii. Failure to complete a summary.
iii. Failure to complete an inventory.
iv. Failure to notify Indian tribes within 6 months after completion of the inventory.
v. Refusal to repatriate.
vi. Repatriation prior to publishing a notice in the Federal Register.
vii. Failure to consult with Indian tribes and/or lineal descendants.
viii. Failure to inform recipients that items have been treated with pesticides.

Allegations of Failure to Comply: A Snapshot

Through FY 2009, 248 counts of alleged failure to comply with the requirements of NAGPRA have been made against 43 museums. The number of counts alleged, by year, is as follows:

Table 6. Total Number of Counts Alleged by Year

Year	Total Counts Alleged
1996	1
1997	7
1998	10
1999	2
2000	4
2001	4
2002	25
2003	11

Table 6. (Continued)

Year	Total Counts Alleged
2004	16
2005	10
2006	3
2007	14
2008	76
2009	65

FY 2009: Investigations and Findings

During FY 2009, 56 counts of alleged failure to comply, made against 1 museum, were investigated. The investigations yielded determinations of failure to comply on 1 count (failure complete an inventory) and determinations that the allegation was unsubstantiated on the 55 counts of failure to repatriate human remains, all of which the museum had determined to be culturally unidentifiable. Determination of cultural affiliation is a matter of fact upon which the Review Committee can assist the parties with findings upon the request of "any affected party."

New Allegations Received in FY 2009

During FY 2009, 65 new counts, made against 3 museums, were received. By the end of the fiscal year, none of these counts had been investigated.

Table 7. Disposition of Alleged Counts of Failure to Comply in FY 2009 and Total

Number of Counts Pending Investigation at the Beginning of FY 2009	New Counts Received in FY 2009	Number of Counts Found to Be Substantiated in FY 2009	Number of Counts Found to Be Unsubstantiated in FY 2009	Number of Counts Remaining to be Investigated at the end of FY 2009
113	**65**	**1**	**55**	**122**
Running Total Number of Counts Alleged as of the Beginning of FY 2009	New Counts Added During FY 2009	Running Total # of Substantiated Counts as of the End of FY 2009	Running Total # of Unsubstantiated Counts as of the End of FY 2009	Running Total # of Counts Remaining to be Investigated as of the End of FY 2009
183	**65**	**18**	**108**	**122**

Table 8. Disposition of Alleged Counts of Failure to Comply in FY 2009 and Total by Museums

FY 2009	# Museums Represented in FY 2009 Allegations	# Museums Investigated in Whole or Part in FY 2009	# Museums Investigated in FY 2009 With at Least One Substantiated Count	# Museums Investigated in FY 2009 Without a Single Substantiated Count	# Museums Remaining to Be Investigated in Whole or Part at the End of FY 2009
	3	**1**	**1**	**0**	**26**
1996-2009	Total # of Museums Represented In Allegations	Total # of Museums Investigated in Whole or in Part	Total # of Museums With at Least One Substantiated Count	Total # of Museums Without a Single Substantiated Count	Total # of Museums to Be Investigated in Whole or Part
	43	**19**	**12**	7	**26**

FY 2006-2009: Investigations and Findings

To date, the investigation of 126 allegations of failure to comply, made against 19 museums, has yielded a determination of failure to comply on 18 counts, involving 12 museums, and a determination that the allegation was unsubstantiated on 108 counts. Of the unsubstantiated counts, 6 counts, alleged against 3 museums, were found to be un-substantiated because the deadline for compliance had not yet passed. Thus, through FY 2009, the percentage of museums that have been determined to have failed to comply with the requirements of NAGPRA is 63.2%, whereas the percentage of alleged counts that have been determined to be substantiated is 14.3%.

The 18 substantiated counts of failure to comply were comprised of 1 count of sale or transfer of NAG PRA cultural items contrary to NAG PRA (43 CFR 10.12 (b)(1)(i)); 1 count of failure to complete a summary (43 C FR 10.12 (b)(1)(ii)); 7 counts of failure to complete an inventory (43 C FR 10.12 (b)(1)(iii)); 6 counts of refusal to repatriate (43 CFR 10.12 (b)(1)(v)); and 3 counts of failure to consult with Indian tribes (43 CFR 10.12 (b)(1)(vii)). The trends in allegations made and violations substantiated are reflected in the following charts.

Table 9a. Alleged Counts of Failure to Comply According to Year and Category

FY	I	ii	iii	iv	v	vi	vii	viii
1996					1			
1997			3				4	
1998	1		7				2	
1999	1	1						
2000	1		1		1		1	

Table 9a. (Continued)

FY	I	ii	iii	iv	v	vi	vii	viii
2001		2	1	1				
2002	3	4	3	3	6	3	3	
2003		1	1	1	6		2	
2004	1		6		5		4	
2005	3		2		1		4	
2006			3					
2007	2		1	2	3	1	5	
2008	7	2	4	2	56	1	3	1
2009	3	55	3	2			2	
Total	22	65	35	11	79	5	30	1

Table 9b. Counts of Failure to Comply Substantiated According to Category

Violation Type	FY 2009	Total
i. Transfer	0	1
ii. No Summary	0	1
iii. No Inventory	1	7
iv. Not Notify	0	0
v. Not Repatriate	0	6
vi. No Notice	0	0
vii. Not Consult	0	3
viii. Pesticides	0	0

Penalty Assessments

A museum receiving a notice of failure to comply has 45 days to take specific action, as set forth in the NAGPRA regulations, after which a penalty assessment may issue. To date, 7 notices of penalty assessment, involving 6 museums, have been issued by the Assistant Secretary. In one case, the Assistant Secretary determined, following informal discussion with the museum, that the institution of a civil penalty was not an appropriate remedy (43 CFR 10.12 (d)). Altogether, the 7 notices assessed penalties in the amount of $38,490. As of the end of FY 2009, $26,170 in penalties has been paid by 5 of the museums ($19,920 of which was paid in FY 2009). The 45-day notice period has not yet run for payment of the $12,320 penalty assessed against 1 museum.

Administrative Hearings

A museum receiving a notice of failure to comply or a notice of penalty assessment has 45 days from the date of receipt of the notice to request an administrative hearing. Thus far, 1 museum has requested a hearing. As a settlement was reached prior to the hearing, a motion to dismiss the case was granted by the administrative law judge assigned to hear the matter.

Upon receipt of a notice, a museum may request an informal discussion with the Assistant Secretary's designees.

Outreach Activity in FY 2009

In addition to investigating allegations and completing penalty assessments, a concurrent priority of the civil enforcement team was the scripting, production, and completion of a NAGPRA training video on civil penalties. This film is one segment of a multi-part series devoted to providing guidance and examples of NAGPRA in action.

Review Committee

During all or part of FY 2009, the following people served on the Native American Graves Protection and Repatriation Review Committee: Sonya Atalay, Donna Augustine, Alan Goodman, Eric Hemenway, Willie Jones, Colin Kippen, Dan Monroe, Vincas Steponaitis, Rosita Worl, and Mervin Wright, Jr. During the course of FY 2009, Ms. Atalay succeeded Mr. Steponaitis, Mr. Hemenway succeeded Mr. Jones, Mr. Wright succeeded Ms. Worl, Ms. Worl succeeded Mr. Kippen as the at-large member, and Mr. Monroe was reappointed.

The 2006 Review Committee charter allowed members to continue serving on the Review Committee until the Secretary of the Interior appointed their replacements. In November 2008, the Review Committee charter reauthorization removed this holdover provision. At the Seattle meeting the Review Committee recommended that the DFO seek reinstatement of the holdover provision and insertion of a quorum provision.

The Review Committee's Designated Federal Official complies with all filings required by the Federal Advisory Committee Act (FACA). For more information on the Review Committee, contact David Tarl er, Designated Federal Official (David_Tarler@nps.gov).

On October 11-12, 2008, the Review Committee met in San Diego, CA. At the meeting, the Review Committee heard a dispute between the Onondaga Nation and the New York State Museum, and made findings of fact and recommendations related to the cultural affiliation of certain human remains and the return of these remains. As a result, the New York State Museum, relying in whole or in part on the expert opinion of the Review Committee, determined that the human remains in question were culturally affiliated with the Onondaga Nation and the federally recognized Indian tribes comprising the Haudenosaunee Confederacy (of which the Onondaga Nation is a constituent member). The Review Committee also heard requests and made recommendations to the Secretary of the Interior regarding the disposition, per an agreement, of culturally unidentifiable Native American human remains and associated funerary objects under the control of Fort Vancouver National Historic Site, the Arizona State Museum, the Detroit Institute of Arts, the Kalamazoo Valley Museum, and the Cranbrook Institute of Science.

On May 23-24, 2009, the Review Committee met in Seattle, Washington. The Review Committee heard requests and made recommendations to the Secretary of the Interior regarding the disposition, per an agreement, of culturally unidentifiable Native American human remains and associated funerary objects under the control of Great Sand Dunes National Park, Hovenweep National Monument, Pecos National Historical Park, Central

Michigan University's Museum of Cultural and Natural History, and the University of Nebraska State Museum. The Review Committee selected a subcommittee to draft the Review Committee's annual report to Congress for 2008, as required by NAGPRA. The Review Committee deferred making recommendations to the drafters of the regulation concerning the disposition of unclaimed human remains and other cultural items discovered on Federal or tribal lands after November 16, 1990 (to be codified at 43 CFR 10.7). Out of consideration for an absent member, the subcommittee of the Review Committee deferred the development and finalization of the consented-to list of persons from which the Secretary of the Interior appoints the at-large member.

On June 8, 2009, the subcommittee of the Review Committee met to develop a consented-to list of persons from which the Secretary of the Interior appoints the at-large member. They met telephonically and finalized the list of persons. The list consisted of three names – Clayton Dumont, Colin Kippen, and Rosita Worl. On September 4, 2009, the Secretary appointed Rosita Worl to succeed Colin Kippen as the at-large member.

Review Committee procedures may be found at www.nps.gov/history/ NAGPRA. A template to assist in submitting a request for a recommendation to the Secretary for approval of disposition of culturally unidentifiable Native American human remains is posted on the National NAGPRA Program website. Review Committee vacancies are noticed in the Federal Register. The information on all of the nominees then proceeds through a review process in the Department of the Interior, culminating in a decision by the Secretary of the Interior.

EXCAVATIONS AND DISCOVERIES

Notices of Intended Disposition

There were 13 Notices of Intended Disposition submitted to National NAGPRA in FY 2009. There are 90 Notices of Intended Disposition reported by Federal agencies to date, accounting for 495 individuals, 4,148 associated funerary objects, 64 unassociated funerary objects, and 4 objects of cultural patrimony. A listing of these notices is available at: http://www.nps.gov/history/nagpra/NOTICES/NID-Table-Current-for-web

REGULATIONS

Three reserved sections of the NAGPRA regulations (43 CFR 10) were pending in FY 2009

- 43 CFR 10.7, Disposition of unclaimed human remains, funerary objects, sacred objects, or objects of cultural patrimony, is in development. A Federal Agency Working Group was established to assist the regulations coordinator to develop a rule. The group is comprised of Federal agency NAGPRA coordinators, who self-nominated to the open group during the Federal Agency NAGPRA Coordinators annual meeting. This Working Group joined contractor Patricia Zell, who was employed to assist the regulations coordinator in rule development. At the beginning of FY 2009, contractor Lesa K osci el ski prepared a disc for use by the Review Committee and the Working Group, which contained the full transcript of all of the prior consultation sessions with Indian tribes, NHOs and science and museum groups, as well as an executive summary of the suggestions. This disc and the ongoing drafts of the Working Group were provided to the Review Committee at each of the two meetings of the Review Committee in FY 2009, to assist the Review Committee in consultation on the developing rule.

- 43 CFR 10.11, Disposition of culturally unidentifiable human remains, was published as a proposed rule on October 16, 2007, with a comment period until January 14, 2008. A total of 153 comments were received from Indian tribes, N H Os, Native American organizations, museum and scientific organizations, Federal agencies, the Review Committee, and members of the public. At the close of FY 2009 the rule passed from consideration in the Department of the Interior to the Office of Management and Budget for review.
- 43 CFR 10.15(b), Failure to claim where no repatriation or disposition has occurred, is held pending the completion of the above noted regulatory sections.

Also, in FY 2009, the NAGPRA Regulations, 43 CFR 10, were renewed for three years in compliance with the Paperwork Reduction Act. The renewal is effective through August 2012. Renewal of the underlying regulations cleared the way for the eventual publication of additional reserved sections of the regulations.

For more information on regulations, contact Richard Waldbauer (Richard_ Waldbauer@nps.gov).

TECHNICAL ASSISTANCE

Training

The National NAGPRA Program provides training offered by the program and hosted by Indian tribes, museums and Federal agencies. During this reporting period, staff has given 15 training programs and other presentations to 612 participants, in addition to supplying materials for training given by others. For more information on training, contact David Tarler (David_Tarler@nps.gov).

In FY 2009, National NAGPRA provided training and program presentations as summarized below, with the number of attendees:

Video Project

The NAGPRA Video Project began in October 2008 with the mission to create a training series that would include grant-writing tips, first-person narratives, program statistics, anecdotal evidence, and in- depth, engaging coverage of the entirety of the law and its consequences. Over the past year the National NAGPRA Program has conducted 50 interviews in 10 cities across the country. These interviews with tribal members, museum officials and Federal agency representatives have created a historic archive of resources on consultation, grants, notices, law making, dispositions, documentation and repatriation. Along with the interviews, the National NAGPRA Program was also able to complete the segment on NAGPRA Civil Penalties with the help of Loras College in Dubuque, Iowa. By the end of 2009, with the help of the DOI National Business Center, the National NAGPRA Program will complete two more segments on NAGPRA Grants and NAGPRA Notices. In addition to the many longer segments to be developed, the National NAGPRA Program will also be developing a shorter piece to be used on its website and as an introduction to the NAGPRA process. As the project moves into its second year, the National NAGPRA Program is pleased to report that the NAGPRA Video Project has already proved to be a useful tool for forging relationships, developing understanding and discussing the future of NAGPRA.

Date	Location	Sponsor/Course	Number of Attendees
Oct. 10	CA	National NAGPRA: "NAGPRA Basics"	76
April 16-17	VA	National NAGPRA and Manassas Battlefield NP: Enforcing the Archaeological Resources Protection Act Criminally and Civilly"	20
May 20-21	WA	National NAGPRA and National Preservation Institute: "Writing a NAGPRA Grant"	25
May 22	WA	National NAGPRA: "NAGPRA Basics"	62
May 27	CA	San Francisco State University: "NAGPRA Basics"	25
June 2	CA	Sixth Annual Society of American Indian Government Employees (SAIGE) Training Conference: "NAGPRA Basics"	15
June 13	IA	Cultural Resources Teachers' Workshop for Area Educators (IA, MN & WI): "Cultural Resources Protection"	65
June 30	DC	National NAGPRA Webinar: "How to Write a Successful Federal Register Notice for NAGPRA: Types, Process & Content	30
July 27-31	WV	National Park Service: Cultural & Natural Resources Management Training for NPS Superintendents	35
Aug. 10	OK (by telephone from DC)	11th Annual Meeting of the National Association of Tribal Historic Preservation Officers: National NAGPRA Program Databases"	60
Sept. 14	IL	National NAGPRA and National Preservation Institute: "Determining Cultural Affiliation"	35
Sept. 15-16	IL	National NAGPRA and National Preservation Institute: "Writing a NAGPRA Grant"	23
Sept. 23	DC	National NAGPRA Webinar: "Managing Your 2009 NAGPRA Grant"	40

(Continued)

Date	Location	Sponsor/Course	Number of Attendees
Sept. 22-25	CA	National NAGPRA, Dept. of Interior – Indian Arts and Crafts Board and Dept. of Justice: "Cultural Resources Protection Law: Enforcement"	31
	NM	National Park Service and U.S. Forest Service: "Native American Cultural Property Law"	70
TOTAL			612

Interviews	
Affiliation	**Number**
Indian tribes	21
Museums	15
Federal Agencies	6
Review Committee	5
Other	3
Total Interviews	50

Interview Locations
Denver, CO
Flagstaff, AZ
Phoenix, AZ
Syracuse, NY
Boston, MA
Martha's Vineyard, MA
Seattle, WA
Washington, DC
Juneau, AK
Dubuque, IA

Partners
National Preservation Institute
Dept. of the Interior, National Business Center
National Portrait Gallery, Smithsonian Institution
Sealaska Heritage Institute
S. Margaret Spivey, Harvard University
Megan Keller, George Washington University
Lauren A. Trice, University of Mary Washington
Jim Boyd, National Park Service
B Creative Group, Inc.
Loras College

Outreach

During this reporting period the National NAGPRA Program provided information to the following:

News outlets and media enterprises:
Associated Press
Indian County Today
Charleston Gazette
Columbus Dispatch
Salem Oregonian
Native America Calling (radio live broadcast)
National Public Radio

Legislative and public information:
Library of Congress
Senator Dorgan
Senator Hastings
Senator Inouye
Senator Murkowski
Representative Rahall

In addition to responding to telephone inquiries and email correspondence, including mail sent to the website on a daily basis (in total for FY 2009 approximately 2,000 inquiries), the National NAGPRA Program receives requests for assistance from college students and faculty conducting research projects which rely on program information. Aides to research by institution are:
University of Arizona, Rogers College of Law
Harvard University
American University College of Law

Website

The National NAGPRA website provides an opportunity to supply training and technical guidance on a range of NAGPRA matters. The web pages and training materials began a wholesale review in FY 2008, which is continuing. See www.nps.gov/history/NAGPRA.

For information on the website contact: Mariah Soriano (Mariah_Soriano@nps.gov).

Databases

The National NAGPRA Program maintains several databases and will be adding additional public access databases in the near future. The National NAGPRA Program receives the compliance documents from Federal agencies and museums, including:

- inventories of culturally affiliated Native American human remains,
- inventories of culturally unidentifiable Native American human remains,
- notices of inventory completion published in the Federal Register of Native American human remains, either culturally affiliated for repatriation or culturally unidentifiable for disposition,
- summaries of Federal agency and museum collections,
- notices of intent to repatriate items from the summaries, per agreement with Indian tribes, and
- newspaper notices published by Federal agencies for new finds on the land and intended disposition.

The National NAGPRA Program supports consultation between Federal agencies and museums with Indian tribes in furtherance of the NAGPRA process by making this information publicly available on the web. In addition, other tools to assist consultation are posted on the Program website. The following databases exist, are in development, or updating as follows:

Native American Consultation Database (NACD): This long-standing database provides the names and contact information supplied by each Indian tribe for their NAGPRA contact for consultation. The database has recently undergone structural updating with a software contractor and will undergo an update of the information in FY 2010.

Consultation efforts are further supported by maps accessible on the Program website, including maps of tribal lands, treaty areas, and the 1906 ethnographic maps of tribal aboriginal areas. Once the area of an item in a collection, or new discovery on the land, is determined, these maps can be used to locate the Indian tribes with a possible interest in human remains or items from an area. The NACD will supply the contact information for the Indian tribe.

Notice Database: There is currently available on the website a database of published notices, which is updated as new notices are published. This information is helpful to aid in information sharing and informing consultation on other notices.

Culturally Unidentifiable Native American Human Remains Database (CUI): This database was launched in 2005 and has informed disposition decisions on CUI, as well as bringing to public view the contents of CUI inventories from which thousands of individuals have been subsequently listed in amended inventories as culturally affiliated, placed in published notices and made eligible for repatriation. The database is in continual update from newly submitted records as well as to reconcile program data to ensure accuracy.

Culturally Affiliated Native American Human Remains Database (CA): This database of CA inventories should launch as a public access item in early FY 2010. Full population of data will enable accurate reports of the individuals culturally affiliated but not yet in notices.

Summaries Database: By posting summaries on a public access database, Indian tribes will have easily accessible information on those Federal agencies and museums that list them as having an interest in items, as well as to disclose locations of items when summaries were not sent to a particular Indian tribe. The database should foster consultation and inform claims decisions of Indian tribes, as well as provide information to museums of similar collections.

Notice of Intended Disposition Database (NID): This notice database will complete the disclosure and public access of the NAGPRA compliance documents for public use, with new discovery information.

Review Committee Decisions by Topic: A report of Review Committee decisions has been supplied in Program reports for several years. These reports have given historical accounting of the parties in a dispute, the general dispute item and the resolution. For purposes of assisting parties, researchers and the general public, having an interest in the varied issues and determinations on the matters, a more issue specific database is needed. A searchable-by-topic database of Review Committee opinions has been evolving and has been the project of several volunteer law school student interns. This project is not yet ready for release and will be in continual development in FY 2010.

Future Database Development: Planned in the future are public access tools including: listings of training opportunities by government, tribal and private providers; resources to support the NAGPRA process for Federal agencies, Indian tribes and museums such as providers of toxic substance detection; listings of state/NAGPRA protocols approved by the Secretary of the Interior; and other products as may be suggested by the Review Committee to support the NAGPRA process.

State Burial Laws Project: This massive, multi-year project is an undertaking with the partnership of the American University, Washington School of Law. Each year, for the last four years, 8-10 law students under the direction of David Tarler have made a comprehensive accumulation of every law in each state that pertains to the regulation and enforcement of human remains and burials. When all the state canvassing was complete, the students then turned to the next stage of the project: the annotation of each state according to a set list of questions, to enable research across the states or within a state. With the annotation of fifteen states almost complete, the public launch of this database may occur early in FY 2010. The database will be housed on the website of the Washington School of Law Library. American University has made a commitment to maintain and update the database, once launched, and have funded Dean's Fellows dedicated to this project. The product of this partnership will assist states in the resolution of repatriation and protection of human remains discovered on state lands, and will support further development by states of repatriation protocols consistent with NAGPRA. It will be a useful tool for developers and those who work in the field of NEPA and NHPA compliance.

Illegal Trafficking

NAGPRA provides criminal penalties for violations of 18 U.S.C. 1170, Illegal Trafficking in Native American Human Remains and Cultural Items. The cases are investigated by Federal law enforcement agents and handled by United States Attorneys throughout the country. National NAGPRA offers training for attorneys and agents and provides technical assistance upon request. For more information on cultural property law and enforcement, contact David Tarler (David_Tarler@nps.gov).

PROGRAM OPERATIONS

Operational Management

The National NAGPRA Program employed a software contractor in FY 2007-2008 to develop a stable format. That contract is complete. A second contract is underway to develop specific programmed report functions for each of the program tasks. The contract began in 2008, and by the end of FY 2009, the contractor, NuAxis, had developed, and put into operation, programs to support reporting of notice processing, grants processing, civil penalty file management and reporting, a database of culturally affiliated Native American human remains, a database of notices of disposition and updates to the culturally unidentifiable Native American human remains database. To be completed are programs to support a database of summary information and updates to the consultation database.

For more information on technical reporting capacity of the National NAGPRA Program, contact M ariah Soriano (Mariah_Soriano@nps.gov).

Externs, Interns

The National NAGPRA Program forms partnerships with the National Center for Preservation Education (NCPE), law schools and universities, and the Cultural Resources Diversity Program within NPS, through the Student Conservation Association (SCA), to offer internships in government service and externships from law schools where students earn course credit. Intern/extern projects provide numerous benefits to the National NAGPRA Program and the communities that it serves.

The externs/interns and the projects in progress in FY 2009 were:

Project: *A Survey of State Laws Affecting Burials,* under the direction of David Tarler

Externs/Interns: Second and third year law students, American University Washington College of Law, Abbey Baker, Samantha Cardenas, Ernest Edwards, Kate Halloran, Christine Peterson, Courtney Schumacher, Dan Zagoren

Project: Culturally Affiliated Native American Human Remains Database, under the direction of M ariah Soriano

Externs/Interns: Mathew Estes, graduate of the Anthropology Department, SUNY Oswego Sarah Stanton, undergraduate, Native American Program, Dartmouth College

Project: *NAGPRA Video,* under the Direction of Sangita Chari and David Tarler

Externs/Interns: Margaret Spivey, graduating senior, Anthropology Department, Harvard University

Lauren Trice, graduate of the Historic Preservation Program, University of Mary Washington Megan Keller, graduate student, Museum Studies, George Washington University

National NAGPRA Staff

The National NAGPRA staff roster as of September 30, 2009 is:
Program Manager: Sherry Hutt
Program Secretary: Robin Coates
Program Officers: David Tarler
Sangita Chari
Mariah Soriano

In February 2009, C. Timothy McKeown left the National NAG PRA Program for a career-enhancing position in the Department of the Interior. On October 1, 2009, Richard Waldbauer will assume the position in the National NAGPRA Program of technical documents and reports coordinator, which will include drafting regulations, special reports, developing new training products with regard to regulations, coordinating the interagency NAGPRA coordinators working group, as well as providing technical assistance to constituents and providing webinars and video segments. Dr. Waldbauer comes to the National NAGPRA Program from the Federal Preservation Institute and with experience in the early days of the National NAGPRA Program in NPS.

The program is assisted by contractors:
Jaime Lavallee
Lesa Koscielski
Patricia Zell
NuAxis
Lauren Trice

The civil penalty investigator is Bob Palmer, in cooperation with NPS Law Enforcement, Resource and Visitor Protection and Effigy Mounds National Park. The National Park Service is accommodating the National NAGPRA Program on an ongoing basis with law enforcement agents across the country to assist Bob Palmer in collecting information on allegations of failure to comply, as needed.

In addition, the National NAGPRA Program receives support from other NPS employees:

Hampton Tucker and Vedet Coleman, grants administration
Kathleen Murphy, IT support
Jane Fu, IT support
Randall Bohnert and Lesa Weissman, finance
Joe Wallis, finance, long-range planning

FY 2009 Budget

The National NAGPRA Program receives appropriations from Congress for grants and grants administration. Funding is also provided through the National Park Service. The figures below are in thousands and are approximate pending final invoices.

Grants Appropriations:

Congressional appropriation	$2,300
Used for National NAGPRA Program	450
Available for Grants FY 2009	1,850
Grants Awarded FY 2009	$1,850

National NAGPRA Program Funding:

National NAGPRA Program support	450
Grants administration appropriation	191
Operations funding from NPS Cultural Resources accounts	329
Funding from NPS Law Enforcement for enforcement support and training	45
Total of funding sources:	$1,015

Operational Expenses:

Personnel Compensation:	$ 651
Contractors and interns:	120
Publication (Fed. Reg. & printing)	90
Travel NAGPRA staff, Review Com. (training & Review Committee meetings)	65
Equipment, supplies	15
Review Committee meeting events	12
Review Committee transcripts	32
Review Committee fees	30
Total Expense	$ 1,015

See page 3 of this chapter for a summary of the products achieved.

APPENDIX

Recipients of Training Grants

Tribes/NHO's

Absentee Shawnee Tribe
Agua Caliente Band of Cahuilla Indians
Buena Vista Rancheria
Central Council Tlingit & Haida Tribes of Alaska
Eastern Shawnee Tribe of OK
Elk Valley Rancheria
Greenville Rancheria
Hawai'I Maoli
Hui Kakoo
Iowa Tribe of Kansas & Nebraska
Kalama'ula Mauka Homestead Assn.
Kenaitze Indian Tribe
Kona Historical Society – Pulama Ia Kona
Lac Vieux Desert Band of Lake Superior Chippewa
Lac Vieux Desert Band of Lake Superior Ojibwe
Las Vegas Paiute Tribe
Lower Elwha Klallam Tribe
Ohana Keohokalole
Organized Village of Kake
Pawnee Nation of Oklahoma
Penobscot Nation
Pueblo de San Ildefonso
Pueblo of Zuni
Saginaw Chippewa Indian Tribe of Michigan
San Xavier District of the Tohono O'odham Nation
Santee Sioux Nation
Seal aska Heritage Institute
Squaxin Island Tribe
Three Affiliated Tribes
White Mountain Apache Tribe
Wiyot Tribe
Wrangell Cooperative Association

Museums

Alutiiq Museum & Archaeological Respository
Eastern WA State Historical Society

The Friends of ʻIolani Palace
University of Denver Museum of Anthropology

Other

American Indian Center of Chicago
UC-San Diego

In: Native American Graves and Repatriation
Editor: Kathy J. Bergmann
ISBN: 978-1-61122-410-8

Chapter 5

WHO ARE THE CULTURALLY UNIDENTIFIABLE?

Andrew Kline

INTRODUCTION

Pursuant to 25 U.S.C. 3003(a) each Federal agency and museum which has possession of or control over human remains is required to compile an inventory which identifies the geographical and cultural affiliation of items in its possession based on documentary evidence. The inventories provided by the Federal agencies and museums in compliance with 25 U.S.C. 3003(a) resulted in the classification of over 118,000 individuals as culturally unidentifiable. According to 25 U.S.C. 3001, cultural affiliation is defined as, "a relationship of shared group identity which can be reasonably traced historically or prehistorically…" between a current day federally recognized Indian Tribe or Native Hawaiian group. According to the reporting institutions and agencies 118, 833 Native American human remains cannot be found to have a group identity with any existing federally recognized Indian Tribe or Native Hawaiian Group.

This chapter compiles information regarding the culturally unidentifiable remains which are held in federally funded museums and Federal agencies across six states of the United States. The six states which are examined in this chapter account for 53,182 culturally unidentifiable remains, roughly 44.75% of all the culturally unidentifiable remains in the United States as of February 2, 2007. In addition to holding nearly half of the CUI in the United States, this group of states held a small number of culturally identified individuals. The six states of this study geographically comprises a swath of land which runs from the Gulf of Mexico to the Ohio River Valley.

The intent of this chapter is to give an in-depth description of CUI in these six states (Alabama, Florida, Ohio, Tennessee, Kentucky, and Illinois) from a number of perspectives to aid future consultation and identification efforts. The first round of inquiry focused on the provenience, modality, and age of the CUI. After completion of the preliminary inquest, a second round of investigation was conducted which analyzed the date of excavation, affiliated funerary objects found, and the quantity of remains uncovered. From the statistical data compiled in this chapter a greater understanding of the nature of the CUI population can be gained. It was not the intent of this chapter to attempt to determine cultural affiliation; the goal was merely to provide the National NAGPRA Review Committee with refined statistical analysis from which further discussion can be made regarding culturally unidentifiable individuals.

The figures used to create the tables and charts included in this chapter are derived from the inventories provided to National NAGPRA as of February 2, 2007. These inventory reports are available to the public on-line, via the National NAGPRA website, http://www.cr.nps.gov/nagpra.

I. PROVENIENCE

The first section of this chapter examines the provenience of the culturally unidentifiable Native American human remains from the sample population; specifically investigating the current location of the individuals. Comparison of the state in which the individual was excavated, with the current location where they are held may provide clues as to why the remains have yet to be culturally affiliated.

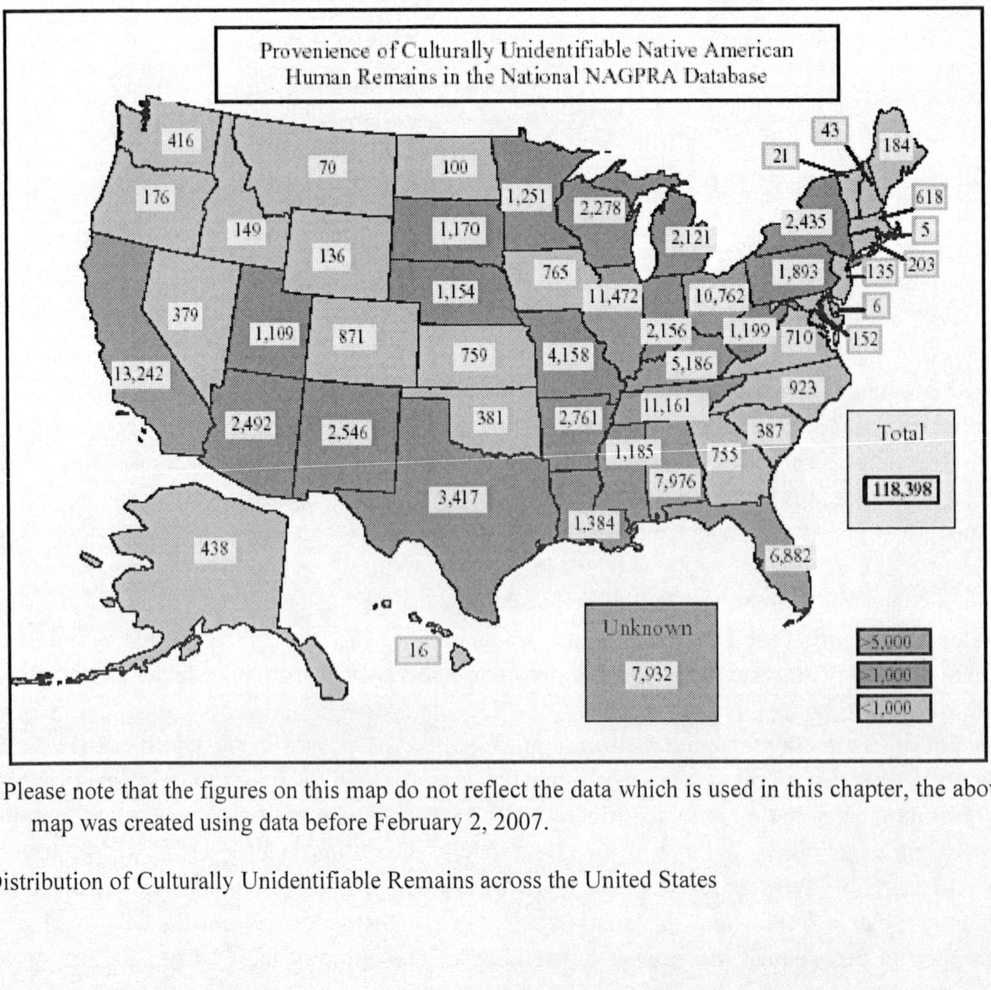

* Please note that the figures on this map do not reflect the data which is used in this chapter, the above map was created using data before February 2, 2007.

Distribution of Culturally Unidentifiable Remains across the United States

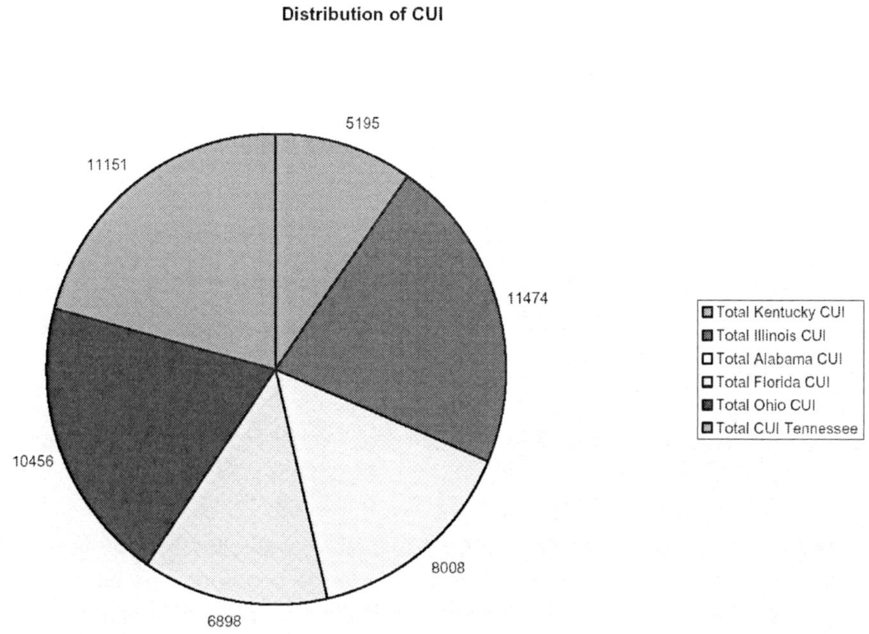

Figure 1.

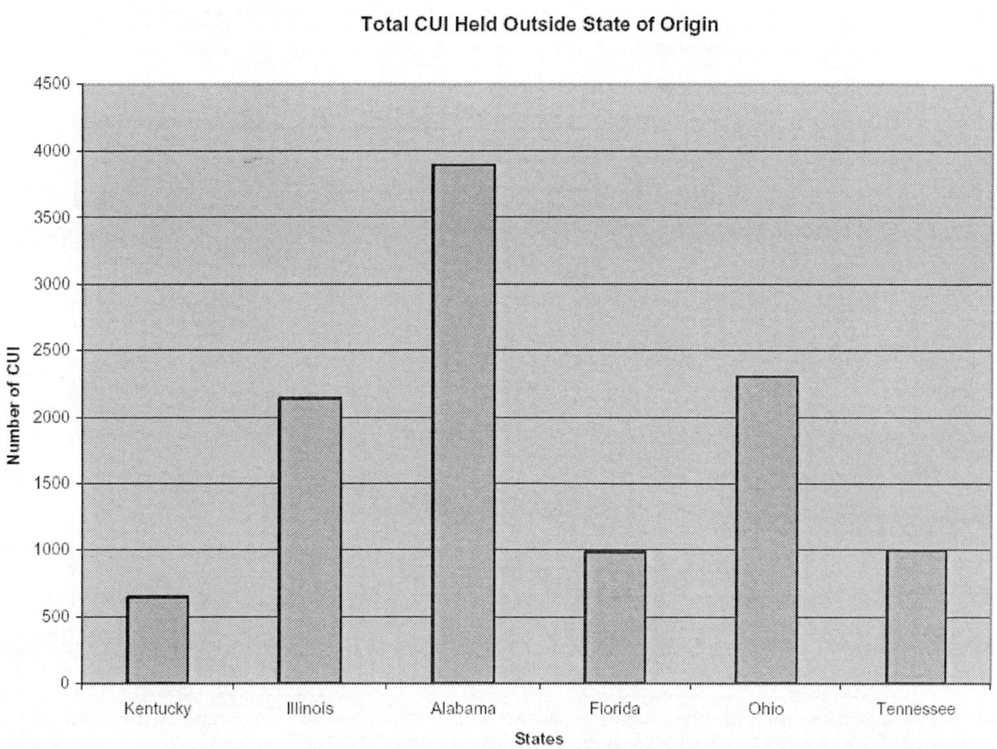

Figure 2.

Table 1.

State	Total CUI Held Out-Of-State	Percent Held Out-Of-State	Average CUI Held Out-Of-State	Median CUI Held Out-Of-State
Alabama	3892	48%	353.85	4.5
Florida	987	14%	39	3
Ohio	2305	22%	144.06	5
Tennessee	999	9%	62.43	5
Illinois	2139	19%	101.85	5
Kentucky	650	13%	38.2	5.5

Assessment of existing data shows that the largest number of individuals determined to be CUI were excavated in Illinois, followed by Tennessee, Ohio, Alabama, Florida, and lastly Kentucky. Further analysis reveals that 21% of all the CUI in this chapter are currently located outside the state in which they were excavated. Examination of the current location of the CUI located out of provenience reveals that they are predominately held in Tennessee. Over 3,700 individuals who were excavated from Kentucky, Illinois, Alabama, Florida, and Ohio are located in Tennessee. Massachusetts currently holds the second largest number of individuals excavated from Kentucky, Illinois, Alabama, Florida, Ohio, and Tennessee with 3,595 individuals.

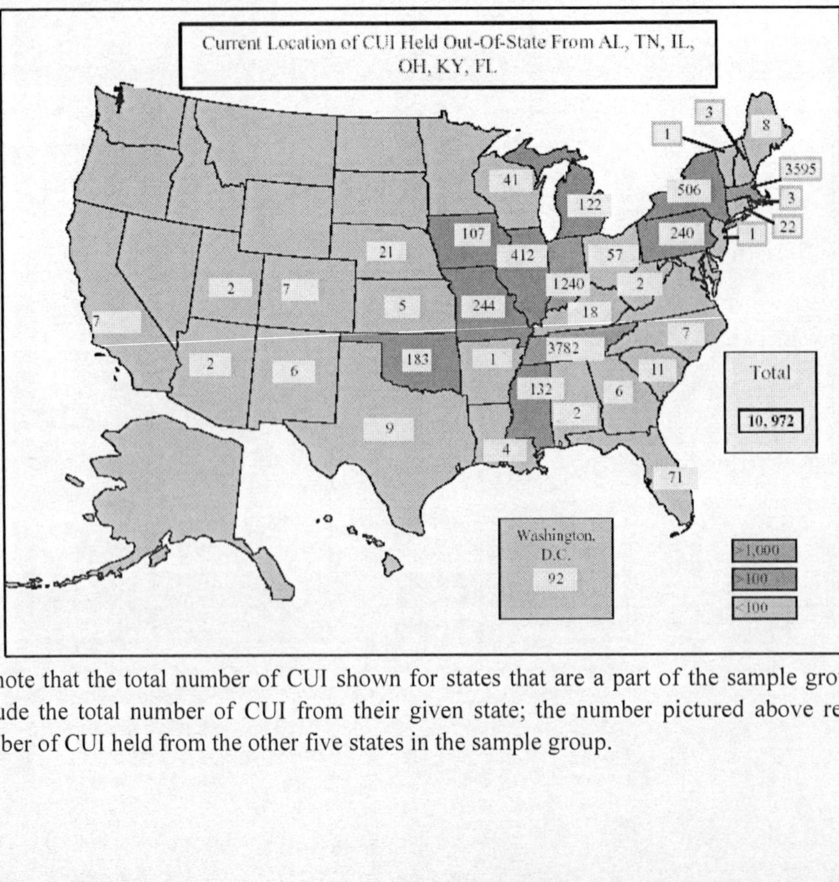

*Please note that the total number of CUI shown for states that are a part of the sample group do not include the total number of CUI from their given state; the number pictured above reflects the number of CUI held from the other five states in the sample group.

Completion of a distribution breakdown of the CUI held out-of-state from the study group across the United States shows that the average number of individuals held in each state appears to be considerable, averaging 123 CUI per state. However, this information is skewed significantly. [1] Outliers have affected the data for each state, meaning that one or two states possess an abnormally high number of CUI in comparison to other states in the set, causing the average number of CUI to be drastically higher than actually is the case. To eliminate the effect of the outliers on the data set the median number of CUI held out-of-state has been tabulated.

In total 10, 972 CUI from the study group are currently held outside their state of provenience. Spread across 36 states these CUI account for roughly 21% of all culturally unidentifiable individuals in the sample population. Examination of the 36 states in which the CUI are located reveals a concentration of CUI in 17 of the 36 states. Concentrated within these 17 states is 59% of all CUI held out of provenience, accounting for 6,484 CUI in total. Proximity to the states in the sample population appears to be the key to understanding this distribution, as all 17 states in question border at least one of the states in the study group.

II. DATE EXCAVATED

Examination of when the culturally unidentifiable individuals were excavated may not assist directly in the interpretation of who the CUI are, however, it will assist in understanding why they have been determined to be culturally unidentifiable. Modern archaeology in the United States can trace its origins to the early 1800's; outlining the development of modern archaeology from its beginning allows for comprehension of period paradigms and research practices. Analysis of the date of excavation in comparison to research practices and period paradigms will allow for a better comprehension of why the individuals are CUI. [2]

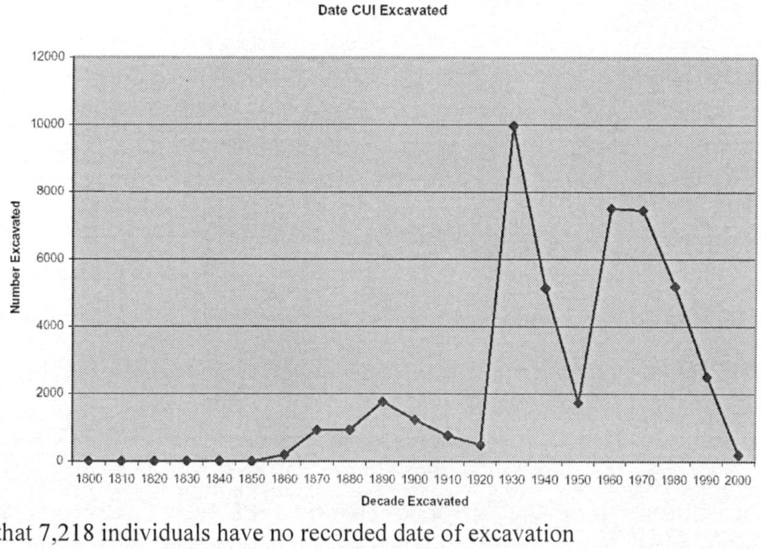

*Please note that 7,218 individuals have no recorded date of excavation

Figure 3.

As illustrated in the graph above, the number of culturally unidentifiable individuals spiked three times over the past two hundred years, once in the 19th century, and twice in the 20th century. The first significant increase in CUI occurred from 1890 to 1899; of the Native American human remains excavated at this time 1,758 of them were found to be culturally unidentifiable. After the spike in the 1890's the number of CUI which were excavated each year made a steady decline until the 1930's. Between 1930 and 1939 the largest percentage of Native American remains were found to be culturally unidentifiable, roughly 9,957 individuals in all. Thirty years later, in the 1960's, another spike in the number of CUI would occur, as 7,508 persons would subsequently be found to be culturally unidentifiable.

Table 2.

State	Decade Most CUI Excavated/ Recorded	Percent of Total CUI Excavated During Decade	Percent Date of Excavation Unknown
Alabama	1930-1940	63%	6%
Tennessee	1930-1940	31%	8%
Kentucky	1940-1950	43%	6%
Ohio	1960-1970	24%	6%
Illinois	1960-1970	22%	28%
Florida	1980-1990	19%	26%

III. Associated Funerary Objects

Examining the number of associated funerary objects, items which as part of the death rite or ceremony of a culture were placed at the burial site, sheds light on the amount of information which is available to assist in the identification of the culturally unidentifiable individuals. Analysis of the data has found that 18,816 CUI, roughly 35% of the CUI in the study group, were excavated with no associated funerary objects. However, this means that 34,366 culturally unidentifiable individuals were excavated with at least one associated funerary object. Of the 34, 366 that were found to have at least 1 associated funerary object 5,066 were excavated with over 2,000 associated funerary objects.

IV. Modality

Examination of the methodology used in the excavation of the CUI, as with the data of excavation, may not assist directly in the interpretation of who the CUI are. However, it will assist in understanding the auspices in which the remains unearthed. Investigation of the modality in which the CUI were excavated reveals that nearly half of the CUI, which were disinterred from the sample group, were done so in a scientific manner under the guidance of academia, either directly through a university or a field school.[3] The second largest group, scientific excavation conducted by institutions other then university/field school accounts for roughly a quarter of all the CUI in the sample population. It is important to note here that

71% of the culturally unidentifiable remains were excavated in a scientific manner, not by amateur archaeologists.

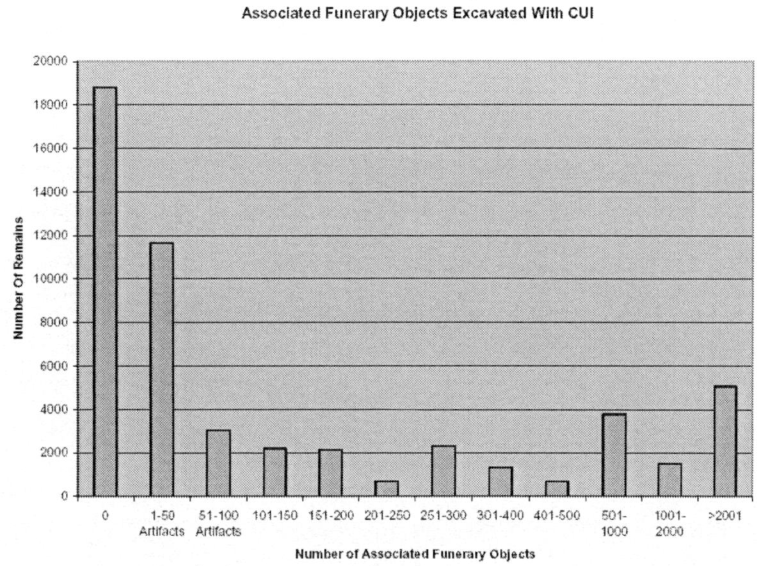

Figure 4.

V. SIZE

Reflecting upon the concentration of CUI which were found at each site, the data reveals that majority of the CUI were found in either small burials that comprised between 1 and 10 individuals or they were buried in mass graves which held more then 500 individuals.

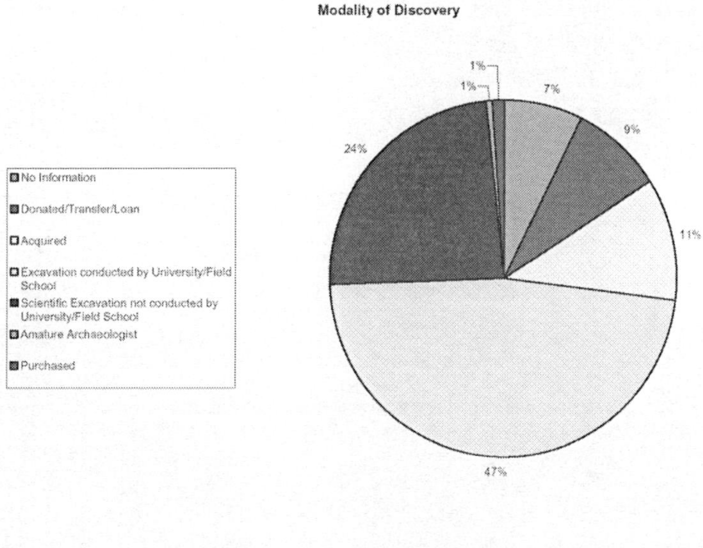

Figure 5.

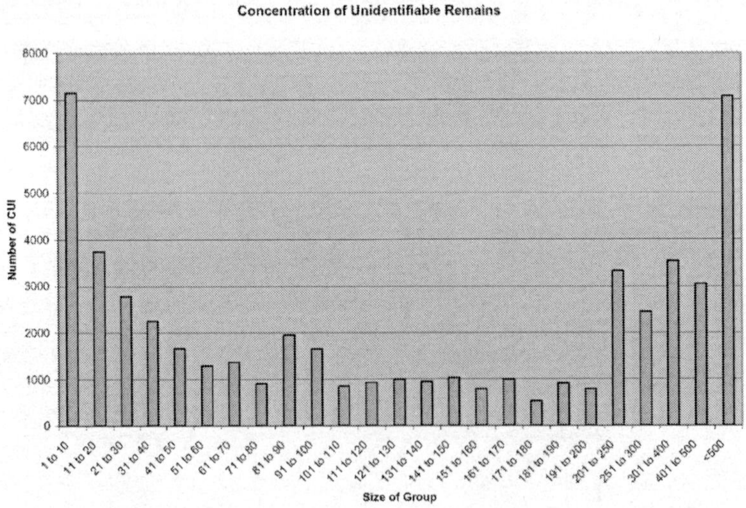

Figure 6.

I. AGE

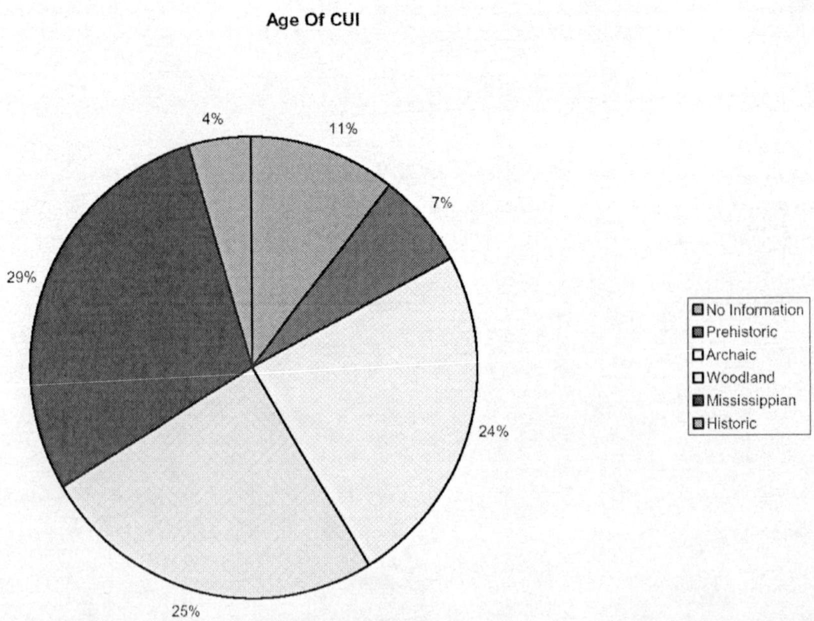

Figure 7.

Table IV.

State	No Information	Donated	Acquired	Scientific Excavation By University/Field School	Scientific Not Conducted by Academia	Amateur Archaeologist	Purchased
Alabama	70	52	105	7627	152	2	0
Kentucky	86	202	69	4819	7	11	1
Tennessee	802	224	1429	7981	708	2	5
Ohio	455	491	2	2770	6526	102	110
Illinois	2053	3290	960	767	3902	47	455
Florida	421	287	3385	1274	1384	144	3

Examination of the time period when the CUI were believed to have been alive presents a near even spread of CUI between 8000 B.C.E. and 1400 C.E. The largest percentage of CUI has been dated to the Mississippian period, which spanned from 1100 C.E. to 1400 C.E.[4] In total 15,554 of the 53,182 CUI from the study group were alive during the Mississippian period. The second largest group, the Woodland period, had a projected total of 13,252 CUI. Only 3,478 of all the CUI from the sample population were believed to have been alive during the prehistoric period; only a 3% difference separates the number of individuals that lived during the prehistoric period and those who lived in the historic period, which spanned from 1500 C.E. to 1715 C.E. Currently a total of 5,678 CUI have not been associated with a time period, accounting for 11% of all the CUI.

End Notes

[1] Please note that the figures "Average CUI Held Out-of-State" and "Median CUI Held Out-of-State" examine the states which have federal agencies and/or museums which currently have possession over CUI which were excavated in either AL,FL,KY,OH,TN, or IL.

[2] It is important to note that the date of excavation was not always provided in the inventories produced by the federal agencies and museums. This is due to large part to poor documentation by both the institutions and individuals who excavated the remains, and the museum for not documenting when the remains came into their collection. In cases in which the date of donation was known that date was used by the museum.

[3] The number of CUI excavated in a scientific manner by universities and field schools is inaccurate and shown to be lower then actually is the case. This is due in large part to the practices of higher education institutions in transferring their holdings to other museums. As a result of this, the proper collection history is not provided in the inventory summary and the CUI appear under categories such as donation or acquired, instead of scientific excavation conducted by a university or field school as is a more accurate description.

[4] Please note that each state does not have the same begin and end date for the Archaic, Woodland, and Mississippian period. In order to compile this data a general date range was applied to all of the states: The Prehistoric date used ranged from 15,000 B.C.E. -8,000 B.C.E. the Archaic period date ranged from 8000 B.C.E. to 1000 B.C.E. the Woodland period used a date range from 1,000 B.C.E. to 1,000 C.E. while the Mississippian period used a date range from 1100 C.E. to 1400 C.E. the Protohistoric and Historic periods were combined into the Historic period for this graph, the date range used for this figure spanned from 1500 C.E. to 1715 C.E.

In: Native American Graves and Repatriation
Editor: Kathy J. Bergmann
ISBN: 978-1-61122-410-8

Chapter 6

NATIVE AMERICAN GRAVES PROTECTION REPATRIATION REVIEW COMMITTEE

CHARTER NATIVE AMERICAN GRAVES PROTECTION AND REPATRIATION REVIEW COMMITTEE

Official Designation

The official designation of the Committee is the Native American Graves Protection and Repatriation Review Committee (Committee).

B. PURPOSE.
The purpose of the Committee is to monitor and review the implementation of the inventory and identification processes and repatriation activities required under sections 5, 6 and 7 of Public Law 101-601.

C. DUTIES AND RESPONSIBILITIES.
The duties of the Committee are solely advisory. Specifically, the Committee will be responsible for:

1. Monitoring and reviewing the implementation of the inventory and identification processes and repatriation activities required under sections 5, 6, and 7 of Public Law 101-601 to ensure a fair and objective consideration and assessment of all available relevant information and evidence;
2. Reviewing and making findings relating to the identity or cultural affiliation of human remains, funerary objects, sacred objects, and objects of cultural patrimony, or the repatriation of such items, upon the request of any affected party;
3. Facilitating the resolution of any disputes among Indian tribes, Native Hawaiian organizations, or lineal descendants, and Federal agencies or museums relating to the repatriation of human remains, funerary objects, sacred objects, and objects of cultural patrimony, including convening the parties to the dispute, if deemed desirable;

4. Compiling an inventory of culturally unidentifiable human remains that are in the possession or control of each Federal agency and museum and recommending specific actions for disposition of such human remains;

Consulting with Indian tribes, Native Hawaiian organizations, and museums on matters pertaining to the work of the Committee affecting such tribes or organizations;

6. Consulting with the Secretary in the development of regulations to carry out Public Law 101-601;
7. Performing such other related functions as the Secretary may assign to the Committee;
8. Making recommendations, if appropriate, regarding future care of human remains, funerary objects, sacred objects, and objects of cultural patrimony which are to be repatriated; and
9. Submitting an annual report to Congress on the progress and any barriers encountered in carrying out the Committee responsibilities during the year.

D. MEMBERSHIP.

1. The Committee will be composed of seven members appointed by the Secretary as follows:
   (a) Three members appointed from nominations submitted by Indian tribes, Native Hawaiian organizations, and traditional Native American religious leaders, with at least two of such persons being traditional Native American religious leaders;
   (b) Three members appointed from nominations submitted by national museum organizations and scientific organizations; and
   (c) One member appointed from nominations developed and consented to by the other members of the committee.
2. Members are appointed as Special Government Employees.
3. Terms of appointment will be for 4 years. Reappointment of current members will be for a term of 2 years. All appointments will terminate upon the termination of the Committee. Any vacancy on the Committee will be filled in the same manner in which the original appointment was made within 90 days of the occurrence of such vacancy.
4. Any member who fails to attend two successive meetings of the Committee, or who otherwise fails to substantively participate in the work of the Committee, may be removed from the Committee by the Secretary and a replacement named.
5. Members of the Committee will serve without pay, but will be reimbursed at a rate equal to the daily rate for Level IV of the Executive Schedule for each day (including travel time) for which the member is actually engaged in Committee business. While away from their homes or regular places of business in the performance of services of the Committee, members will be allowed travel expenses, including per diem in lieu of subsistence, in the same manner as persons employed intermittently in government service are allowed such expenses in accordance with Sections 5703 of Title 5 of the United States Code.

6. The Secretary will establish such rules and regulations for the Committee as are necessary. The Secretary may not appoint Federal Officers or employees to the Committee.

E. ETHICS RESPONSIBILITIES OF MEMBERS.

All members will comply with applicable ethics rules and regulations. The Department of the Interior will provide materials to those members appointed as Special Government Employees, explaining their ethical obligations and with which the members should be familiar. Consistent with the ethics requirements, members will endeavor to avoid any actions that would cause the public to activities, or advice. The provisions of this paragraph do not affect any other statutory or regulatory ethical obligations to which a member may be subject.

F. ADMINISTRATION.

1. CHARTER. The Committee is subject to the provisions of the Federal Advisory Committee Act (FACA), 5 U.S.C. Appendix (1994). The Committee will take no action unless the charter filing requirements of sections 9 and 14(b) of FACA have been complied with.
2. DESIGNATED FEDERAL OFFICIAL. The Committee reports to the Secretary of the Interior, United States Department of the Interior, 1849 C Street, NW, Washington, DC 20240. The Manager, National NAGPRA program, National Park Service, or a designee will serve as the Designated Federal Official (DFO) required by section 10 of FACA to oversee the management of the Committee.
3. CHAIRPERSON. The Committee will designate one member to be Chairperson.
4. SUPPORT AND COST. Support for the Committee is provided by the U.S. Department of the Interior, National Park Service, Office of the Director. The estimated annual operating cost of the Committee is $163,000, which includes the cost of 0.5 work-years of staff support.
5. MEETINGS. The Committee will meet approximately three times a year, although it may convene more often if there is an immediate need for consultation, advice and review. All meetings of the Committee will be subject to the provisions FACA, 5 U.S.C. Appendix (1994). No Advisory Committee member, and no member of any subgroup of this Committee, shall participate in any matter in which the member has a financial interest.
6. SUBCOMMITTEES. The Committee may, in consultation with the DFO, create subcommittees from among its membership supplemented when appropriate by members of the public, provided that the role of such subcommittees will be solely to gather information or conduct research for the Committee, to analyze relevant issues and facts, or to draft proposed position papers for deliberation by the Committee. Membership on all subcommittees will be determined by the Chairperson, subject to the concurrence of the DFO. Subcommittees will meet as necessary, subject to the approval of the DFO.

G. DURATION AND DATE OF TERMINATION.

In view of the objectives, scope and purposes of the Committee, it is expected to continue into the foreseeable future. The Committee will terminate at the end of the 120-day period beginning on the day the Secretary certifies, in a report submitted to Congress, that the work of the Committee has been completed.

H. AUTHORITY.

The Native American Graves Protection and Repatriation Review Committee is established by authority of Section 8 of Public Law 101-601, November 16, 1990.

/s/ Dirk Kempthorne____/November 24, 2008
Secretary of the Interior   Date Signed
DATE CHARTER FILED November 24, 2008

CHAPTER SOURCES

The following chapters have been previously published:

Chapter 1 – This is an edited, excerpted and augmented edition of a United States Government Accountability Office publication, Report Order Code GAO-10-768, dated July 2010.

Chapter 2 – This is an edited, excerpted and augmented edition of a Native American Graves Protection and Repatriation Review Committee Report to the Congress, dated 2008.

Chapter 3 – This is an edited, excerpted and augmented edition of a United States Department of the Interior publication, dated August 2009.

Chapter 4 – This is an edited, excerpted and augmented edition of a United States Department of the Interior publication, dated 2009.

Chapter 5 – This is an edited, excerpted and augmented edition of a publication written by Andrew Kline, dated March 22, 2007.

Chapter 6 – This is an edited, excerpted and augmented edition of a Native American Graves Protection and Repatriation Review Committee Charter.

INDEX

D

E

F